65- 25488 (7 - 18-66)

NATIONS OF THE MODERN WORLD

CEYLON
S. A. Pakeman
Formerly Professor of Modern History, Ceylon University College. Appointed Member, House of Representatives, Ceylon, 1947–1952

MODERN INDIA
Sir Percival Griffiths
President, India, Pakistan and Burma Association

MODERN IRAN
Peter Avery
Lecturer in Persian and Fellow King's College, Cambridge

IRAQ
Brig. S. Y. Longrigg
Formerly of the Government of Iraq and the Iraq Petroleum Company and one time Political Officer, Iraq
and
Frank Stoakes
Director of Middle Eastern Studies, St. Antony's College, Oxford

JAPAN
Sir Esler Dening
H.M. Ambassador to Japan, 1952–1957

MALAYA
J. M. Gullick
Formerly of the Malayan Civil Service

PAKISTAN
Ian Stephens
Formerly Editor of The Statesman *Calcutta and Delhi, 1942–1951 Fellow King's College, Cambridge, 1952–1958*

SOUTH AFRICA
John Cope
Formerly editor-in-chief of The Forum

TURKEY
Geoffrey Lewis
Senior lecturer in Islamic Studies, Oxford

THE UNITED
STATES OF
AMERICA

H. C. Allen
*Commonwealth Fund Professor of American
History, University College London*

YUGOSLAVIA

Muriel Heppel
and
F. B. Singleton

SOUTH AFRICA

SOUTH AFRICA

By

JOHN COPE

FREDERICK A. PRAEGER, *Publishers*
NEW YORK · WASHINGTON

BOOKS THAT MATTER

Published in the United States of America in 1965
by Frederick A. Praeger, Inc. Publishers
111 Fourth Avenue, New York 3, N. Y.

© J. P. Cope 1965

Library of Congress Catalog Card Number: 65–25488

Printed in Great Britain

THIS BOOK IS DEDICATED TO
MARGARET NANCY, MY WIFE,
WITHOUT WHOSE ENCOURAGEMENT
AND HELP IT COULD NEVER HAVE
BEEN WRITTEN

Foreword

No COUNTRY in the world is more absorbing to the student of inter-racial affairs than South Africa. No country suffers so stubborn a problem of human relationships, yet offers so tantalising a prospect of progress and development. Here is a vast country, largely under-populated, blessed with a healthy and temperate climate, extrava-gantly endowed with material resources, yet full of uncertainty and fear. All the qualities are there, among the different peoples of the Republic, to mould a sturdy, enterprising, confident nationhood. English and Afrikaners spring from among the finest stock in Europe and have repeatedly proved their courage, resourcefulness, dour tenacity, organising and administrative ability. To the pool of human qualities the Africans add their remarkable patience, their laughter, basic intelligence and great eagerness to learn and pro-gress, while from the East the Asians bring their quick understand-ing, their craftsmanship and shrewdness. The one ingredient that is lacking is the willingness to share, and the one disturbing element that prevents a rich amalgam is racial prejudice.

How is it that this nation which fought so well on the side of democracy in two world wars is today regarded by many as tyran-nical? Worse still, a tyranny based on skin-colour? How could this land, which played a leading role in creating the Commonwealth, become one of the first to leave it? What has happened to turn so smiling, so proverbially hospitable and carefree a country sour? What are the real origins of the crisis in South Africa, and how will it all end?

In this book an attempt has been made to answer some of these questions by setting forth the historic, economic and sociological factors of the situation as simply and as objectively as it is possible for anyone to do who has been intimately concerned with public affairs in this land of sharp and sometimes violent controversy for more than thirty years. The author has not sought to praise or to con-demn any particular policy or special point of view. The facts, he believes, speak eloquently for themselves.

Contents

xiii

Maps

Sources

MUCH of the information in this book was drawn from the author's personal notes, records, and press-cuttings dating from 1930 to the present time. In addition he has consulted various government blue-books and publications including the important report of the Commission for the Socio-Economic Development of the Bantu Areas (Tomlinson Report) and several editions of the South African Official Year Book. He wishes to acknowledge the following further sources: Hugh Ashton, *The Basuto*; Edgar H. Brookes and J. B. Macaulay, *Civil Liberty in South Africa*; Rev. A. T. Bryant, *Olden Times in Zululand and Natal*; *Cambridge History of South Africa*; R. K. Cope, *Comrade Bill*; Anthony Delius, *The Fall*; Ifor L. Evans, *Native Policy in Southern Africa*; H. E. Hockley, *The Story of the British Settlers of 1820*; Jan H. Hofmeyr, *Life of Jan Hendrik Hofmeyr*; Ralph Kilpin, *The Romance of a Colonial Parliament*; Sir J. G. Kotze, *Memoirs and Reminiscences*; President S. J. Kruger, *Memoirs*; Colin and Margaret Legum, *South Africa – Crisis for the West*; Julius Lewin, *Politics and Law in South Africa*; Graham Mackeurtan, *The Cradle Days of Natal*; Prof. S. J. Marais, *The Fall of Kruger's Republic* and *The Cape Coloured People*; L. Marquard, *The Native in South Africa* and *The Peoples and Policies of South Africa*; Thomas Mofolo, *Chaka*; B. G. Paver, *Zimbabwe Cavalcade*; M. Roberts and A. E. G. Trollip, *The South African Opposition*; Nancy Rouillard, *Matabele Thompson*; Prof. L. Shapera, *The Bantu-speaking Tribes of South Africa*; S.A. Institute of Race Relations – Reports and Annual Surveys; C. M. Tatz, *Shadow and Substance in South Africa*; *The Forum*, bound volumes 1939–1951.

PART ONE

Chapter 1

The Land

TWO MIGHTY ocean currents, one sub-tropical and tepid and the other cold with a tang of the Antarctic, meet at the Cape of Storms. And where they meet the sea is troubled and the sky is filled with wind and scudding cloud. Like a gnarled and crooked finger, a vast granite ridge claws into this maelstrom at the ships that cross in unending procession from Atlantic ports to the east. The finger begins at Table Mountain, where a cascade of white mist driven by the prevailing south-east gale pours down to melt into the higher levels of Cape Town, oldest and fairest city in the Republic of South Africa.

Table Mountain together with the crooked finger and its warts and callouses – Lion's Head, Devil's Peak, Chapman's Peak and the Twelve Apostles – form a geological complex of their own, boasting a distinct climate, a rare and unique flora, and a storehouse of fossilised remains yet to be fully explored. There seems little doubt that in comparatively recent times, reckoned geologically, Table Mountain and its attendant peaks and ridges were an island apart from the mainland, and that the great land-mass of the sub-continent began at the mountain range of the Hottentot's Holland some fifty miles to the north. Even today, though joined to the mainland by the low-lying and sometimes flooded expanse of the Cape Flats, Table Mountain has managed to retain an almost mystical air of aloofness.

Perhaps it is this air of detachment, this suggestion of standing apart from the restless sequence of events in the brash young territories to the north, that has cast a spell over so many South Africans, including two such famous men as Cecil Rhodes and General Smuts. Rhodes became an avid devotee of the Mountain, and he bought up thousands of acres on its flanks, presenting them to the nation. Upon these estates there now lie the famous Kirstenbosch Botanical Gardens, the grounds of the University of Cape Town, the homestead and grounds of Groote Schuur, official residence of the Prime Minister, and many acres of parklands. A memorial to Rhodes stands on a shoulder of the Mountain where

3

he used to sit dreaming of a great federation of British states stretching from the fair Cape to beyond the Zambesi.

General Smuts spent every hour he could spare climbing the rugged heights of Table Mountain, and he knew all the paths and crevices, the crystal springs that bubble out of the bracken, and the long flat rocks pock-marked where the rain is caught in glimmering pools. He was an authority on the many unique plant-species growing on the crests and slopes. Carrying a long staff, wearing bush-shirt, too-short khaki trousers and heavy boots, and with a haversack slung over his shoulder, this bearded patriarch was a familiar figure to week-end climbers who would greet him respectfully and leave him to trudge his solitary way, peering among the shrubs and pulling grasses and leaves for scientific examination in his study. General Smuts used to say that the idea of writing his philosophical book *Holism and Evolution* was born as he was climbing Skeleton Gorge and that he thought out most of his arguments while on the Mountain. At one point beside the path that twists from the top of Skeleton Gorge to the mountain hut where stragglers shelter if the mists catch them unawares there is a soft, grassy ledge backed by a granite boulder facing north-east. Here General Smuts often sat gazing at the blue ridge of the Hottentot's Holland, beyond which rose the high plateau of the Karoo.

This is a good point from which to study the topography of this rich and diversified land. In shape the sub-continent is rather like a cluster of swarming bees hanging from a branch in a mimosa tree and pushed a little to one side by the wind. The area of the Republic is 472,370 square miles, to which must be added the 318,000 square miles of South-West Africa, administered as part of the Republic and directly represented in the Parliament at Cape Town. The grand total of 890,360 square miles is ten times the size of Britain and about a quarter as big as the United States of America. But almost half of South Africa is semi-desert. In the remaining half the rainfall ranges from 8 to 20 inches per annum in the central and western regions and from 30 to 60 inches mostly east of the Drakensberg Mountains. There are some points on the mountain ranges where the rainfall exceeds 100 inches, but in comparison with many other parts of the world South Africa is a dry country. In the long run, lack of water is likely to prove a major economic problem. Already it presents an exciting challenge to the engineering enterprise of a country richly endowed with material resources.

Over most of South Africa the climate is healthy and congenial. With its lush vineyards and orchards and rolling wheatlands framed between mountain and sea, the Cape Peninsula must surely be rated as one of the lotus-lands of the world. The rainy season is in the winter months of June, July and August, and spring bursts forth with a blaze of multi-coloured wild flowers. Proteas and heaths tint the flanks of the mountains and the flatlands are often carpeted with a riotous profusion of arctotis, iscias, lanchenalias and gladiolus. Cool breezes from the Atlantic keep the temperature down in the dry summer months while the warm Agulhas current flowing down the Indian Ocean to Cape Point prevents a freeze-up in wintertime. Snow falls only occasionally, on the tops of the mountains, and frost is rarely recorded in the valleys and flatlands below. This region, which extends round the coast roughly from Cape Town to Port Elizabeth, is known as the 'winter-rainfall area'.

If you take a map of South Africa and draw a line northwards from Port Elizabeth to the sources of the Limpopo River, on the borders of Bechuanaland, all of the Republic lying eastwards to the Indian Ocean falls within the 'summer-rainfall area'. Here the winters are dry. Here, too, the rainfall during the summer months is more variable and uncertain. There is nothing like the monsoon that brings its annual deluge with clockwork precision to the high plateau of Ethiopia or the highlands of Kenya. Instead, there appears to be a kind of guerrilla warfare in the upper atmosphere between the dry airs of the Kalahari Desert and the moist winds of the Indian Ocean, with unpredictable intrusions of tropical currents from Central Africa. As a result, so the experts put it, 'precipitation in the summer-rainfall zone is largely due to instability showers'.

Days will pass without rain, then big clouds will roll up and there is a storm, with lightning and thunder. Sometimes a mealie-crop is wiped out with hail. A great luxury is a three-day soaking rain. It is not uncommon for the farmers in one district to suffer a serious drought, with their crops wilting and springs drying up, while their neighbours in an adjoining district enjoy abundant rain from passing showers. A celebrated occasion is recorded when, during the hearing of a bill before Parliament to authorise the payment of relief for drought in a certain area, a clause had to be inserted to provide compensation for damage caused by floods.

Most of the countryside in the summer-rainfall area consists of a high plateau varying in altitude from 4,000 to 6,000 feet, bordered or crossed with mountain ranges. There are hundreds of square miles of flat, featureless grassland or cultivated fields like the mealie-triangle of the Free State and the Transvaal and the arid plains of the western Free State. Natal and the southern Free State, bordering the Drakensberg Mountains, are hilly and grass-clad. The climate is comparatively cool and healthy, and frost and sometimes even snow occur in the wintertime.

There is a third climatic region in the Republic known as the lowveld, in extent comparatively small. This consists of land lying below 1,000 feet from Durban on the east coast, northwards and inland, including parts of Zululand, Swaziland, and the Eastern and Northern Transvaal. It is tropical country, bush-clad and lush. Plagued with malaria and nagana and heart-water among cattle, the lowveld was long considered unhealthy and until recently was little developed. But modern methods of mosquito and tsetse-fly control have brought about a revolution and today the lowveld is being opened up to agriculture in a spectacular way.

A question that has frequently been asked is whether South Africa is really suitable for white people to live in, or whether, in the course of time, the whites will not gradually deteriorate physically as a result of excessive sunlight, and lack of bracing, snow-bound winters. This question was considered of sufficient importance to prompt the Government, some thirty years ago, to commission an eminent authority from Holland to investigate the effects of the South African climate upon human beings of European or Nordic stock. The result of the inquiry was entirely reassuring. During World War II when thousands of recruits were put through rigorous medical tests the general physical standard was found to be high. Incidentally, the fittest and best-developed recruits were found to come from sun-drenched cities like Kimberley in the Karoo and Pretoria in the centre of the Transvaal.

However, there are two factors at present worrying those who are concerned with the physical welfare of whites and blacks in South Africa alike. One is the grave extent of soil-erosion and the other is the alarming spread of bilharzia. The menace of soil-erosion was recognised a quarter of a century ago when a soil-conservation Act was passed by Parliament providing for financial and organisational means to fight erosion. At the request of General Smuts, who was Prime Minister at the time, a civilian body known as the National Veld Trust was formed to awaken the public to the soil-erosion threat. Today there are few farmers who are not aware of erosion and how to fight it, and strict conservation measures have been applied over thousands of acres of veld and plough-land. Nevertheless South Africa as a whole is still losing the fight against soil-erosion, as a recent assessment of the situation showed. The incidence of erosion is particularly bad in the territories and reserves set aside for occupation exclusively by Africans. The major causes are overcrowding and ignorance. The Department of Bantu Affairs spends much time and money on its campaign to apply conservation measures and to teach Africans how to prevent erosion but there are formidable difficulties in the way of success. Rural Africans are still mainly an ignorant, peasant folk suspicious of change and clinging tenaciously to old customs such as the cattle-cult and lobola, through which a man's status in the tribe is measured by the number of stock he owns and he is compelled to buy his wives with cattle. Government measures to limit herds of cattle and goats to the numbers that can be safely grazed on the veld have been received with sullen resentment and on one or two occasions have provoked open hostility.

The problem is seriously aggravated by overcrowding in the African reserves. Though Africans occupy some of the most fertile areas in the Republic, the total extent of their land is a little over 13 per cent, and most of this is seriously eroded. In order to apply adequate conservation measures at least a million out of the four millions who inhabit the African reserves ought to be drawn off the land, but under the Government's Bantustan policy the plan is to crowd even more into the reserves. Here we go to the crux of what is fast becoming the most explosive problem in South Africa – a question that will be discussed in greater detail as our story unfolds.

Bilharzia is caused by a minute parasite picked up by human beings bathing in infected waters, or drinking or even washing in infected rivers and dams. The parasite burrows through the skin and finds its way eventually to the bladder or some other organ where it proceeds to lay eggs. These eggs return to water where certain types of snails become hosts in order to complete the cycle. Efforts to fight the disease are generally directed at eliminating the snails, but in recent years the scourge has spread from the lowveld and east-flowing rivers, to which it seemed originally to be confined, into most parts of South Africa. Bilharzia is rarely fatal to human beings but has serious debilitating effects and is considered by many sociologists to be responsible for the lassitude shown by so many Africans. One of South Africa's leading health authorities, Dr. Eustice Cluver, recently described bilharzia as South Africa's No. 1 health problem, and there is no doubt that a scientific breakthrough on this front would be an event of major economic importance to the Republic.

There are other health problems too, such as the presence of amoebic dysentery in certain areas, but to keep the picture in perspective South Africa must be rated a healthy country and likely to become increasingly so with the march of scientific progress.

Scenically, the Republic cannot compete with many other countries in the world. Though parts of it are beautiful, and even a vast
and arid region such as the Karoo has a subtle charm all its own,
South Africa has no snow-bound mountain areas like the Alps, no
fiords, no lake-districts – nothing to compare with the forest-country
of Canada, the rugged grandeur of the Himalayas, or the overwhelming beauty of the mountain regions of China. Nor is there
anything like the intimate and fertile landscape of Southern France
or Italy, or the soft loveliness of the English countryside. Yet with
its backdrop of mountains, its two warring oceans, its bays and
incomparable beaches, its oaks and pines, its wild-flowers, heath
and lush vineyards, the Cape Peninsula is a most pleasant place to
live in. And a motor trip over the 1,200 miles of coastal road from
Cape Town through the forests of George and Knysna to Port
Elizabeth, then over the bush-clad hills of the Ciskei into the highlands of the Transkei Territory, across the wilder and more rugged
Pondoland into Natal, will prove an enjoyable experience.

From Natal one should fly along the Drakensberg, the mountain-
divide that dominates the eastern hinterland of the Republic. Climbing to about 12,000 feet, the plane is soon weaving between the
grassy and rock-strewn peaks of the British protectorate of Basutoland, and it is easy to understand why the Basutos managed to defy
the waves of white settlers who trekked into the hinterland over a
hundred years ago. Crossing Basutoland we follow the border
between Northern Natal and the Transvaal, where the mountains
are lower and less clearly defined, until we reach the British protectorate of Swaziland. Here the Drakensberg curves northwards
and westwards, becoming wilder and more spectacular until it ends
at Haenertsburg, near the mountain-fastness of Mojaji the Rain
Queen.

Not far from here, over against the border of Portuguese East
Africa, is the Kruger National Park, probably the greatest attraction
that South Africa has to offer to the tourist. In low-lying tropical
bush-veld, the Park stretches from the Limpopo River in the north
to the Crocodile River some 200 miles southwards, and is about
40 miles wide. Here almost every species of wild animal indigenous
to South Africa is to be found. Around the heavily-scented wood-
fires at the rest-camps there yet lingers, despite gramophones and
portable radios blaring the latest hit-parade, something of the Jock
o' the Bushveld atmosphere of a hundred years ago.

Westwards from the Drakensberg, rolling for hundreds of miles
into the semi-desert of the hot and waterless Kalahari, is a great
plateau, decreasing in fertility the further we go. On this plateau,

at an altitude of between 5,000 and 6,000 feet in the centre of the
Transvaal, is South Africa's most important industrial complex, the
Pretoria-Witwatersrand-Vereeniging triangle where a fifth of the
total population of the Republic is now concentrated. Airline pilots
who fly the world's routes say that a night-landing at Jan Smuts
Airport, at the centre of the triangle, is one of the most spectacular
night-landings to be found anywhere in the world. The furnaces at
Iscor steelworks belching molten metal, the coloured neon lights,
hundreds of miles of brilliantly-lighted highways, the mine-dams
and reservoirs reflecting lights, all form a brilliant kaleidoscope in
the dry air.

Such, then, is the land of the Republic of South Africa. It is an
ancient land, geologically, undisturbed by volcanic shocks and not
unduly troubled by violent extremes of weather. It has its scenic
attractions, but they are not as breath-taking as the beauty-spots
in many other parts of the world. Nature somehow forgot to diver-
sify so much of the land of South Africa. Yet if Nature gave the
Republic a rather plain exterior, it made amends by endowing her
with a rich storehouse of material resources, the like of which can
be found in few other countries.

Chapter 2

The Resources

NOT FAR from the commercial centre of Johannesburg, on the edge of Motortown, there is a municipal beer-hall for Africans. On the pavement beside the beer-hall squat the Dingaka, the traditional medicine-men, offering their charms and potions to the throng of Africans flowing ceaselessly up and down the dusty street. Stand among these primitive vendors with their weird assortments of roots, sticks of pungent-smelling woods, horns, calabashes, bladders of fat, powders and liquids, then lift your eyes to the serried skyscrapers that dominate the horizon above the corrugated-iron roofs of the sheds near the beer-hall. The contrast is startling.

Yet this is typical of South Africa, this strange mixture of superstition and sophistication, this curious blending of itinerant vendors of herbs and weird potions with the chromium and plastic supermarket.

As a concession to modern times one of the Dingaka wraps his roots and charms, his bones and strips of dried flesh in cellophane, unconcerned by the fact that over there in the skyscrapers sit the real enemies of tribalism and superstition, the financiers and technicians who plan to dig deeper into the earth, to set up new and intricate machines in industry, to launch fresh economic empires, and so relentlessly to draw more and more Africans into the towns, despite apartheid and influx-control. And what a vast storehouse of raw materials there is for the men in the skyscrapers to exploit !

Take gold, to begin with. If you consult a geological map you will find the gold deposits marked in a great sickle starting near the little village of Devon on the dreary highveld of the Transvaal and curving down through Springs, Benoni and Boksburg; through the important rail junction of Germiston and the restless city of Johannesburg; through Roodepoort, Krugersdorp and Randfontein; southwards to Westonaria and Klerksdorp; then into the Orange Free State to stop at the rapidly-growing town of Welkom, centre of the new southern goldfields. Along this 200-mile sickle-belt some 50,000 whites and 300,000 Africans burrowing in a vast underground labyrinth of shafts, drives and stopes – probing down in places more than 11,000 feet below the surface of the earth – win gold worth about £225 millions per year. The tube-mills and extraction plants also produce the world's biggest supply of osmiridium, a sizeable quantity of silver and an important strategic supply of uranium together with the gold they grind out of the conglomerates.

Then, of course, diamonds. 'Land of gold and diamonds' – that is South Africa's romantic image. The drama of the diggings where a fortune can lie in a sieveful of gravel; the greatest man-made hole in the earth at Kimberley; skeleton-coast off South-West Africa where police and smugglers hunt one another among the sand-dunes – the reverie is shattered when we learn that the industry, today, is one of the most tightly-controlled in the world, highly mechanised, scientifically-planned and organised on the most modern technological lines. Though highly important, it ranks well down the list in economic precedence. South Africa has long ceased to enjoy a monopoly of diamonds; in fact, the combined production of other lands is much greater than the South African output though the best gems still come from the Republic and South-West Africa. It has been reckoned that during the 75 years from 1883, when records were first kept, until 1958 the total value of diamonds recovered from the mines and diggings of South Africa was £507,929,000. It takes the gold mines of the Republic a little over two years to produce gold to that value.

The diamonds are found mainly in pipes and alluvial deposits in the North-Western Cape Province, the Free State and the Transvaal. There are rich deposits on the shore and under the sea off the mouth of the Orange River, which flows right across the subcontinent to empty itself into the Atlantic Ocean. Mining operations are now carried out from specially-equipped ships to recover gems from the sand under the sea and there is a good deal of prospecting north and south of the Orange River mouth.

The stability of the diamond industry rests largely on marketing control. Thirty years ago, during a world slump which coincided with rich new discoveries in various parts of Africa, the diamond market was flooded and the industry was threatened with collapse. The industry was saved by the imagination, drive, and persuasive ability of a financier who left his mark on the pages of South African history, Sir Ernest Oppenheimer. Sir Ernest persuaded the leading interests involved – the South African Government, the Administration of South-West Africa, De Beers, the Diamond Corporation and the Consolidated Diamond Mines of South-West Africa to form the Diamond Producers' Association which controls diamond sales through two subsidiary companies, one for gems and the other for industrial diamonds. From time to time during the intervening years agreements were made with producers in other parts of Africa, and the industry as a whole has been maintained on a stable basis. In South Africa, as a by-product to mining, a modest diamond-cutting industry has been developed, with factories in Johannesburg and Kimberley.

Platinum is mined in various parts of South Africa – at Potgietersrust on the Great North Road, at picturesque Lydenburg in the Drakensberg Mountains of the Eastern Transvaal, and in the drowsy, citrus-growing district of Rustenberg, west of Pretoria. Antimony and beryllium are also present in fair quantities, their extraction depending upon a somewhat erratic world demand. Chrome in sufficient quantities to supply the steel industry in the manufacture of alloys is found along a belt stretching from Britz in the Western Transvaal to the Crocodile River. Copper has long been mined at the tropical town of Messina, near the Limpopo River, which is the border with Southern Rhodesia. It is also mined on the far side of the sub-continent, a thousand miles away at Okiep in the Namaqualand desert, not far from the Atlantic Ocean. A large mass of low-grade copper ore is known to exist in the Letaba area of the Eastern Transvaal, while copper has been mined on a small scale at different times in the Warmbad district of the Transvaal and the Mount Ayliff district of East Griqualand.

South Africa has rich deposits of manganese ore. Proved reserves over about 130 miles of the hot, arid country between Kimberley and the Kalahari Desert have been estimated at over a thousand million tons. South African industries use about 100,000 tons per annum and a further 500,000 to 700,000 tons are exported.

And so the recital of mineral resources goes on : mercury in the Murchison Range, nickel in sizeable quantities near Rustenberg, tin in the lowveld of the Transvaal, asbestos worth £12 millions mined every year; phosphates, so important in the production of fertilisers, extracted in the Transvaal; corundum, graphite, gypsum, magnesite, mica, sulphur and vermiculite – the list seems unending.

Then, of course, coal, the very foundation of heavy industry. South Africa has enormous resources of coal, believed by some geologists to be the most abundant coalfields in the world. At least 25,000 million tons have been proved beyond doubt and a further 45,000 million tons are conservatively estimated to lie beneath the soil awaiting the prospector's drill. Generally speaking the seams are near the surface and are therefore easily mined. African labour is abundant, wages are low, and costs of production must be among the lowest in the world. Quality varies from anthracite and coking-coal of high value to brown coal used for raising steam. Cheap and abundant coal has made it possible to generate power at exceptionally low rates, and this in turn has been of great value to mining and industry generally. Most of the important rail routes are electrified, so that cheap power has lowered transport costs. The practice is to build power-stations on top of the coal seams so that coal can be mined directly into the furnaces that heat the boilers.

About the only really important raw material not yet discovered in South Africa is oil in any appreciable quantities, though oil-bearing torbanite is found in the Transvaal, Natal and the Cape Province. This is mined and the oil extracted on a commercial scale, but the yield is limited. To fill this gap in the economy a big oil-from-coal industry known as SASOL was set up by the Government on a coalfield near Vereeniging, some forty miles south of Johannesburg. The cost of establishing SASOL was almost double the original estimate and the plant suffered teething troubles, but despite gloomy forecasts that it would prove to be a failure it is now a going concern. The industry produces large quantities of motor spirit together with a wide range of by-products of great value to secondary industries.

That Nature should have placed a seam of coal so considerately at Boksburg, right in the middle of the Witwatersrand, was an important factor in the early development of the goldfields. There is little timber to be found on the highveld of the Transvaal, and the problem of carting firewood from the kloofs and valleys beyond the Magaliesberg to feed the furnaces of the first primitive steam-engines used for driving the stamp-mills, not to mention the forges where picks and drills were sharpened, and the campfires and cooking-stoves, must have been formidable. In any case, not all the timber to be found within hundreds of miles around could have sufficed for more than a few years.

Next to coal, iron is the most important raw material upon which to found a thriving industrial economy. Deposits of iron-ore are found all over South Africa, and they were worked long before the white man came with his advanced technology. Today South Africans point with pride to Iscor, the state steelworks that produce more than two million tons of rolled and finished steels every year, but Iscor was not the first state 'steelworks' on the sub-continent. Tshaka, king of the Zulus, who ruled from 1816 to 1828 undisputed over a land bigger than Britain, had an industry for manufacturing spears for his warriors, and hoes for the womenfolk to cultivate the fields. He had his expert quarrymen who knew the seams of iron-ore and dug ore out of the hillsides. Long trains of women carried the ore in baskets on their heads, walking for miles along the twisting paths that led through kloofs and around the shoulders of hills to the smelting-places. Then there were the coke-producers, men and women who lived on the fringes of the forests. They cut trees and branches of hardwood and dried them in the hot sun. Great piles of faggots were heaped up and set alight, and when they had burnt a while the flames were extinguished with water. The wood-coke thus manufactured was also carried by the womenfolk in baskets on their heads to the smelting-places.

Tshaka's furnaces were ingeniously designed. There was a large cone of baked clay in the centre, and out of this, like the spokes of a wheel, led three or four clay pipes, to each of which was attached a bellows of raw oxhide, worked something like a concertina. A man would squat on the ground pumping the bellows, fastened with a thong to the palm of each hand. First a fire of dry twigs and chips of hardwood was lighted in the cone, then, when this was blazing furiously in the blast from the bellows, a mixture of charcoal and iron-ore was packed on to the flames. After a while a clay plug was knocked from the bottom of the cone and a thin trickle of molten iron ran into a clay mould. As soon as the iron had set, it was turned out on to a flat stone which served as anvil and was hammered into shape. Some of these old spear-heads have been tested and the iron has been found to be of surprisingly good quality.

The story of Iscor, the state steelworks at Pretoria and Van der Bijl Park, near Vereeniging, is interesting. In 1924 the Nationalist Party of General Hertzog, almost exclusively Afrikaans and pledged to work for the independence of South Africa, formed a coalition with the Labour Party led by an old-time socialist, Colonel F. H. P. Creswell. This coalition defeated the South African Party led by General Smuts at a general election and General Hertzog became Premier. The Labour members of the new coalition government had dreams of nationalisation, but the ruggedly-conservative Nationalists, most of whom led patriarchal lives on their farms in the rural areas, were only interested in state-enterprise where it furthered the cause of independence. A steel industry was the perfect compromise. Almost all of South Africa's requirements of steel were imported, most of them from the traditional enemy of Afrikaner nationalism, Great Britain. Efforts by private enterprise in South Africa to found a steel industry had not proved very successful, but – as General Hertzog's advisers insisted – until South Africa could produce her own iron and steel she could never really become economically independent.

So in 1928 the Iron and Steel Industry Act was passed by Parliament, setting up the Iron and Steel Corporation. As Chairman was appointed an Afrikaner of great vision and ability, Dr. H. J. van der Bijl, who chose as one of his technical managers another young South African fresh from advanced scientific training in Europe, Dr. Hendrik van Eck. Shares in the Corporation were offered to the general public, but so poor was the response that the Government had to take up most of them in addition to its own controlling interest. It is ironical, today, to recall the speeches in Parliament against the establishment of Iscor, denouncing it as socialistic folly and prophesying failure and loss of public funds. The steel importers organised a vigorous lobby, the Press wrote critical articles and editorials, and speeches were made throughout the country attacking the Government for its dangerous essay in socialism. Undeterred, Dr. van der Bijl, Dr. van Eck and their technical colleagues went ahead planning the steelworks, ordering the plant and erecting the furnaces and mills. The coke oven was fired in 1933 and a few months later the blast furnaces were blown for the first time.

Soon the Iron and Steel Corporation, known as Iscor, was manufacturing rails for the state-owned South African Railways. Rumours began to circulate that they were of inferior quality and that they were inclined to split on curves where traffic was heavy. A whispering-campaign was set on foot, suggesting that Iscor had run into technical difficulties, that costs were out of proportion to those of the major steelworks overseas, and that Iscor products did not come up to specifications. R. J. Kingston Russell, a vigorous, impulsive and hard-hitting Irishman who was then editor of *The Natal Mercury*, issued a challenge to Iscor to allow its steel to be tested by some independent body, and greatly to his surprise the challenge was immediately accepted. The newspaper then arranged for a surprise visit to be made to the steelworks, where samples of steel were selected at random and taken to the laboratories of the Natal Technical College in Durban for metallurgical tests. The tests proved highly favourable and the rumours that had been circulating with regard to the alleged inferiority of Iscor steel quickly died down.

South Africa departed from the gold standard in 1932 and the gold industry boomed as never before. The gold boom sparked off an era of industrial development which wiped out unemployment, pushed the national budget from £35 millions annually to £150

millions a decade later, and brought secondary industry into first
place as the greatest contributor to the national income. In this
boom Iscor steel played a vital role. Iscor itself flourished beyond
the most optimistic expectations of its founders and expanded its
works to a site near Vereeniging where the new town of Van der
Bijl Park rose almost overnight from the brown veld. During World
War II Iscor became strategically important to the Allied cause,
providing steel for the manufacture of large quantities of war
equipment and ammunition used in the Western Desert and Italy.
When the war ended the factories were mostly switched to the production of civilian goods and the industrial boom continued apace.

South Africa has, in fact, never really paused in her industrial
stride since the era of development began with the increase in the
price of gold in 1932. The gold industry has been the great primer,
pouring over £150 millions annually into the economy in the shape
of wages and purchases, paying something like £20 millions in
direct taxes to the Treasury, and distributing double that figure in
dividends. Before 1932 there were confident forecasts by mining
experts that the gold industry would reach its peak by the middle
of the century and would thereafter decline as the mines were
worked out. Today it is clear that the industry will continue to
flourish for a century and more, so long as gold remains security
for the currencies of the world. Fresh mining areas are being opened
up every few years. Exciting technological discoveries give new
lives to the old mines. Refrigeration has made it possible to go down
almost 12,000 feet; cementation has solved the problem of holding
back vast floods of underground water; mechanisation has lowered
costs and speeded shaft-sinking and development-work in the stopes.

The story of the South African gold industry is a saga with
political and sociological aspects and a striking record of material
advancement. Gold certainly played a role in the outbreak of the
Anglo-Boer war. Yet without the gold industry, which stabilised the
economy and helped to balance the budget, Afrikaner Nationalism
could not have remained in power long enough to declare an independent republic and pursue the ideology of apartheid against the
opposition of the rest of the world. What gold lost for Afrikanerdom
in sparking off the Anglo-Boer war at the beginning of the century
it more than doubly repaid sixty years later. Who can say what
historic role gold may not yet again play for the South African
Republic during the fifty years that lie ahead?

Chapter 3

The Africans

I N THE early aftermath of the last Great War few people realised that a new problem of race relations, based on the colour of a man's skin, was soon to explode across the world. One of those who did read the portents correctly and was much disturbed was the late Jan H. Hofmeyr, the last of the old school of Cape Liberals. Hofmeyr was Minister of Finance in the Smuts government and the author recalls a conversation in his office at Union Buildings, in Pretoria, late one Friday afternoon in the year 1947. Signs of the overwork that killed him two years later already showed in his drawn face. He had been to address the Natives' Representative Council, a body created in 1936 to serve as a forum for African leaders to express their views, and there he had suffered a rebuff. There was a mood of deep frustration among Africans. They were sick of making requests and giving advice to which nobody listened, and they demanded rights and powers. They refused any longer to be treated as perpetual wards under white trustees and they insisted on taking part democratically in the machinery of government. They brushed aside a plea for patience from their great friend Hofmeyr and delivered an ultimatum : either some tangible notice must be taken of their demands for more effective representation in the councils of state or they would adjourn the Natives' Representative Council indefinitely.

Jan Hofmeyr was deeply troubled. The war had been fought to destroy the doctrine of race-supremacy, and Africans everywhere were demanding equality. Hofmeyr could sympathise with the demands but he saw great difficulties in conceding them. There were ominous rumblings throughout the continent, while in South Africa, among both blacks and whites, a more radical leadership was arising. Hofmeyr had on several occasions described South Africa as 'the world's most important laboratory of human relations' and now he realised with terrible clarity that the laboratory itself was in danger of blowing up.

When this book went to press, sixteen years after Jan Hofmeyr's untimely death, the total population of the Republic was a little

over sixteen millions, five millions larger than the population of
Australia and three millions smaller than that of Canada. There
were eleven million Africans, three million whites, one and a half
million coloureds, and half a million Asians, most of whom were
Indians. By government decree under the apartheid policy the
Africans had been divided into eight national units or 'ethnic
groups': Xhosa, Zulu, North Sotho, South Sotho, Swazi, Tsonga,
Tswana and Venda. The Xhosas, numbering about 31 per cent of
the total, were the most advanced group, and they lived in the
Transkei Territory, the first of the Bantustans. The Zulus, of kin-
dred stock and speaking a similar language, were scattered throughout Natal and Zululand. The Basuto, speaking a distinct language
of their own, inhabited the British protectorate of Basutoland and
spilled over into the Orange Free State (South Sotho) and some
districts of the Transvaal (North Sotho). The Swazis, akin to the
Zulus, lived in the British protectorate of Swaziland, spreading into
the Transvaal. The Tswanas, with their own distinct language,
inhabited the North-Western Cape Province and Western Transvaal, while the Tsongas and Vendas were found in the Transvaal.

But the pattern of distribution of these various tribes was nothing
like as tidy as might be supposed. With the exception of the Transkei, most of the tribal 'homelands' consisted of scattered pockets
with white-owned farms and villages between them. Moreover, only
about 37 per cent of the total African population actually inhabited
the rural 'homelands'. Roughly 32 per cent lived and worked in the
industrial towns of South Africa as a whole, such as Johannesburg,
Pretoria, Durban, Port Elizabeth and Cape Town, while the remaining 31 per cent lived on farms and in villages in the white-owned
rural areas. This distribution of Africans between the towns, the
white-owned farming areas and the reserves is an important fact to
bear in mind. Another significant fact, so frequently overlooked
when considering the situation in South Africa, is that according to
official census returns only 35 per cent of the total African population of the Republic is literate. As might be expected, the literacy-
rate is highest among the 32 per cent who live in the industrial
towns. In the urban areas a little over 50 per cent can read and
write, whereas in the 'homeland' reserves and the rural areas the
literacy-rate is only 22 per cent. Curiously enough African women
are more literate than their menfolk. The reason may well be that
the women are more realistic and see the value of education more
clearly than their menfolk do.

Let us now consider the life of an average rural African, one of
the 37 per cent in the 'homeland' reserves. We will take an infant

born in, say, a kraal in the Melmoth district of Zululand. His father has two wives, a dozen cattle, a few goats and two horses. He cultivates a patch of land that slopes a little too steeply to prevent furrowing by the tropical storms that rumble up from the Indian Ocean. The family live in a cluster of beehive grass huts on the slopes of a grassy hill falling away to a stream in the valley two hundred feet below. The hillside is criss-crossed with paths and scarred with soil-erosion. Close to the huts is a clump of aloes and here and there a thorn-tree waves its arms defiantly at the sky.

Should the infant Zulu succeed in avoiding dysentery, enteritis, pneumonia or one of the many other health-hazards that face him, he will run about naked until he is old enough to wear his first set of skins. The child-mortality rate among Africans in the rural areas is high, but precisely how high is not known since statistics are not available; compulsory registration of births and deaths was not extended to Africans until 1952 and has only been calculated for the urban areas. As soon as he is old enough, our young Zulu will go out to herd the cattle and goats. His father and older brothers must go into the towns in search of work – that is, if they can get permits from the Bantu Commissioner at Melmoth, twenty miles away. It is becoming increasingly difficult to obtain permits to seek work in the towns, since government policy is to limit the number of Africans there. Those already living in municipal houses in the townships, many of whom were born in the towns and know nothing of tribal control, naturally get first preference for the jobs that are going. If a rural African is fit enough he can go to work in the mines, and he may also seek work in the rural areas, in the villages and on 'white' farms. Even farm-work is not so easy to find, excepting during the seasonal rush, because too many families are living in the farming areas and many of them will have to find homes elsewhere.

However, let us hope that two or three menfolk in the kraal do succeed in obtaining work in the towns, on the mines or on a farm, for without the cash they send home the family would starve. The Tomlinson Commission, reporting in 1955, assessed the average income per rural African family of six at £100 per year, and half of this was reckoned to be earned by males working in the towns. The figure has probably increased since then to about £120 which works out at the pitifully small sum of £10 per month to keep a family and pay taxes and tribal levies. The harsh fact is that most of the African reserves are hopelessly overcrowded, seriously eroded and quite incapable of supporting their natural increase in population. In 1960 it was estimated that there were 505,000 'economically inactive' Africans in the Republic of whom 300,000 were in the rural areas and reserves. To put it more bluntly, there were 505,000 Africans unemployed, and this must be regarded as one of the most significant figures to be found among the economic statistics of South Africa. Its implications will be more fully explained in a later chapter.

If our young Zulu lives within walking or riding distance of a tribal school he will be given an opportunity of being educated within the framework of the Government's 'Bantu education' system. He will discard his skins and don a shirt and possibly a pair of shorts as well. He will be taught in his own language, and later on English and Afrikaans will be introduced as subjects. If he is bright enough and his parents can afford to keep him at school, he will be able to go through to matriculate at the age of about 18. He can then move on to one of the new tribal colleges where he can obtain a university degree. But a little over half those who enter the primary school drop out by the time they reach Standard II, while only one in forty reaches junior certificate level and only about one in 400 gets as far as the matriculation examination. Total matriculation passes in 1962 were 362. In the same year it cost about £6 10s. per head to teach African children in state and state-aided schools in the Republic compared with £72 10s. per head for white children. The Bantu education budget in 1963 was £10,765,000 of which £6,500,000 was a fixed statutory appropriation from the general revenue account of the national treasury. The Government refuses to increase this statutory contribution, declaring that the African people must pay for educational expansion out of their own pockets. In 1963 a sum of £3,900,000 was paid out of the general taxes levied on Africans, and the balance of £365,000 came from boarding fees and other sundry receipts.

Africans criticise the Bantu educational system for various reasons. First they object to the fact that it is run on an apartheid basis. They argue that principles of education are the same for all and that their own schools should be run and financed as part of the general educational system of the Republic as a whole. They want to be taught in English or Afrikaans from a much earlier age. They complain that school facilities are inadequate and that teachers' salaries are too low. In 1963 the Bantu education department employed 28,350 African teachers and 450 white teachers. Top salary-scale paid to married African teachers with matriculation and a professional certificate was £774 per annum, increased to £894 if he had a university degree. White teachers with university degrees were paid from £1,320 to £2,175 per annum.

When our young Zulu reaches the age of 16 he must obtain a

reference-book. This will dominate the rest of his life. It has a hard cover and looks something like a British passport, containing photograph, finger-prints, details of tribe and parents. There is space to be filled in by the employer whenever he obtains a job or is discharged. Every month the book must be initialled by the employer. All official endorsements, such as permission to enter a town in search of work, or an injunction that he may only work in a rural area or in a mine, must be stamped in the book. This reference-book must be carried at all times, and failure to produce it instantly on demand generally results in arrest and a night or so in gaol. Cases have been quoted in Parliament where Africans have been arrested outside the places where they work and have not been allowed to go inside and fetch their reference-books. This little brown book is used to enforce the system of influx-control, so deeply resented by the vast majority of Africans.

Life in the African 'homelands' is much the same throughout South Africa. The beehive grass huts of Natal and Zululand give way in other areas to mud-brick and even stone huts, some with thatched and others with corrugated-iron roofs. In some parts elaborate designs are painted on the mud walls. Climatic conditions vary strikingly, but almost everywhere the pattern of too little land, too great a degree of soil-erosion, overcrowding and poverty, is the same. The Government is making strenuous efforts to replan the rural areas, moving scattered kraals together into villages, contouring the land, and instructing the people on how to fertilise with cattle manure and compost. But it is an uphill fight against the traditional cattle-cult, against ignorance and a general spirit of suspicion and hostility to the authorities. In any case, it is difficult to see what prospect there can be of winning the fight against soil-erosion while the reserves remain overcrowded.

For the 3,500,000 or so Africans who live on white-owned farms conditions and prospects vary considerably. In Natal and the Transvaal, mostly in districts bordering reserves, there is a labour-tenant system under which an African is allowed to live on a farm with his family, to cultivate a plot of ground and graze a certain number of cattle on condition that he and his family work for the farmer for a specified period. Usually a small wage is paid and rations of maize-meal, sugar and meat are given. In between working for the farmer, such an African is free to seek work in the towns – if he can obtain a permit to enter a town. Where the farmer is progressive and well-disposed towards his labour-tenants, life for the African family concerned can be fairly congenial. But there are serious objections to the system. Some landowners allow unrestricted squatting, especially on what are known as 'labour farms', with the result that the land is soon eroded and destroyed, and a rural slum arises. The Government has tried for many years through legislation and other means to stop this practice, but the problem always is what to do with the surplus Africans crowding the labour farms. With the reserves overcrowded and Africans not allowed to move freely into the towns, where must they go?

However, farmers are increasingly moving away from the labour-tenant system to payment of cash wages supplemented with rations. Sometimes the African workers are given a share in the market prices obtained for crops. Where skilled work is involved, such as driving tractors and lorries, operating and repairing machinery, the tendency is to pay good wages. Furthermore, a great deal has been done in recent years to improve housing on the farms, and Africans living with their families under these conditions are among the most fortunate in the Republic. Most farmers supplement their regular labour with migratory labour at peak seasons, housing the migratory labourers in compounds.

In some areas, only migratory labour is employed, frequently obtained through recruiting-agents. Inevitably this has led to abuses by farmers and agents alike, exploiting rural unemployment due to influx-control. Almost half a million Africans working on farms and in small towns in the rural areas are foreigners who enter the Republic from Portuguese East Africa, the Rhodesias and Malawi. The fact that these foreign Africans continue to stream into the Republic in search of work despite apartheid and the pass-laws is often cited by supporters of the present regime as evidence that by and large the African is better off in the Republic than he is in any other neighbouring territory.

A serious blot on the farm-labour system, amounting to a scandal, is the procedure of hiring out African prisoners as labour to farmers. This is done mainly in parts of the Cape Province and the Transvaal. The procedure is that a group of farmers band together to build a gaol to specifications laid down by the Prisons Department. Africans convicted of minor offences, frequently under the pass-laws, are drafted out to the farms where they are housed in compounds, sleeping under lock and key, and working under African 'boss-boys' or foremen. The farmer provides rations and pays a small wage, part of which goes to the prisoner. There have been complaints of harsh treatment of prisoners and a number of cases of assault and even homicide have been heard by the courts. Allegations of assaults, bad food and poor quarters have been made in the Press and in Parliament. The Government seeks to justify the practice on the score that it is better to have prisoners gainfully employed in the open air than to keep them locked in cells.

So much for the rural African. Let us take a look at the 3,600,000 or so who live and work in the towns : in the Pretoria-Witwatersrand-Vereeniging industrial complex; in the major port of Durban; in the motor-manufacturing centre of Port Elizabeth; in the rapidly-expanding factory areas of the Cape Flats, and in smaller towns throughout the Republic. This total of around 3,600,000 does not include the half-million labourers employed in the mining industry, more than half of whom are recruited outside the borders of the Republic. Save for an insignificant fraction of family-men employed on surface operations, the mines are allowed to engage only migrant labourers who must return home when their contracts expire. Leaders in the mining industry like Mr. Harry Oppenheimer are not happy about this rigid insistence on migratory labour, and Mr. Oppenheimer himself led a movement to introduce family life to the gold-mines in the new developing areas of the Free State. The reaction of the Nationalist Government was sharp and emphatic : save for the surface-workers mentioned above, only migratory labour might be employed.

These African mine labourers live under hygienic conditions in large compounds and are adequately and scientifically fed, clothed and cared for. A fleet of aeroplanes is used to transport those who come from distant places like Barotseland and Northern Bechuanaland. An African miner returning after a six-months spell in the gold-mines can take back £50 to his family, and though this amount may appear small by overseas standards, the industry has no trouble at all obtaining recruits.

It is the policy of the Nationalist Government to reduce the total of Africans living and working in the urban areas. Inexorably, however, the number continues to rise as the population increases and industry makes its insatiable demands. The 3,600,000 in 1965 will almost certainly be over 4,500,000 ten years hence, no matter what steps may be taken to maintain influx-control and to open up factories on the fringes of the reserves.

Earlier in this chapter we discussed the living-conditions of a typical African born in one of the reserves. By contrast let us now consider the probable life of an infant born in the towns – say, in the sprawling complex of townships known as Soweto on the fringes of Johannesburg. The father of our infant is a Msuto, a member of the Sotho tribe living among the grassy, boulder-strewn mountains of Basutoland. He was one of those hundreds of thousands of Africans sucked into the towns during the early years of the last world war by the labour vacuum created by massive industrial development. There was nowhere for this great influx of workers to live; neither materials nor labour could be spared for housing, and in any case there were influential people who were firmly against building houses for Africans. After the war, they said, the Africans would have to go back to their reserves. But of course the Africans have never gone back and never will. They form an integral part of the economy of the towns. So our migrant Msuto joined the homeless throng which in desperation marched out to the fringes of the industrial cities and squatted on the bare veld, throwing up shacks of hessian, wattle poles, flattened paraffin tins, packing-cases and any other materials they could lay their hands upon. Our particular Msuto built himself a shack at Moroka, near Orlando in Soweto. His was one of the hundreds of shacks that mushroomed almost overnight. Hard on the heels of the men came the womenfolk, single women also seeking work, prostitutes and teenagers fleeing from parental control. Our Msuto took into his shack a Zulu girl who cooked for him, brewed beer as a sideline, and took custom in other ways. In due course a child was born, and nobody bothered to inquire too closely into his parentage. There were other children, too, and after a few years, when the Msuto man and the Zulu girl went on living together, they were generally accepted as being married. There are various ways for Africans to marry : they can merely live together for long enough, or, where tribal custom survives, the man can pay 'lobola' for the girl in cash or cattle, or the marriage can be registered. More rarely still, there can be a church wedding. Illegitimacy is rife and the infant-mortality rate is extremely high, though there has been an improvement in this regard since the shanty-towns have been cleared away.

It was in Moroka that the Rev. Michael Scott built his church of hessian and lived like the Africans in a shack, sharing their hardships and squalor through a particularly bitter winter. He strove to counter the inevitable racketeering and gangsterism that arose and to do the best he could to minister to the sick. There were times when he walked in serious danger of his life.

For the average child born in Moroka life was a stark and precarious affair. If he were lucky enough to escape the death-hazards of enteritis, pneumonia or one of the other prevalent diseases, he would play around among the rubbish-littered alleys between the shacks. When the parents went away to work or left on some errand, he remained unattended or was locked in the shack, if it could be made secure. The remarkable thing was how the Africans themselves, as the months went by, strove to better their own conditions and create congenial homes out of so very little. Working at the week-ends, the Africans in Moroka made bricks of mud which were then baked in the sun, and they built walls inside the tin and hessian of their shacks. Sometimes the hessian, plastered with mud, was used ingeniously for a ceiling to keep out the heat and cold. Where a man could afford to buy second-hand corrugated-iron he could boast a good roof, otherwise he made his roof of flattened tins, odd pieces of damp-course salvaged from building-sites at the factories, and thatch if he could get hold of it. Linoleum was laid on the earth-stamped floor. Walls were plastered and colour-washed. About every hundred shacks was served by a block of communal pit-lavatories, hastily erected by the local authorities and filthy in the extreme. In due course, as part of a post-war slum-clearance project, the shacks and self-built homes of Moroka and of other similar shanty-towns around Johannesburg and the other industrial centres were demolished and the families moved to new Council-built three-roomed and four-roomed brick houses, each with its own water supply and water-borne sewerage. The Municipality of Johannesburg built over 60,000 such homes and continues to build at the rate of about 2,000 a year. Africans themselves have built a further 2,000 under supervision. In Soweto there are 110 schools catering for about 75,000 children. Street-lighting has been provided and electricity is being introduced to some of the homes.

African workers living in the townships travel into the industrial and commercial areas of Johannesburg by train and bus and the fares are subsidised. Extensive housing schemes on similar lines have been completed or are in the process of being carried out in other towns of the Witwatersrand, in Durban, East London, Port Elizabeth and on the Cape Flats. At the time of writing about £5 millions a year is being spent on housing schemes for Africans. Broadly speaking it may be said that a considerable degree of success has been achieved by the Government, which provided most of the money, and by local authorities who carried out the construction work. But there is one grave flaw in the whole scheme. Under the apartheid policy no African is allowed to own land in a so-called 'white' area. He cannot obtain freehold title, and the longest lease is 30 years. Moreover the conditions under which he is allowed to remain in a town are uncertain. He can be ordered to leave if he is out of a job for too long, or if he fails to pay his rent, or if he commits a serious crime. Home-ownership is, accordingly, most difficult to achieve. In all the newer townships the Government insists on Africans being grouped according to their tribal affiliations, even when they no longer owe allegiance to any particular tribe. The average African has little choice of where to live and must take what house he is lucky enough to have allocated to him. A very few wealthier Africans – traders, doctors or professional men – have built their own homes to their own designs. Rent for the ordinary home varies between £3 10s. and £5 per month depending upon the size of the house and the man's income.

Single, migratory Africans not in domestic service in one of the 'white' suburbs are, for the most part, housed in compounds built by the municipality. Some of the older compounds are squalid and overcrowded, while those more newly-built are uncongenial and austere. Another important group of 'single' Africans occupies the servants' quarters of the comfortable homes owned by whites in the residential suburbs. Almost every white householder employs one or two, and sometimes three African servants. There may be a maid who looks after the children, or who does the cooking or general housework. As often as not she takes in a lodger who is introduced as her 'husband'. The man-servant, known invariably as 'the boy' no matter how old he may be, cooks, or cleans floors, or works in the garden and waits at the table. He, too, generally takes in a lodger, a 'brother' or some other relative or friend. All this is quite illegal, but most householders turn a blind eye to it for the sake of peace in the servants' quarters. The authorities are trying to clear surplus Africans from the servants' quarters of white-owned homes through police raids and by threatening to prosecute householders, and the policy of the Government is to limit the number of servants who may reside on any property to one.

Wages of African domestic servants vary in different towns and suburbs, ranging from about £5 to £12 per month, all found. The general practice is to give a servant one free day per week, or two half-days off, working-hours being from about 6.30 a.m. until 8.30 p.m. with a two-hour break in the early afternoon. No recreation facilities of any kind are provided in the 'white' suburbs for African domestic servants and efforts by sympathetic whites to organise educational classes or some other form of leisure-time occupation have been prohibited by legislation. Prostitution is rife and despite strenuous police activity there is an extensive traffic in *dagga* (marijuana).

During recent years a great deal of public attention has been given to the question of wages earned by Africans in urban areas. An organisation known as the Bantu Wage and Productivity Association, created by businessmen, industrialists, and other interested

persons, reported towards the end of 1963 that the average monthly
income earned by the heads of African households in the townships of Johannesburg was around £21 10s. per month. The
poverty-datum line was reckoned to be £23 per month. This meant
that the majority of families were living well below the bread-line.
A movement to raise the wages of Africans is on foot among industrial and commercial men, but it is making slow headway.

The most important factors holding back the economic advancement of the African are the colour-bar in industry and lack of adequate training facilities. The colour-bar is applied in two ways.
Under a job-reservation law the Government issues proclamations
reserving certain categories of work for whites, while Africans are
simply not engaged as apprentices in a wide range of trades. Africans are not recognised under the Industrial Conciliation Act.
African trade-unions are not actually prohibited but are ignored by
the Government, and everything possible is done to discourage
them. A system of works committees for Africans has been created
to handle disputes and it is illegal for Africans to strike. Nevertheless a number of unofficial African trade-unions do exist and many
employers work with them.

Despite job-reservation and other restrictions, in practice the
colour-bar is being breached at many points. Demands for skilled
and semi-skilled labour in an expanding economy are so great that
Africans are engaged to do many jobs not controlled by white
trade-unions or which have so far escaped job-reservation. Even
where it is illegal to employ them, ways are often found of getting
round the regulations. Discreetly out of sight, they work as clerks,
typists, operators of computors and calculating-machines, mechanics
and operatives. Some fortunate few earn up to £100 per month.
Over 500 Africans in Johannesburg pay income tax in addition to
the special taxes and levies imposed on all adult Africans.

Though government policy is to maintain a tribal form of
authority in the townships as well as in the reserves, tribalism is
breaking down rapidly. There is extensive intermarriage, for one
thing. The urge of the African in the towns is to get away from
tribalism and develop along Western lines. Most homes in the townships are filled with modern furniture and many have radios and
some even refrigerators. There are separate cinemas for Africans
since under the apartheid laws no African may enter a 'white'
cinema, theatre, concert-hall, restaurant or tea-room. The African
cinemas are patronised by surprisingly well-dressed audiences.
Dances and socials are held in the townships at which many Africans wear immaculate evening-dress. There are beer-halls at which

both African and European types of liquor are consumed. Football, cricket, tennis and other games are played at the week-end.

Among Africans there is a great thirst for education and knowledge. Demands for reading material of all kinds, ranging from newspapers and magazines to paper-backs and library books, are increasing rapidly. Most of the schools work in two shifts, and even then the school facilities are woefully inadequate. The 'typical child' mentioned earlier – the son of a Msuto man and Zulu girl – will have gone to school until the age of 11, if he was lucky enough to avoid becoming a juvenile delinquent and was able to get a place in a school. On leaving he may have found work as a newspaper delivery-boy, and the next step would be a job in a factory, or in the municipality or on the railways, or as a labourer in a score of different industries, or as a messenger, or selling petrol at a filling-station. Though pay-rates are comparatively low and jobs artificially restricted, the wage-trend is upward and the African is pressing insistently against the barriers of job-reservation.

Chapter 4

The Others

A N IMPOSING new block of latest design stands among a cluster of State and semi-official offices at the foot of Union Buildings in the tree-lined capital city of Pretoria. It is the Population Registry. It contains the particulars of every man, woman and child within the Republic, recorded on cards and in files, classified, mechanised, and filed in modern steel cabinets, so that a man's identity number can be extracted with a minimum of delay and his race and ethnic group determined for a dozen different purposes.

This new building is the inner shrine of apartheid, the remote, immutable authority that fixes every human being in the racial category in which he must work and play, choose his friends and marry, travel and make his home. It was created by one of the earliest measures of the Nationalist regime, the Population Registration Act of 1950. The Act provided for a national register to contain the name of every individual 'who shall be classified as either a white person, a coloured person or a Bantu ... and every coloured person and every Bantu shall be further classified according to the ethnic or other group to which he belongs'. A white person was defined as a person who was obviously white in appearance or was generally accepted as white. A more scientific definition would have been awkward for many people, even in high places, since there are well-known families with a forbear or so who could not have been classified white even within the broad terms of the Population Registration Act.

The Registrar, whose duty it is to compile the register, has on the whole been generous with those who had managed to crash the colour-barrier, but obviously it was impossible to avoid stark tragedy to hundreds on the borderline. To be 'white' in South Africa carries such privileges, such legal and economic advantages, and such social status that the temptation to try for white must have been overwhelming. There were a few – very few – instances where individuals offered 'white' classification declared proudly and even defiantly that they preferred to share the lot of their own coloured folk. There were hundreds who protested bitterly that they had been classified 'coloured' when they ought to be white. To be pushed down a class meant social degradation, having to move out of a 'white' suburb and even the loss of a job.

Provision was made in the Act for a board to consider doubtful cases and for an appeal to the law courts from the board's decision. During the past decade, while the Register has been in the process of compilation, there have been some heartrending cases before the board and the courts, and the full extent of human misery involved in these proceedings may never be known. If a man were lucky enough to be classified 'white' he would receive an identity card four inches long and three inches deep, made of two sheets of cellophane fused together over a square of special green paper on which an automatic machine with a 'memory' device had printed the name, a number running into nine digits, and the all-important letter 'W' denoting white. In the top left-hand corner was a photograph, the size of a postage-stamp. This card is needed for a marriage certificate, a passport and a wide range of official documents. When the law can be suitably amended it will be needed to vote at an election.

Let us now consider how and where the privileged holders of the green identity cards, the three million whites, men and women, live and work. The largest concentration, as might have been expected, is to be found in the Pretoria-Witwatersrand-Vereeniging industrial complex in the Transvaal, which has roughly a third of the white population. The other two-thirds are spread around the industrial towns of Natal and the main economic centres of the Free State and Cape Province. The farming community is most dense where the rainfall is highest and where there are irrigation settlements. The ratio of town and country population is roughly seventeen whites in the towns to two on the land.

Living-standards of the whites in South Africa are among the most comfortable and luxurious to be found anywhere in the world. Almost every family owns at least one and very often two cars and has one or more domestic servants. The long rows of terraced houses in which most Londoners live are utterly unknown in the Republic. Most houses are of the bungalow type, standing back in their own half-acre or quarter-acre plots, and the few that are semi-detached belong to a past era in building. Apartments range from one-roomed bachelor flats, each with its own kitchenette and bathroom, costing around £15 per month to rent, to luxurious six-roomed flats in fashionable areas rented at £100 per month.

The average white artisan earning from £80 to £120 per month, married and with, say, two children, lives in a four-roomed or five-roomed bungalow-type house which he buys through a building-society for £3,000 to £5,000 or rents for £15 to £25 per month. Income tax is low, rates and taxes to local authorities are modest, and costs of food, fuel and clothing average out to about the same level in Johannesburg as in London. Sport and entertainment generally cost far less in South Africa than they do in Britain. Education is free unless a child is sent to a private school, and a university training can be had for as little as £120 per year. There is a State unemployment benefit fund to which employers contribute and most employers offer medical and pension funds on a contributory basis.

The policy of the Government is to protect white workers through job-reservation, and, as explained in the last chapter, a colour-bar is maintained through the operation of the Industrial Conciliation Act and the procedure through which apprentices are admitted into most of the trades. Some idea of the spread of work between the different races and of comparative incomes may be obtained from a series of reports published by the State Bureau of Census and Statistics in 1963, covering industries and professions. As might be expected, whites dominated the skilled occupations and non-whites the labouring jobs. In professional and technical posts there were 132,546 whites, 13,830 coloureds, 5,124 Asians and 48,714 Africans. Moving over to manual labour the count was: farmers, fishermen, lumbermen and farm-labourers 115,765 whites, 126,093 coloureds, 10,061 Asians and 1,480,762 Africans. For miners and quarrymen the figures were: 31,633 whites, 3,287 coloureds, 182 Asians and 524,716 Africans.

The wide gap in earnings between whites and other races is shown by figures published in the official *Bulletin of Statistics* for 1962. In mining, for example, whites earned an average wage per year of £1,217 compared with £205 for coloureds and Asians and £74 for Africans. The figure for Africans, however, did not include the value of free housing, food, medical attention and other benefits which probably amounted to an additional £100, bringing the figure for Africans up to around £174. In manufacturing, the earnings per annum were: whites £977, coloureds and Asians £301, and Africans £196. On construction work: whites £995, coloureds and Asians £400, and Africans £183. Average yearly wages paid in the great State-owned railway administration were: whites £934, and non-whites £163. For the Public Service: whites £819, coloureds £285, Asians £366 and Africans £193. It may be of interest to mention that in the 1961–62 tax-year, 887,150 whites paid £77,898,000 in income tax; 103,046 coloureds paid £836,000; 21,089 Asians paid £676,000; and 556 Africans paid £23,000.

When considering the appalling gap in earnings disclosed by such figures it must, of course, be remembered that the whites brought their skills and knowledge, won over many centuries of industrial experience, to South Africa, and that without their initiative and drive the country would in all probability have remained a primitive backwater. The Africans, on the other hand, have only comparatively recently emerged from their tribal way of life. More than half of them are still illiterate and live under the influence of the witch-doctors. These facts, of course, in no way justify the colour-bar in business and industry, nor is it the only reason for the frightening disparity in the living-standards of whites and non-whites.

What the economic position would have looked like today had there been no official and unofficial colour-bars in commerce and industries, and had Africans been apprenticed, trained and allowed to rise to their full capabilities, is not easy to determine. Would costs of mining gold and coal, smelting steel, and producing food have risen to uneconomic heights? Or would it have been possible without hampering economic development to level out earnings and profits, lowering the extremely high living-standards for whites and raising the unduly low living-standards for non-whites? There is a school of economists who hold that the industrial revolution in South Africa would have been faster, broader and more massive had there been no colour-bars and had employers been free to recruit and train whatever labour was available.

Job-reservation and the colour-bar were designed to protect whites against competition from non-whites. In other words the inefficient white is being propped up at the expense of the more capable non-white, and this must be a drag on progress. Apartheid and the migratory-labour system are also being used to ensure a supply of cheap manual labour to the mines, commerce, industry and agriculture, and who knows what price is being paid in social disruption, discontent and inefficiency?

But we must return to the conditions under which the majority of whites live. The climate is agreeable in most parts of the country and South Africans are keen on outdoor life. They motor many miles to picnic at week-ends and on the many public holidays. There are hundreds of attractive resorts in the mountains, beside the rivers, and all around the long coastline. Places such as the Kruger National Park, with its excellent camping facilities, are crowded to capacity during the season. South Africa has a splendid network of national and secondary roads and it is possible to travel fast by car to all parts at all times of the year. Petrol costs less than in Europe and the prices of most cars are about the same as they are in Britain. This is explained by the fact that there is no purchase-tax in the Republic as in Britain. Both rail and air travel are comfortable and relatively inexpensive. The best hotels are not as luxurious or well-appointed as in Europe or the United States but generally speaking the hotels are comfortable and the traveller gets very good value for his money. Catering standards are high and if one knows one's way around one can get as delicious a meal, with excellent South African sherries, wines and brandies, as can be found almost anywhere in the world. A Mecca for gourmets is the small village of Albertinia, in the wheat-country of the Western Cape. The local hotel, built round a square off the main street, and looking for all the world like a dozen other nondescript hotels in the rural towns, prides itself on traditional South African dishes, and no connoisseur of food should hasten by.

All these excellent holiday resorts and travelling facilities are available to South Africans if they are lucky enough to be included in the green-card section of the Population Register. But if they happen to be coloured, Asian or African it is a different story. Few holiday resorts are open to the non-white. There are only a very few hotels for him, in the larger centres, and no hotel, motel, guest-house or camping-sites for whites will take a non-European. Apartheid is enforced on the beaches. Africans may not travel on the luxury trains and when they do travel by train they must use separate coaches or compartments reserved for them. A non-white must enter a railway station, post-office or Government department through separate doorways reserved for him. In most towns he must travel in a separate bus and he may not enter a cinema, concert-hall, restaurant, bar or tearoom reserved for whites. In a big city such as Johannesburg there are few places where a mixed gathering of any kind can be held and the policy is to limit such places. An anomaly is that Africans can still shop freely wherever they care to go, and they patronise the bazaars, department-stores and most exclusive shops. So far the sharp eye of a colour-conscious Government has not fallen upon the shops, and possibly business considerations may have been responsible for this oversight. The spending-power of the African section of the population was reckoned in 1963 to be about £400 millions a year, and there is no doubt that without their African custom many so-called 'white' shops would close.

White South Africans, especially supporters of the Nationalist Government, resent the accusation that the Republic is a 'police state'. Look at the Parliament, they declare, where comment is free and aspects of apartheid are frequently and unrestrainedly condemned by opposition speakers. Look at the English-language Press which does not hesitate to denounce the policies and actions of the Government. Consider the fact that there is no internal or external censorship of news. Consider also the law courts, in which all races are given a fair hearing. How, in the face of these things, can it possibly be said that South Africa is a 'police state'?

The answer depends, firstly, on what precisely is meant by the term 'police state', and, secondly, whether or not one happens to have a white skin. For the non-white, and especially for the African, South Africa is undeniably a 'police state' by any interpretation of the term. The African must carry a pass and is liable at all times to be stopped by a policeman and asked to show it. If he does not have it on him or if the policeman is not entirely satisfied with the answers to his questions, the African is bundled into a police van. An African's home is liable to be raided by the police at any time of day or night. An African may be banished indefinitely to some remote place if the Special Branch of the Police consider him to be an 'agitator'. This is done by ministerial edict and there is no appeal to the courts. Under one or other of various restrictive laws and regulations an African may be held almost indefinitely without a specific charge being framed against him. The Asian and coloured man have more rights and are not harassed in the same way under the pass-laws, but for them the Republic is unquestionably a 'police state' too.

The average white is inclined to regard democracy as one of the privileges, but what he fails to see is that in imposing restrictions on non-whites he has been steadily curtailing his own democratic freedoms. How serious this erosion of rights has been during the past fifteen years was shown in a book by Dr. Edgar Brookes and Mr. J. B. Macaulay Q.C. on *Civil Liberty in South Africa*. After making an exhaustive study of restrictive legislation since the Nationalists assumed power, these eminent authorities wrote :

'Whether or not we agree with the principle of the rule of law, we must agree that immense inroads have been made into it in South Africa especially (though by no means solely) during recent years. . . . The rule of law has in fact been challenged extensively on points that affect intimately the lives of thousands of citizens. That fact cannot be challenged';

'Almost the whole of the African's life is now governed by administrative decisions, appeal from which to the courts has been deliberately denied by Parliament';

'The new concept of the police function tends to clothe the police force with the character of the political police of authoritarian rule';

'That these conditions [in the various laws analysed by the authors] have inhibited freedom of discussion and speech is certain. ... Both the individual and the Press must necessarily exercise warily the right to express opinions, with a caution which cannot be healthy and conducive to a proper working of parliamentary government. ... That legal avenues and media of expression continue to remain open is not enough if intimidation and fear of the sanctions of administrative disapproval so rule his mind that the subject will no longer take the risk of using even these media.'

Dr. Brookes and Mr. Macaulay wrote their book before the African National Congress and Pan-African Congress were banned and before the law was passed which enables the police to hold a man of any colour for ninety days at a time for questioning. For the privileged white it may be arguable whether, semantically, South Africa can be termed a 'police state'. But if a white believes that he is living even in a 'whites-only' democracy he is suffering from a delusion. The fact is that it is easier and far more comfortable to conform with the conventions of apartheid, and that is precisely what the vast majority of South Africans do. The result is that though most whites have African servants and though whites and non-whites work alongside one another and talk to each other throughout the day, a great gulf yawns between them. For example, the average white has never even seen Soweto, where most Africans in Johannesburg live. No white person may enter an African township without a permit. Moreover, too close an interest in the African could prove intellectually and even physically uncomfortable, since it might invite the attentions of the Special Branch of the police.

For the white living in the rural areas it is different. Unless he lives in the Western Province of the Cape and employs coloureds, his farm-workers will be Africans living in houses, huts or compounds on the farm. As a rule he speaks their native language as fluently as they do. In all probability he played with African piccaninnies when he was a child. Relations between white and black are friendly, in a feudalistic kind of way, so long as the African understands his place as a servant and keeps it.

South Africa has two official languages, English and Afrikaans, a simplified and modified form of the Dutch spoken by the early settlers of the Cape. Of the three million whites about 60 per cent speak Afrikaans in their homes and approximately 40 per cent English. A child is taught in his home-language at school and he takes the other

official language as a compulsory subject. According to a recent
census some 73 per cent of whites speak both languages and the percentage is steadily increasing. Both English and Afrikaans are used
in Parliament, the Provincial Councils, the majority of town councils, the courts, and at meetings of a wide range of semi-official and
private bodies. English is still the predominant language in commerce, while Afrikaans is spoken mostly in the civil service, police,
railway administration, in the armed forces, on the mines and in
many industries. It is the language mainly used in the rural areas.

Afrikaans is also the language spoken by most of the million and
a half coloureds, who are classified as a distinct racial group and
are to have a form of self-rule under the apartheid plan. The origin
of the coloureds is interesting. They are not, as is sometimes
assumed, the progeny of whites and Bantu, though there has, of
course, been intercourse between whites and blacks, accounting for
a small percentage of coloureds in more recent times. The first
white settlers in South Africa arrived in 1652 when Jan van Riebeeck was sent out by the Dutch East India Company with three
ships to set up a depot at the Cape. The countryside around Table
Bay was at that time inhabited by a few Bushmen, with whom the
early whites had almost no contact, and some scattered tribes of
Hottentots. Labour was needed by the whites, and since the Hottentots were reluctant to work, ships were sent to fetch slaves from the
Guinea coast. As the years passed, further batches of slaves were
brought from Madagascar and the Malay Archipelago, and by the
year 1700 the population of the Cape settlement consisted of about
1,600 whites of mixed Dutch, German, French, Danish and Swedish
stock, with the Dutch predominating, and 1,100 slaves from West
Africa, Madagascar and Malaya.

Intermarriage between whites and non-whites was officially encouraged in the early years of the settlement, and many of the
whites took Hottentot, Malay and Negro women as their wives.
At one period there was a considerable importation of Malays and
their womenfolk, so that the Malay strain is strong in the blood
of the coloureds. The Malays also succeeded in preserving their own
exclusive community, with its distinct culture and food, and its
music and songs which help to give Cape Town so attractive a
personality of its own.

For something like 200 years the coloureds have formed the main
labour force of the Western Cape. Bantu from the north did not, in
fact, reach the Cape Peninsula until modern times, as will be
related in a later chapter. Coloureds worked in the vineyards and
on the wheatfields; they were the builders and carpenters, the

manual labourers at the docks, on the roads and on the railways. They were the gardeners and domestic servants. After the liberation of the slaves they were given the rights of citizens and they voted for the old Cape Parliament and other public bodies. Some of them rose to positions of high standing in the community. But, in general, they were regarded as a less-intelligent, less-dependable, somewhat inferior segment of the community. This was due, partly, to their humble origins and to the fact that they were, in the main, the labouring class. It may also have been due to the pernicious effects of the 'tot system' that came to be adopted by the farming community, under which part of a coloured labourer's wage was paid to him in daily rations of cheap but often potent wine. The system persists to this day and is responsible for a great deal of drunkenness and degeneracy. But fortunately other and more constructive forces are at work among the coloured people, who are fast becoming recognised as a human asset of great value to the Republic. They have been caught up in the industrial boom that brought a vigorous crop of new factories to the Cape Peninsula. Their incomes and living-standards have risen dramatically in recent years and the time is fast approaching when their demands for equality with the whites will be impossible to resist.

The greatest concentration of coloureds is in and around the Cape Peninsula, with settlements in Namaqualand, along the Orange River, at Kimberley in the North-Western Cape Province, in the towns of the Karoo, in and around Port Elizabeth and the towns and villages of the Cape Eastern Province; in Johannesburg, and, to a small extent, in a few areas of Natal. Nine out of every ten coloureds speak Afrikaans in their homes.

The half-million Asians consist mostly of Indians with a small sprinkling of Chinese who are mainly traders and live quietly and unobtrusively unto themselves. Officially the apartheid laws apply to them as well as to other non-whites, but in practice there has been a tendency to be lenient with this group. Nobody bothered too much if they slipped quietly into cinemas or restaurants, and a few managed to live unobtrusively in 'white' suburbs, sending their children to exclusive white schools. However, the Chinese fall under the Group Areas Act in relation to their business activities, and the various other limitations imposed on non-whites by the apartheid policy are steadily closing in upon them.

Indians were introduced to the British colony of Natal in 1860 as labour for the sugar industry. Zulus were reluctant to work in the canefields and a serious shortage of labour developed. Many of the planters had connections with the sugar-growing island of

Mauritius, in the Indian Ocean, which at that time was booming as a result of the importation of indentured labour from India. Why, asked the planters of Natal, should not they, too, employ indentured labour from India? The Government of India was most reluctant to entertain the idea, but in the end the Indian labourers were allowed to come over, followed by their families and by traders who set up stores in Natal and the Transvaal.

By the time the flow of Indians was stopped fifty years later a large, vigorous, and permanent community had established itself in Natal. It has spread into the Transvaal and Cape Province but Asians are not allowed to enter the Free State. Unlike the Chinese, who are so small in number, the Indians are both vocal and politically active. It was in Natal that Mahatma Gandhi carried out his first passive-resistance campaign and succeeded in wringing important concessions from the government of the day.

Of all sections in race-conscious South Africa, Asians have aroused the greatest hostility and have suffered most through discriminatory legislation. Relations between them and the Africans are uneasy and the Indian community in Durban were brutally attacked by Zulus in one of the worst riots in recent years. Politically, the strongest organised body of Asians aligned itself with the Africans, but this has not prevented an underlying hostility between Africans and Indians based largely on personal relationships. Asians are charged, probably quite unjustly, with exploiting Africans in their trading activities, and with associating with African women. Moreover, Asians can be made to play the role of scapegoat. Whereas the white man is strongly armed and backed by the police, the Indian, whom nobody loves, is more open to attack.

The Group Areas Act, designed by the Nationalist Government to sort out the different races into the areas where they may reside, own businesses and establish factories, has hit the Indian community most severely of all. In many large and small towns of Natal, the Transvaal and the Cape Province, they are in the process of being moved out of homes and businesses which they have occupied for many years. The new areas where they are settled are generally far from the centres of economic activity upon which they have hitherto depended. An idea of the size of the operation may be gleaned from the fact that out of the 231,000 Indians in the town of Durban alone, 100,000 had been affected by Group Areas proclamations up to the end of 1963. Some 70,000 were already living in a state of great uncertainty, expecting at any moment to be ordered to move elsewhere.

There is machinery for compensation for properties that have to be evacuated and for financial assistance in building homes and shops in the new areas to which Indians have to move. But the compensation is usually inadequate and nothing is paid for loss of trading goodwill. For most traders the order to move means in effect an order to close business. In Johannesburg, to give an example, Indians from various parts have to move to a new township called Lenasia, twenty miles away. At the time of writing it had no street lights, no water-borne sewerage, no hospitals or clinics, and no recreational facilities excepting at the schools. Many families settled there are already behind with their rents and there is a good deal of unemployment. A typical suburb in Johannesburg from which non-whites had to move was Martindale, which contained 70 Indian traders with more than 500 persons dependent upon them. Some had lived there for over 40 years. Of 31 traders who had left by the end of 1963, only 7 succeeded in finding other premises. Eleven became unemployed, one died and the rest managed to find jobs as waiters and shop-assistants.

With the exception of a very small number of relatively wealthy merchants, Indians in South Africa are poor, and many of them live in slum conditions. Their progress in industry is restricted by the colour-bar, they may not buy land and property outside the areas proclaimed for their own use, and they may not move without permission from one province to another. If an Indian should marry outside South Africa he may not bring his wife into the Republic, nor may he bring in any children born outside the borders. Indians work as labourers, small farmers, waiters, shop-assistants and traders and in a variety of industrial and commercial jobs not yet closed to them by the laws of apartheid. They are an industrious, intelligent people capable of making a considerable contribution to the economic development of South Africa, if only given an opportunity to do so. The Government would like them to move to India and promises to meet the costs of such a migration, but most of them have been in South Africa for two or three generations and they refuse to go.

Politically, the Indian community are both active and vocal. They are divided into two movements, the S.A. Indian Congress and the S.A. Indian Organisation. Congress is by far the larger and more militant body, claiming 'mass support', while the Indian Organisation includes a smaller but wealthier section of business and professional men. Owing to the fact that many of their leaders and officials have been placed under restrictive orders by the Government, both these bodies have been relatively inactive in recent months. They opposed the creation by the Government in

1964 of a National Indian Council, arguing that acceptance of this purely advisory body would imply endorsement of apartheid and would destroy the hopes of the Indian community of ultimately obtaining representation in Parliament and the other legislative bodies. However, after a great deal of heart-searching, 21 prominent Indians agreed to serve on the National Council, arguing that this at least might provide an opportunity for presenting the grievances of the Indian people to the Government.

Chapter 5

The Apartheid Plan

THE NATIONALIST PARTY rode to power on the slogan of 'apartheid'. It was a broad term meaning separation of the races, but all those who voted for it knew that it also implied *baasskap*, which is the political term in South Africa for white domination. The word 'apartheid' was coined by Mr. Paul Sauer, who was chairman of a special sub-committee of the Nationalist Party appointed to draw up a programme for the 1948 general election.

Mr. Sauer's committee made no attempt to prepare a detailed plan indicating how apartheid was to be applied. Many leaders of the party were, in fact, opposed to any attempt being made to announce details. It was in its detailed application that all the difficulties would obviously arise. The leader of the party, Dr. D. F. Malan, was an old and experienced political campaigner and he knew the value of generalisations that could not be so readily attacked by his opponents. In any case, the Nationalists did not expect to win the election, but having done so they had to make a show of delivering apartheid. So Dr. Malan began with some of the more obvious and spectacular forms of separation that could be enforced without too many difficulties. Separate entrances were decreed for whites and non-whites to railway stations and public buildings. Railway passengers were ordered to ride in separate coaches, and bills were introduced in Parliament providing for separate group-areas and amenities of various kinds. When questions were asked about the increasing number of Africans in 'white' towns, about territorial separation, political rights and how the coloureds and Asians would be fitted into the scheme of things, Dr. Malan became vague. He publicly reproved a deputation from a group of Afrikaans churchmen and intellectuals who called for territorial apartheid in the true sense of the term. Nothing, he said, would be done that might have an adverse effect on the economy.

It was left to another man who at first was not even a member of the Government to give form and content to apartheid. He was Dr. Hendrik Verwoerd, formerly Professor of Psychology at the

University of Stellenbosch and at the time editor of the Nationalist newspaper in the north, *Die Transvaler*. Tall, blond and heavily-built, with a forceful and aggressive personality, Dr. Verwoerd was born in Holland, migrated to South Africa with his missionary parents, lived for a few years as a child in the Orange Free State, then moved to Southern Rhodesia where he attended high-school. Studying first at the University of Stellenbosch and later in Germany, he obtained a doctorate in Psychology and returned to become Professor of Psychology at Stellenbosch. There he soon identified himself with the radical intellectual wing of the Nationalist Party and joined the secret and influential Broederbond society. Leading a movement to oppose the admission into South Africa of Jewish refugees from Nazi Germany shortly before the war, he caught the eye of J. G. Strydom, who was leader of the Nationalists in the Transvaal. Strydom was looking for someone to edit a new Nationalist daily newspaper in Johannesburg, *Die Transvaler*, and he offered the post to Dr. Verwoerd, who took it, to the surprise of everybody.

Dr. Verwoerd quickly became a power within the ranks of Nationalists in the north. Applying his professional knowledge of psychology with skill and determination, he not only established *Die Transvaler* as a crusading newspaper, but he planned and directed a propaganda campaign that helped to consolidate the Party as a formidable political movement. His mind worked on blue-print lines. He spent long hours late at night drawing diagrams and drafting involved memoranda to explain them. He sat on the inner executives of both the Broederbond and the Party and is reputed to have been the author of the strategic plan of campaign that returned so many Nationalists to Parliament in the Transvaal, thus securing the triumph of 1948.

He disagreed with Dr. Malan that apartheid should remain a vague concept. He had spent the war years drafting a republican constitution for South Africa modelled on that of the old Transvaal under Paul Kruger, and he set about preparing a detailed blue-print for apartheid complete with 'bantustans' or separate Bantu states. He gathered about himself a group of enthusiasts, some of whom later helped him implement the plan. The first step was to get himself appointed Minister of Native Affairs, and he then set about reorganising the Department into a state-within-a-state with its own educational, agricultural, labour, social-welfare, justice and propaganda activities. His was the most insistent, most persuasive voice in the Cabinet and in Parliament. He introduced bill after bill, establishing tribal authorities, tribal courts, a separate system

BANTUSTANS

of 'bantu' education, African labour bureaus, tighter control over movement into the towns, control over African businesses, more efficient administration of the pass-laws, and other measures to enforce the system of 'autogenous development', as he called it. Methodically, step by step, he unrolled his apartheid blue-print, but the plan could not be seen in its entirety until after he became Prime Minister in 1958 and his position in supreme control of the Party was assured.

The apartheid concept is based on the assumption that different races – more especially whites, blacks and coloureds – cannot live harmoniously together as an integrated community. The plan is to separate the races at every point where this can be done without creating economic difficulties for industry, commerce, mining and agriculture. Each 'ethnic group' must be allowed to develop as far as it is capable of progressing, on its own lines and within its own sphere of activity. If there is no separate territory in which a group can have its 'heartland', then the group must as far as possible evolve a separate way of life within the territory it shares with another group. This means separate tearooms, transport, homes, churches, recreational facilities and places of entertainment. The groups can work together but they must drop into their own spheres when the shift is done. Even at work they will come under different controls, enter the factories through different doors, use different lavatories, change and eat in different rooms.

The African reserves lie in a great fragmented horseshoe, with the right leg resting on the Great Fish River north-east of Port Elizabeth, and the curve of the horseshoe extending up between Basutoland and the sea through Natal and Zululand, over Swaziland through the eastern and northern Transvaal, then downwards again between Bechuanaland and the Orange Free State to form the left leg resting almost on the Orange River. The total extent of 'scheduled' and 'released' areas plus land still to be bought for occupation by Africans amounts to 19,611,000 morgen, or about 65,000 square miles out of the Republic's total area of 472,000 square miles – roughly 13.8 per cent of the area of the Republic. The idea is to tidy up all these fragments into eight 'consolidated' blocks, each to be the 'heartland' of a tribal unit. The British protectorates of Basutoland, Swaziland and Bechuanaland are visualised as eventually forming part of the overall Bantustan scheme, which would then mean that Africans would occupy an area of 357,421 square miles, or approximately 47 per cent of the total area of South Africa. At the present time the Government is not pressing for the inclusion of the Protectorates in the Republic, but the assumption is that ultimately they will of their own accord link up with the Republic.

A map has been officially drawn showing what the eight 'heartlands' will be like when consolidated. Even after they have been tidied up, there is only one with any pretensions to being a solid, contiguous territory. This is the Transkei, the first Bantustan to be set up. The rest will remain scattered clusters of African settlements interspersed with white-owned corridors and blocks of farms and looking for all the world like a ragged archipelago spread around the northern areas of the Republic.

An Act of the South African Parliament passed in 1959 laid down how each of these tribal units was to be governed. At the head of the administration, rather like the governor in a British colony, is a white commissioner-general. He represents the Republican Government and is the political link with the African authority in the tribal unit. Inside the unit is a three-tier system of representation of Africans, with tribal authorities at the bottom, regional authorities in the middle, and a territorial authority or tribal parliament at the top. A tribal authority consists of a chief or headman and his councillors, elected according to tribal custom but requiring the endorsement of the Republican Government. They conduct tribal courts, allocate land for cultivation, supervise soil-conservation measures and generally manage the affairs of the clan. Fines and any tribal levies that may be agreed upon are paid into a tribal treasury.

A regional authority is the next senior body and exists for two or more tribal areas. It consists of the chiefs in the region together with a sprinkling of councillors nominated by each tribal authority. The regional authority elects its own chairman. It also has a treasury into which are paid levies and fees and its main tasks are to provide school buildings, construct by-roads, set up clinics and supervise agriculture and soil-conservation. It can pass by-laws to control these activities.

Then at the top is the territorial authority for the whole area of the tribal unit or 'heartland'. It consists of the chiefs of the tribal authorities plus a proportion of elected members. It serves as a co-ordinating body for the tribal unit and has limited powers to legislate on tribal affairs, to establish markets and pounds, keep an eye on tribal justice and the courts, the schools and by-roads, and to operate a treasury. A more responsible form of 'home-rule' has been given to one of the eight 'heartlands'. In the Transkei, where an elected council known as the Bunga had existed for many years, a new form of legislative assembly combining features of the Bunga and of the Bantu Authorities system has been created. The assembly consists of the paramount chiefs of the four main tribes in the territory, 60 chiefs and 45 members elected by popular vote. There is a Prime Minister and a cabinet of five others selected by the Prime Minister. Each cabinet minister heads a department administered by a white secretary, the intention being to replace these white civil servants with Africans in due course. There are about 2,500 civil service posts in the territory, of which 570 are held by whites.

The official language of the Transkei Parliament is Xhosa, but English, Afrikaans and Sesotho may also be used. All Africans, men and women alike, get the vote over the age of 21 (or 18 years of age if taxpayers). This Parliament controls its own budget and treasury and is responsible for protection of life and property, maintenance of law and order, control of tribal courts dealing with tribal law, control of land-settlement, agriculture, soil-conservation, veterinary services, irrigation, forestry, administration of estates, African local government institutions, education, welfare services, registration of births, deaths and marriages, licensing (other than arms), registration of voters, roads and bridges other than national roads, traffic, African labour, markets and pounds, and any other matters that may be delegated by the President of the Republic. The Republican Parliament at Cape Town retains control over defence, military units, external affairs, postal, telegraphic and radio services, railways, harbours, national roads, aviation, immigration, currency, public loans and banking, customs and excise, and the constitution of the Transkei. The official anthem is that stirring hymn heard all over Africa south of the Zambesi 'Nkosi Sikelel i-Afrika', and the Transkei is to have its own flag.

An attempt has been made to persuade the Zulus to adopt a similar form of 'home-rule', but the majority of Zulu chiefs and headmen are against the Bantustan apartheid plan and have declined to co-operate. The idea has, accordingly, been shelved for the time being and at the time of writing no other Bantustan was being organised on the Transkei model. So far territorial authorities have been set up in six out of the eight tribal units, while some 60 regional authorities and about 450 tribal authorities have been established.

Only about a third of the total African population of the Republic actually lives in these 'heartlands' and the apartheid plan is to link the other two-thirds living outside the tribal reserves closely with the 'heartlands'. Thus in the white man's towns, the first step has been to separate Africans from whites. Here the Group Areas Act was used and the map was redrawn with 'white' and African residential and business areas. Some African townships occupied for many years were declared 'white' and their inhabitants moved to new African townships. Africans were deprived of freehold title to land and they are not allowed to buy land anywhere outside the 'heartlands' reserved for them. A big job of rehousing Africans has been completed and is still going on. Though Africans cannot buy land outside the reserves, they may lease it for 30 years and build their own homes. They must regard themselves as 'temporary sojourners' in the white towns, liable to be moved out if they are unemployed for too long a period or fall foul of the authorities for one reason or another. Wherever possible the new townships are arranged in tribal sections, so that Africans belonging to the same tribal units can live together. Every African must declare his tribal affiliation, and if he does not do so or has long since lost all contact with a chief, or was born in the town and simply doesn't know to what tribe his father or grandfather belonged, he is given a tribal unit.

As far as possible the urban townships are being run on a tribal basis, with tribal courts. Urban Bantu Councils are being established, elected by popular vote and working under the supervision of the local municipality. They are responsible for whatever powers may be assigned to them by the local authority, such as water and sanitary services, maintenance of streets, control of traffic and collection of rates. To illustrate how this works out in practice, let us take the case of a Xhosa family-man living in, say, Orlando Township and working as a 'machine-boy' in a printing firm in Johannesburg. He was born in Johannesburg and has long since abandoned tribal life in favour of the Western way of life, but his father hailed from Tsolo in the Transkei, so he belongs officially to the Xhosa 'heartland' of the Transkei. He has a vote for the candidate in the Transkei Parliament for Tsolo, which he exercises by post since he cannot go to Tsolo and in fact has never been there. He will also get a vote for the local Bantu Council when one is formed to replace the existing Advisory Council for Orlando. Apart from these two votes he has no political rights whatever. In Johannesburg, at work or buying in the shops, or travelling to his township, he falls under the laws of the Republic but will never be allowed to have any say in them. He must orientate himself and his family towards the Transkei. In Johannesburg he is a 'temporary sojourner', little better off than an alien excepting that he has a few very limited rights in Orlando plus the distant rights he may get in the Transkei.

Africans living on white-owned farms, who number about a third of the total African population of the Republic, must also link up with the 'heartlands'. In most cases this is not very difficult since there is likely to be a reserve not very far away. Where an African may have wandered far from his tribe, or for some reason or other may have broken with the tribe, it is just unfortunate. The only rights he will get will be to vote by post in the 'heartland', if that can be organised. Theoretically he can go back to the reserve if he wishes to do so, but in practice that is generally impossible since the reserves are already hopelessly overcrowded.

An interesting question is how far the 'heartlands' – the Bantustans – will be allowed to develop along the road to self-rule and independence. From the list of powers reserved by the Republican Government in the case of the most advanced Bantustan, the Transkei, it will be seen that the authority of the Transkei Parliament is far less than that of a Provincial Council in the Republic. Obviously the Africans will demand more powers, and Dr. Verwoerd has said that from time to time further powers will be conceded. But he is quite emphatic that the Bantustans must remain part of the Republic and that the white Parliament will remain supreme.

Two other aspects of the apartheid plan in its relation to the African people must be mentioned since they are cardinal to the whole Bantustan concept and without them Dr. Verwoerd's apartheid plan would collapse. One is the pass-law system and the other is influx-control. Every African, apart from a few who have been exempted for special reasons, must carry a reference-book at all times. It is the document that controls his movements, residence and employment, and records the taxes he pays. Every year about 385,000 Africans are convicted under the pass-laws for trivial offences like failing to show their reference-books on demand, being in some area or other without permission, entering a town to seek work without permission, or failing to get permission to be abroad at night-time after 10 o'clock. An African cannot move freely from one magisterial area to another in search of employment. A permit has to be obtained and the number of permits issued is strictly controlled. There is an elaborate organisation of labour bureaux which determines the employment situation in every area and fixes the number of permits to be issued. Further, an employer does not enjoy complete freedom to select the African worker of his choice. He must recruit his African labour through the local labour bureau.

The idea is to maintain strict limits to the number of Africans employed in the industrial towns and to draw as many as possible away into the reserves. But the reserves are badly eroded and there is not work enough in them for their existing inhabitants. The only

way to absorb surplus labour is in industry, since the land is already
overcrowded. Dr. Verwoerd has firmly ruled that 'white' capital
and enterprise may not be employed to develop industries in the
reserves, since to do that would merely be to create further 'white'
pockets in the African 'heartlands'. So the plan is to establish
'white' industries on the borders of the reserves. Africans can then
live in their homelands and come out to work in the nearby factories, returning home at night time if the factory is close enough, or
at week-ends. The South African Government has created a special
body known as the Permanent Committee for the Location of
Industry and the Development of Border Areas whose job it is to
promote the establishment of these border industries. Loans, tax-
concessions, special railway tariffs, special power and water supplies
and other attractions are offered to induce industrialists to move to
the borders of the reserves. By the end of 1963 it was reckoned that
some 56,000 Africans were employed in these border industries. A
ten-year project for developing textile industries now under way is
expected to provide employment for 30,000 Africans at a cost of
about £22½ millions, and other schemes are reported to be under
consideration.

Inside the reserves the Africans must create business concerns and
start factories themselves. To help them do so a body known as the
Bantu Investment Corporation has been set up with an initial share-
capital of £1 million. In its first two years of operation some 150
existing businesses were expanded and 43 new ones started.

So much for the African section of the population. The plan has
had to be considerably modified for the million and a half coloureds,
since they began on a much higher scale than the Africans and have
no territorial 'heartland' to which they can be tied. There have
been vague suggestions that an attempt might possibly be made to
create a 'national home' for the coloureds in the North-Western
Cape, but nobody takes the idea very seriously. The greatest con-
centrations of coloureds are in the Cape Peninsula, Johannesburg,
Kimberley, in the Eastern Province of the Cape, and on rural settlements in the North-Western Cape Province. Before the four colonies
of South Africa came together as a union in 1910 the coloureds of
the Cape were on the common voters' roll, voting for Parliament
and the Provincial, Divisional and Town Councils. Coloureds themselves served with distinction on a number of public bodies.

One of the first moves by the Nationalist Government after it
assumed power in 1948 was to introduce a bill to Parliament to
remove the coloureds from the common voters' roll and to place
them on a separate roll to elect four whites to represent them in

Parliament. The bill was fought in Parliament and challenged in the law courts but it became law after a long and bitter struggle. Since then a series of measures has been adopted to separate the administration of 'coloured' affairs from 'white' affairs. A special Department of Coloured Affairs has been created, presided over by a minister in the Republican Government. A Board of Coloured Affairs, nominated by the Government, advises the minister on all matters affecting the coloured people. Such functions as child-welfare, reformatories and education affecting the coloured people have been taken away from the ordinary departments of state administering them and placed under the Coloured Affairs Department.

Meanwhile the Group Areas Board has been at work sorting out areas for coloureds to live in. Many coloureds have been moved out of areas proclaimed 'white' and a few whites have been moved out of areas proclaimed 'coloured'. The plan is to create self-contained townships for coloureds in the urban areas, each with its own board. The idea seems to be to link the councils and boards with a central body which would in time become a kind of parliament for coloureds dealing with whatever functions can be proclaimed as being of special concern to the coloured people. It remains to be seen whether at that stage, if it is ever reached, the four whites representing coloureds in the Republican Parliament will be removed.

The apartheid plan for the half-million Asian section of the community is somewhat similar to that for the coloureds. Like the coloureds, the Asians have no territorial area that could possibly be turned into a 'heartland'. A scheme was once proposed to open up a large and fertile region in the Pongola Valley, where the borders of Zululand, Swaziland and the Transvaal meet, as an extensive Indian settlement, but it came to nothing. Proposals to relieve the pressure of Indians concentrated in the Durban area through migration to one of the British colonies had been flatly rejected and the politicians of Natal were pressing for steps to be taken to provide outlets for Indians in other parts of South Africa. However, vested interests proved to be too strong an obstacle to the Pongola settlement idea, but it is interesting to reflect that a 'heartland' might have been available now had the plan been carried out.

Meanwhile a Department of Indian Affairs has been set up, with a cabinet minister at its head. The task of the Department is to administer laws specifically affecting Asians, such as immigration, movement between the provinces, poor relief, registration of births, deaths and marriages, housing and higher education. A Council for Indian Affairs nominated by the Government is being created to advise the Minister. The Group Areas Board has been at work proclaiming residential and business areas for Asians throughout the Republic, excepting in the Free State, and a process of resettlement is taking place which has brought great hardship and misery to the Indian community.

No detailed blue-print of apartheid has been published for the Asians, but the assumption is that it will be similar to that for the coloureds, excepting that Indians will get no representation in the Parliament of the Republic. When they are settled in their own townships and their rural smallholdings have been tidied up, no doubt they will elect councils and boards to be linked in a central body to take the place of the Council for Indian Affairs and to serve as a kind of parliament for Asians, legislating on matters of specific concern to them.

Such, then, is the Nationalist Government's overall plan for regulating race-relations in South Africa. The legislative framework has already been set up but a good deal of detail has still to be filled in. Some of its aspects are still obscure. Nationalists admit that hardships are being inflicted in its application, but they contend that the final result, which they claim will be race-harmony, will justify the suffering entailed in carrying it into effect. 'After all, hundreds of thousands of people suffered when India was partitioned', is a favourite phrase.

Chapter 6

Opponents of the Plan

PARLIAMENT HOUSE stands at the top of Adderley Street, main thoroughfare of the Mother City of South Africa. It is an ugly building, pseudo-Corinthian, with ornate columns and plastered walls, set among lawns and flower-beds and with a long avenue of oak trees running up one side towards Table Mountain. Here in the House of Assembly and the Senate an all-white Parliament has debated and passed all the complex laws that form the structure of Dr. Verwoerd's apartheid plan. Pointing to this parliament, where discussion is free, the Nationalists claim that the Republic is a democracy. But, such as it is, only whites may enjoy the privileges of this democracy. While four-fifths of the population of South Africa are unrepresented and cannot take part in its proceedings, an air of unreality hangs over the Cape Town parliament. A further factor adding to this atmosphere of make-believe is the mechanical and inflexible way the Government goes through the motions of placing its legislation on the Statute Book. Like all the other parts of this rigid political machine, the Nationalist caucus is a well-disciplined body, kept in order by a whole array of powerful sanctions. There are discussions and disagreements in this caucus and occasionally the Government is criticised, but never in such a way as to embarrass the Cabinet or challenge the authority of the Leader. Among Nationalists deviationism is regarded as subversive to the Afrikaner volk, and to take an independent line is to risk the wrath of the powerful Broederbond, the Church, the Party, one's friends and associates. Moreover, a great many Nationalist Members of Parliament are dependent on the Government, or the Party and its associated financial concerns, for incomes or economic favours. To quarrel with the Party hierarchy is not merely to risk one's political future but may even entail financial ruin.

Once a bill is introduced to Parliament it is rarely modified in any way, unless a fault in draftsmanship can be discovered. No plea, no argument by the Opposition has the slightest effect. The whole proceeding bears the stamp of a wearisome formality that has to be gone through merely for the sake of the record. Measures proceed through Parliament, clause by clause, like the mechanical progress of a pile-driver and a sense of utter futility has long since settled over the Opposition.

It was in this atmosphere that most of the apartheid laws were adopted during the past fifteen years. At the beginning of the Nationalist regime there were four whites to speak for the Africans of the Cape Province, and they unequivocally opposed each new apartheid law at every stage. Later this form of representation was abolished and there is no longer anyone elected by Africans to represent them in Parliament. There are four whites to speak for the coloureds, and they have opposed most, though not quite all the apartheid measures.

One of the difficulties of judging non-white opinion about aspects of race-relations is that the two main African political organisations, the African National Congress and the Pan-African Congress, have both been banned, while most of the African leaders have either been gaoled or confined in remote areas, or proscribed, or have escaped to other lands. In the Transkei Territory, where the only free elections for an African body to be held in recent times have taken place, two political factions arose. One was led by Chief Matanzima, and it supported the idea of separate bantustans but demanded additional land and further rights for the newly-independent states. Matanzima was regarded as the Republican Government's protégé. The rival group led by Chief Victor Poto stood for a non-racial order in both the Transkei and the Republic, demanded votes for whites as well as blacks, and opposed the idea of separate states. In the Transkei general election in 1963 Chief Poto won 38 seats compared with Chief Matanzima's 7, and this may be taken as a fair reflection of African opinion in the first bantustan state to be created by Dr. Verwoerd.

But though he had won the popular vote by an overwhelming majority, Chief Victor Poto failed to secure election as Premier of the Transkei. This was due to the preponderant number of chiefs nominated to the Transkei Assembly by the Republican Government. Only 11 chiefs had the courage to support Poto whereas 47 sided with Matanzima and secured his appointment as premier by a narrow majority. From the result of the popular vote in the Transkei and from the known views of such Africans as have managed to speak for their people, there is, however, little doubt that the vast majority of Africans oppose Dr. Verwoerd's apartheid plan, consider it to be repressive and unworkable, and demand equal political and economic rights with all other sections of the population. In particular they resent the pass-laws, influx-control and the colour-bar in industry.

What attitude Africans would adopt towards whites if they were suddenly given the power to determine the political structure of the Republic is impossible to determine since they are not a cohesive, unified group. It is part of the Nationalist Government's strategy to prevent them from uniting, hence the division of Africans into eight separate 'ethnic units'. Hence also the Government's sharp reaction against the formation of any organisation, however innocent it may appear to be, which cuts across these ethnic divisions. Hitherto most responsible Africans have taken the line that they acknowledge the role of the whites in developing South Africa and wish to work with them on a basis of equality. Before it was banned, at no stage did the African National Congress advocate black domination or call for the expulsion of whites from the Republic. On the contrary most dispassionate observers consider that the African National Congress was surprisingly restrained in its political demands.

An example of this restraint occurred shortly before the parliamentary general election in 1953. The African National Congress and the Indian Congress were conducting a passive-resistance campaign against the most recent apartheid laws. Thousands of Africans and many Indians had gone to gaol and white public opinion was unhappy about the campaign and its possible consequences. Responsible voices had been raised demanding that an attempt should be made to ease race-tensions through negotiation and conciliation. Unofficial soundings were taken among leaders of the African National Congress to discover what their terms would be for calling off the passive-resistance campaign on the eve of the parliamentary general election. Such a move, it was considered, would have a reassuring effect on the white electorate which was becoming anxious about the defiance campaign. It would be to the advantage of the United Party to demonstrate that it could influence non-white opinion.

The reply from the A.N.C. was that the United Party should issue a declaration undertaking to repeal all the apartheid laws introduced by the Nationalist Government since it assumed power five years previously. In exchange for such a declaration the passive-resistance campaign would immediately be called off and the A.N.C. would issue a statement indicating its desire to talk over the grievances of Africans at a representative conference. Unfortunately, just then, signs began to appear within the ranks of the United Party of a right-wing revolt against the leadership, and nothing was done about the A.N.C. offer. However, this incident is related not so much to criticise the United Party as to illustrate how modest were the demands of African leaders at that time. They fully understood the political difficulties of the all-white United Party and did not wish to push the Party too far. Though abolition of the pass-laws and removal of the economic colour-bar coupled with the acquisition of political rights were basic objectives then, as they are today, the A.N.C. leaders did not ask for these things as a condition for calling off the passive-resistance campaign. All they demanded was that the United Party, if it came to power, should undertake publicly to halt the tide of apartheid and set the flow in the opposite direction.

What the million and a half coloureds think of Dr. Verwoerd's apartheid plan is easy enough to determine. The coloureds have always regarded themselves as belonging politically to the white group. Most coloureds voted against the Nationalists and were deeply hurt by the action of the Government in placing them on a separate voters' roll. It is fairly safe to say that if the issue could be put to them they would reject apartheid outright and support the establishment of a non-racial order.

The Indian community has long been divided into a small, somewhat conservative section consisting mainly of the traders, and a large, vocal section led by the Indian Congress, which has been the real spearhead of Indian opposition to apartheid. Indians do not always see eye to eye with each other on tactical issues such as whether or not to accept meagre concessions and to co-operate with Government bodies, but they are united in condemning Dr. Verwoerd's plan for separating the races. Their aim is to secure equality of political and economic rights.

The white, privileged section of the population, which holds all political power and runs the country, may be divided, broadly, into three groups. The largest, led by the Nationalist Party, is trying to implement Dr. Verwoerd's bantustan apartheid plan described in the last chapter of this book. The next largest section, represented by the United Party and its followers, stands for apartheid in principle but differs from the Nationalist Party on how it should be applied. The third and by far the smallest group rejects apartheid and stands for a non-racial order in South Africa with equal political and economic opportunities for all sections. Within this third section are the Progressive Party, the Liberal Party, leaders of the English-language churches, and many intellectuals. In the 1962 general election the Nationalist Party obtained 370,431 votes, the United Party 336,453 votes, the Progressives 69,042 votes and the Liberals 2,461 votes in the 86 seats contested. In a further 64 constituencies the members were returned unopposed.

The United Party rejects Dr. Verwoerd's Bantustan apartheid plan. The Party holds that it is unrealistic and impracticable to try to divide the races on a territorial basis. Such a step might have been tried 100 years ago, with a far more appropriate division of land and resources and before the present pattern of economic development had evolved. But as things are, the races have become inextricably integrated in the economy, dispersed throughout the Republic. The United Party argues that to try to merge the fragments of the reserves into cohesive, viable states would entail massive land-purchases and the handing over of many villages and towns to African control, and such an operation would never be agreed to by the white electorate. The Party is definitely against further land-purchases to add to the reserves and has even called a halt to the land-buying programme agreed to in 1936 when a schedule of areas to be added to the reserves was proclaimed. On the other hand Dr. Verwoerd, to his credit, has promised to complete the 1936 programme, and continues to buy land.

As an alternative to Dr. Verwoerd's plan to create separate 'heartlands' for Africans, the United Party proposes a form of apartheid which it terms 'race federation'. The idea is to create a series of communal councils for the different races, one for whites and coloureds, one for Asians, and one or more for Africans. Each council would control whatever functions might be divided out on a group basis, such as local government, education, health and matters connected with personal status and succession. There would be a central parliament in which each racial group would be represented 'in accordance with the standard of civilisation it has reached'. The coloured people of the Cape Province and Natal would be restored to the common voters' roll. Coloureds in the other provinces of the Republic would be given representation in the Senate, voting on separate rolls. Africans would be represented by not more than eight whites in the House of Assembly and six whites in the Senate. Discussions would be held with the leaders of the Asian community to determine in what form they would be represented in Parliament.

Like 'apartheid' before Dr. Verwoerd gave it form and substance, 'race federation' is little more than a political slogan. For the coloureds and Asians it would appear to visualise much the same kind of state-within-a-state contemplated by Dr. Verwoerd. A minor difference is that the United Party promises to restore the coloureds in the Cape Province to the common voters' roll whereas Dr. Verwoerd intends to keep them on separate rolls. The United Party has not yet explained the anomaly in its policy: why it wants coloureds on the common roll only in the Cape Province and not also in the rest of the Republic. With regard to the Africans there are some interesting differences between the two parties. The most obvious flaw in Dr. Verwoerd's bantustan apartheid policy is the assumption that Africans and whites can be separated on a territorial basis. This flaw the United Party avoids. It accepts the fact that Africans are integrated in the so-called 'white' economy and that two thirds of the African population are permanently resident in the so-called 'white' areas.

Another difference between the United Party and the Nationalist Government is purely theoretic, nevertheless it is important politically. Whatever the practical effects of his policies may be, Dr. Verwoerd has again and again stated that all races must be free 'to attain the full political rights of which they are capable'. He promises that no limitations will be placed on the goal of political freedom along the bantustan apartheid trail. Political students may find it difficult to determine how political freedom can be achieved through the apartheid plan, nevertheless that is the principle to which Dr. Verwoerd is committed. The United Party, on the other hand, stands firmly for 'White Leadership'. The white man must remain in control for all time, it says. The United Party is obviously setting the stage, politically, for the day when faith in the practicability of bantustans is destroyed by the inexorable process of more and more Africans being drawn into the 'white' towns and the proportion of Africans in the reserves falling, instead of rising as Dr. Verwoerd's apartheid policy postulates. The United Party also hopes that it will attract support from Nationalists who are uneasy about the doctrine of the non-white achieving full political freedom through apartheid, however theoretical that might be. Incidentally, the United Party is at one with the Nationalists in wishing to retain the colour-bar in industry, and in upholding residential apartheid, the pass-laws and influx-control, though it has opposed measures like the Group Areas Act and the job-reservation clauses of the Industrial Conciliation Act.

Africans have never been consulted about the United Party's 'race federation' plan, but from what those of their leaders not yet proscribed have said, and from the comments of the fairly extensive African Press, it is quite clear that they reject the whole idea as firmly as they do the Government's 'bantustan apartheid' scheme. Thus in the unlikely event of the United Party displacing the Nationalists at a general election, race-relations in South Africa would be no nearer solution.

The Progressive and Liberal Parties both reject the principle of white domination and stand for equal political rights and opportunities for all individuals, irrespective of race. Both would abolish the pass-laws and influx-control. Both would remove the economic colour-bar and admit non-whites to trade-union membership. Both would remove all forms of administrative apartheid, such as having separate government departments for the different races. Both would introduce common voters' rolls and admit all races on a basis of equality to representative bodies. But there are differences between the Progressives and the Liberals on how the principle of equal rights should be applied. The Progressives advocate a non-racial qualified franchise, with the qualifications applying to every individual irrespective of his colour. The argument in favour of a qualified franchise is that only 35 per cent of Africans are literate and have any idea how to run a modern state. The Progressives promise a massive educational programme and maintain that within a generation or so most Africans would qualify for the common roll. The Liberal Party, on the other hand, believes that the franchise should be extended gradually to all adult persons without any literacy, income or other qualifications.

There are differences, too, with regard to residential areas, schools, hospitals and social amenities. The Progressive Party holds that the individual should have the right to decide whether he wishes to live in an area reserved for his own group or in a mixed area, and proposes to have both reserved and mixed residential suburbs. The choice would, in most instances, be left to the township owners. Similarly there would be reserved and mixed schools, hospitals, and social amenities. The Liberal Party would throw all residential areas, schools and other social amenities open to all races. Both the Progressive and Liberal Parties include members of all races. The Progressives command more support than the Liberals do among whites and the position is reversed with regard to non-white support.

To sum up, the Government's apartheid plan is rejected for one reason or another by roughly half the white population of South Africa, and almost the entire African, coloured, and Asian sections of the people. Apart from the moral question of denying rights to people merely on a basis of skin-colour, the main objection to Dr. Verwoerd's plan is that it is impracticable and that much hardship and injustice are entailed in attempting to enforce it. There are growing doubts whether a small minority, however skilful and well-organised, can indefinitely dominate even an unorganised and generally inexperienced, illiterate and impoverished majority by force of arms.

If a real and genuine attempt is to be made to apply apartheid, then there must be a massive redivision of land and economic resources, coupled with a resettlement programme involving millions of people of all races. To believe that eleven-sixteenths of the population can be squeezed into 13·8 per cent of the total area of the Republic is plain nonsense. Yet the white electorate, which Dr. Verwoerd handles with such psychological skill, would obviously not tolerate such a redivision and resettlement programme.

Finally, it should be pointed out that neither Africans, coloureds, nor Asians have ever been consulted about the apartheid plan. To them it is merely an elaborate façade to cover white domination. It began as a political slogan, was turned into a burning ideology and was given shape and substance by the most powerful man in the Republic, Dr. H. F. Verwoerd. Whether he himself really believes that it can succeed is a subject of perennial discussion among South Africans.

PART TWO

Chapter 7

Trek South

A s though swept up by some primeval storm and left there to harden when the waters subsided, the long range of the Magaliesberg and the broken ridge of the Witwatersrand lie side by side like twin ramparts across the high plateau of the Transvaal. And in the broad valley between them is an insignificant koppie crowned with a few straggly mimosa trees and a heap of boulders. Between two of the boulders is the entrance to the Sterkfontein caves, a great underground labyrinth eaten out by rainwaters seeping down through the subsoil for hundreds of thousands of years. Here, a great many centuries ago, man's earliest ancestors took refuge from the wild beasts and the violent weather, and here in the limestone have been found various fossilised skulls and bones from which a story of evolution can be told. These bones belonged, so the scientists tell us, to Australopithecinae, the so-called 'missing link' between the apes and the first of the true hominids. From these remains, and from other bones found in the limestone quarries at Taungs and at the Matapan Hills, it is possible to reconstruct the scene, as it may well have been, when those half-men, half-apes roamed the lush plateau during one of the warmer intervals between the great winters of the Pleistocene Age.

There are eminent anthropologists who hold that the human race was created in this geologically old and settled region between the Kalahari Desert and the curve of Southern Africa bordered by the Indian Ocean. It may well have been here where Australopithecinae evolved into the earliest forbears of the Bushmen who came to inhabit most of the African Continent south and east of the Sahara. One great migration of these earliest humans probably spread into the Near East, fanning northwards through Europe and Asia, and evolving into the white men of the north and the brown men around the eastern Mediterranean. At some stage, possibly when the Bushmen were evolving down in the south of Africa, the Negro race began in the broad basin of the Congo River. This area of habitable soil was completely cut off from the south by the Kalahari Desert, which at that time was far more extensive than it is today, stretching from the Atlantic Ocean right across to beyond where the mighty Zambesi now plunges over the Victoria Falls. More barren and more lifeless than they are today, the Kalahari in the south and the Sahara in the north confined the Negroes for thousands of years. At some stage they came in contact with the brown men of the eastern Mediterranean and north-eastern Africa, probably around Abyssinia and the Great Lakes, and from this mixture evolved the Bantu, who for many centuries lived in Central Africa between the Equator and the Zambesi.

Meanwhile in the south, below the barrier of the Kalahari, the Hottentots evolved from the Bushmen, spreading all over the subcontinent from the Cape Peninsula right up to the Limpopo and driving the Bushmen into their mountain caves and the deep kloofs of the forest country. The Bantu in Central Africa were more advanced than these Hottentots of the south, employing tools and weapons of iron which they obtained from the traders who came in by sea from the east. The Hottentots and Bushmen, on the other hand, used bone, hardwood and stone for their implements, arrows and spears. It has been suggested by several historians that the dependence of the Bantu on outside traders for tools and weapons of iron was one of the main reasons why they did not push down into Southern Africa sooner than they actually did. The traders came in ships from the Red Sea and the Persian Gulf, and we are told in Ptolemy's guide-book to the Indian Ocean for Greek sailors, the *Periplus* written about A.D. 60, that 'in exchange for lances, hatchets, daggers, awls, glass, wine and wheat' the ships that traded with the east coast of Africa brought back 'ivory, rhinoceros horn, tortoise-shell, palm-oil and slaves'.

There is still much to be discovered about the early history of Central Africa, where the Bantu originated. A great question-mark hangs, for example, over the ruins of Zimbabwe in Rhodesia, with its terraced gardens and ancient gold-mines on the plains and among the hills round about. The British Association for the Advancement of Science sent Miss G. Caton-Thompson there in 1929 to carry out investigations, and a short while later the German archaeologist, Professor Leo Frobenius, made some further excavations on the site of the ruins. It was interesting to see how these two authorities disagreed. Miss Caton-Thompson considered that the ruins were of Bantu origin, dating from about A.D. 1400, while Professor Frobenius declared emphatically that the earlier parts of the ruins, which were altered and rebuilt at a later stage, were of ancient origin. He linked them with the Sabaeans, whose trading ships ventured down the east coast of Africa some 2,500 years ago

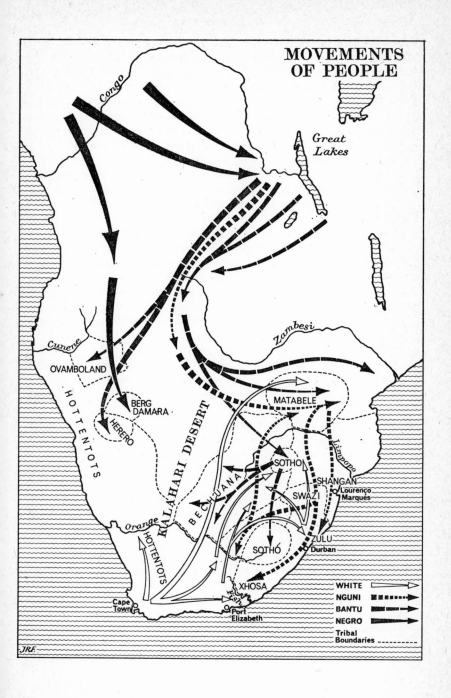

MOVEMENTS
OF PEROPLE

Congo

Great
Lakes

Cunene

OVAMBOLAND

Zambesi

HOTTENTOTS

BERG
DAMARA

MATABELE

HERERO

Limpopo

KALAHARI DESERT

SOTHO

SHANGAN

BECHUANA

SWAZI

Lourenço
Marques

Orange

HOTTENTOTS

ZULU

SOTHÓ

Durban

XHOSA

WHITE

NGUNI

BANTU

NEGRO

Cape
Town

Port
Elizabeth

Tribal
Boundaries

JRf.

and who may well have founded the ancient port of Sofala, near Beira, where a small fishing village stands today.

From Sofala there is an ancient trail, not easily followed on the ground but clearly visible from the air, leading in almost a straight line inland over the escarpment to Zimbabwe. At regular intervals, each two a day's march apart, there was once a chain of small forts, and several of these are now villages occupied by Africans. It could well have been that some enterprising people from another land – Sabaeans, Phoenicians, Arabs, or whoever they were – mined gold in Mashonaland, using Zimbabwe as a central point of communications. There the ore from the mines was smelted and the gold was stored in the acropolis on the hill facing the temple until it could be sent down by convoy along the trail of forts to Sofala. Most experts agree that the old mine-workings were not of Bantu origin. The mines were cleverly engineered, with a most ingenious ventilation system, and the shafts and stopes were too narrow for the average Bantu to enter. Rock was blasted by lighting fires in the shafts, raking out the hot embers and pouring cold water on the hot quartz, which splintered and crumbled. An interesting discovery has been a pick made of copper but tempered hard by a process said to have been known in ancient times.

Could some of King Solomon's gold have come from Mashonaland? We read in the Old Testament (1 Kings, Chapter 10) how the Queen of Sheba gave to King Solomon 'an hundred and twenty talents of gold', and how the navy of Hiram set out from Eziongeber on the shores of the Red Sea and brought back 'gold from Ophir' to swell Solomon's treasury. 'And he made three hundred shields of beaten gold.... And all King Solomon's drinking vessels were of gold, and all the vessels of the house of the forest of Lebanon were of pure gold....' All that can be said with certainty at the present time is that considerable quantities of gold were mined around Zimbabwe, and that there is a good deal of evidence to support the theory that it was mined by some invading people or series of peoples who had no desire to settle there and were forced to protect themselves against the local inhabitants. Who the miners were, when the mining took place, and whether or not the Zimbabwe ruins were linked with the mining operations have yet to be established.

If the mines were very ancient, it must have been Bushmen or Hottentots and not Bantu against whom the invading miners had to protect themselves. The Bantu are believed to have begun their southward and eastward migration somewhere between the years A.D. 300 and 500. The great Zambesi River, infested with crocodiles,

more than a mile wide above the Victoria Falls and a raging torrent
in the gorges below the Falls, would have been an impassable barrier to the south. The first Bantu trek south must have crossed the
Zambesi somewhere above the Falls. They would then have swung
eastwards into the high plateau of Rhodesia, advancing as far as the
coastal belt and driving the Bushmen and Hottentots to flee further
southwards or retreat into their caves. By the year A.D. 600 the
Kingdom of Monomatapa had been formed, with its capital either
at Zimbabwe or somewhere in the neighbourhood. By that time the
people who worked the gold-mines had long since disappeared, but
traders came in from Sofala and other points on the coast. It may
be that in this Kingdom of Monomatapa – shown on early maps –
the Bantu first learnt the art of smelting iron and forging their own
spears and implements. When the Bantu first moved into Rhodesia
from around the head-waters of the Zambesi, they of course left
other Bantu behind them, and we can well imagine that from time
to time inter-tribal wars must have taken place. It is even possible
that the Kingdom of Monomatapa at some stage extended westwards and northwards to include what is now Zambia and possibly
Uganda. Later the Bantu split into different clans, from each of
which, at different times, migrations trekked off to the south.

According to A. T. Bryant, in his *Olden Times in Zululand and
Natal,* the great Nguni clan which in the end occupied all the
territory in South Africa east of the Drakensberg from the Limpopo
down to the Great Fish River, originated in the land now called
Zambia. Following the old trail round the headwaters of the
Zambesi, the Ngunis first attacked Monomatapa, then swung southwards across the Limpopo. This was probably in the year A.D. 1300
or thereabouts. Already some Bantu from Monomatapa had settled
in the Eastern Transvaal and Swaziland, and the Ngunis fell upon
these in a series of tribal skirmishes and southward thrusts. Some
fled westwards to found new clans in later years. Others merged
with the Ngunis to form the Swazis, Zulus, Pondos, Xhosas and
Tembus. By the year 1500 the foremost Ngunis, who later became
the Xhosas, had reached the Great Fish River which flows into the
Indian Ocean north-east of Algoa Bay. There the slow southward
migration seems to have halted for roughly 250 years. It may be
that the movement did proceed further to the south and was swept
back by some disaster such as a plague of rinderpest or East Coast
Fever which wiped out the cattle, or a succession of droughts,
which have at times so sorely afflicted that part of the country. Or,
as several historians have suggested, the Hottentots living at that
time in the Eastern Province may have been better organised and

stronger than they were in most other parts of Africa, and they may have turned back the van of the Nguni migration. Or it may just have been that the whole southward migration had lost momentum and become stabilised.

So far as can be gathered from the shreds of history passed down from generation to generation by word of mouth and from the reports of shipwrecked mariners who were by then sailing regularly round Africa to India, no movements of any great significance were taking place along the east coast of Africa between Algoa Bay and Delgoa Bay in the year 1600. The various tribes were living in a state of relative peace, herding their cattle, cultivating patches of land, indulging in occasional faction-fighting, prospering when the seasons were good and suffering in times of drought, or when there were outbreaks of rinderpest, East Coast Fever, malaria or nagana.

Somewhere about 1620, in the Mhlatuzi valley, not far from Melmoth in Zululand, there was born a Nguni child named Zulu. According to legend he became the head of a small tribe living in that part of the valley that is bordered by the Mtonjaneni hills, and he ruled the tribe so well that it flourished and grew into the aba-kwa-Zulu clan, destined to become the most powerful nation of Africans to emerge south of the Limpopo. But the man who turned the clan into a powerful nation and wrote a dramatic page of history was Shaka, born in 1787. His mother was Nandi, daughter of Bebe, chief of the eLangeni clan. One day Nandi was waylaid by a chief of the Zulu clan, Senzangakona, as she was on her way to the stream to fetch water for her kraal. We can picture the scene, with the maiden walking along a path through the bushes, clay pitcher on her head. She is attacked and overpowered by Senzangakona, and because he is a chief and too powerful to be accused, the maid flees with her parents to another kraal in a distant part of the country, where Shaka is born.

For about 20 years Shaka and his mother moved from kraal to kraal, leading a precarious existence. Shaka himself grew into a powerful man, unusually adept with the fighting-sticks, cunning and resourceful. Joining the household of a headman named Dingiswayo, generally recognised as the most powerful chief in that part of the world, he soon made himself indispensable. Placed in charge of the chief's troop of fighting-men, he drilled them and introduced the technique of fighting at close quarters with short spears instead of hurling long spears from a distance as had always been the practice before then. He himself was so formidable a fighter that he soon became known and respected far and wide. To Dingiswayo he revealed that Senzangakona was his father, and when Senzangakona died in 1816, Dingiswayo decided to make him chief of the Zulu clan. This was done in a swift operation carried out with the aid of the warriors Shaka had trained.

Having disposed of the legitimate heir to the chieftainship, Shaka set about organising the Zulu clan with remarkable skill and vigour. His first step was to mobilise and train a small army with which he subdued several neighbouring clans in the name of Dingiswayo, to whom he continued to profess allegiance. One day Shaka and his troops were away on an expedition to a more distant part of the country when Dingiswayo was ambushed and killed in a surprise raid from an unexpected quarter. Returning to hear the news and to find a state of confusion, Shaka immediately proclaimed himself chief of Dingiswayo's tribe as well as his own and was again able to dispose of Dingiswayo's legitimate heirs. Shaka's next move was to announce the creation of the ama-Zulu nation which would rule the whole land from the Drakensberg to the sea. He built himself a capital city, organised a large army split into 'impis' (regiments), created an effective form of army command, established an industry for smelting iron and forging weapons and implements, created a system of tribal law, and appointed an administration responsible for organising agricultural activity, storing grain in underground storehouses, and keeping his capital city clean and tidy. He had his secret police, a body of informers who kept him remarkably well advised of the sentiments of his captains and officials and events throughout his kingdom. He even sent spies to discover what was happening in distant parts of the country, and they brought back reports from as far distant as the Cape Province and the Portuguese settlement of Lourenço Marques.

Introducing a new strategy of attack known as the 'horned cres-cent', a kind of pincer-movement, Shaka quickly subdued all the clans in Zululand and Natal and became undisputed overlord of a territory bigger than Great Britain. He ruled for only twelve years, and it was a reign marked with great cruelty. In more than one instance he ordered an entire tribe to be butchered. If an 'impi' showed cowardice, every warrior in it was clubbed to death. Men and women suspected of indulging in witchcraft, or cheating, or lying, were summarily flung over a precipice. Thousands of tribes in more distant parts did not wait to be attacked but fled, sometimes falling upon other tribes in their way and sometimes joining up in a fugitive horde, causing far-reaching migrations and movements of people.

Shaka was first visited by a white in 1825 when the traveller Isaacs made a journey through Zululand. Secret instructions had been given to allow Isaacs to travel unmolested through Zululand, since Shaka was curious to see one of those strange white folk who came in ships across the seas. He had heard about the English and the Portuguese, and on being assured that the English were more powerful, he decided to negotiate a treaty of friendly alliance with the King of England. About that time the first English adventurers arrived at Durban to establish a settlement there, and Shaka sent word that one of them was to visit him. He was duly called upon by several of them, including Lt. King, whom Shaka selected to lead a deputation to the Governor of the Cape Province in order to secure his treaty. King and several Zulu headmen travelled by ship to Cape Town, where they were not taken seriously and were sent back after a long delay with a few trivial presents and some vague promises that filled the Zulu king with uneasiness.

In 1828 Shaka was murdered by his two half-brothers, Dingane and Mhlangana, and according to his biographer, Thomas Mofolo, his last words as he lay dying were : 'You think you will become chiefs when I am dead. But it will not be so, for the white man is coming and you will be his slaves.'

Some weeks later Dingane organised the killing of Mhlangana and proclaimed himself King of the Zulus. Moving the royal capital to a new site further north in Zululand, he proceeded to dispose of various headmen and captains whose loyalty he mistrusted, and he set about reorganising the armies. However, he had neither the fighting prowess nor cunning of Shaka and his reign of ten years could not be counted a great success. The whites were crowding in upon him, both from the sea to strengthen the settlement at Durban, and from the interior, across the passes of the Drakensberg. Constantly haunted by Shaka's dying words, Dingane could not make up his mind whether to drive the whites out of his domain or to cede land to them and try to maintain some form of independence through negotiation. In 1837 he was visited by a party of Boers under Pieter Retief, who were anxious to establish a settlement in Natal. Dingane agreed to sign a treaty to this effect on condition that Retief should recover some cattle recently seized by a chief in the Harrismith area, over the Drakensberg. Retief recovered the cattle and returned with them to Dingane's capital on 3 February 1838. In the party were 69 Boers, some boys and a number of Hottentot servants. After entertaining the visitors and signing the concession, Dingane suddenly and treacherously ordered them all to be killed. This was the signal for war with the whites, and Dingane's armies were decisively beaten by the Boers at Blood River on 16 December 1838 – a date celebrated in the Republic today as

a national holiday. After this setback, Dingane moved his capital
to the upper Ivuna River, but was attacked and again defeated by
a brother, Mpande, who was supported by a party of Boers armed
with guns. Fleeing across the Pongola River into Swaziland, Dingane was caught by the Swazis and put to death. Mpande ruled
with diminishing power until 1872 when he was succeeded by
Cetshwayo, the last of the independent Zulu kings, who clashed
with the white government in Natal, was forcibly removed from his
throne and died in 1884. Thus ended the saga of the rise and fall
of the Zulu nation, who for a short while ruled supreme in the land
stretching from the Drakensberg to the sea.

Meanwhile another Bantu nation was being formed right in
among the massive ranges and rounded, rock-strewn peaks of the
Drakensberg. Founder of this nation was a young chief named
Moshesh, head of the Koena clan of the Basuto people who lived
near where the Caledon River flows out of Basutoland to cross the
broad plains of the Free State. The Basuto were a later branch of
the Bantu migration from the headwaters of the Zambesi, across
the Limpopo into Southern Africa. Finding the Ngunis already in
possession of the fertile country east of the Drakensberg, the Basuto
settled on the high plateau of the Transvaal and the eastern Free
State. They were living with their cattle in relative peace when
Shaka, and later Dingane, imposed a reign of terror in Natal and
Zululand, scattering many tribes over the Drakensberg into the
Free State and the Transvaal. Moshesh retreated with his Koena
clan into the Drakensberg Mountains, and fortified himself in an
impregnable stronghold named Thaba Bosiu. There he was joined
by fugitives from many parts of the country and he organised an
army which defended the stronghold against all attacks. His power
and prestige grew as he remained undefeated and was joined by
more and more people. From their stronghold the Basuto ventured
out in times of peace and soon established themselves throughout
the rugged area now known as Basutoland. Unlike Shaka, Moshesh
had no ambitions to conquer the whole countryside. He was a man
of peace, seeking only to defend himself and his people against
attack. But when forced to fight he proved to be a most skilful
general. He used the rugged mountains to great advantage, and
frequently surprised an enemy with a skilful ambush. On one point
he agreed with Shaka : he realised that the real enemy to the independence of his people lay not among the African tribes, but with
the whites then pressing into the hinterland.

Moshesh met the problem of the whites far more skilfully than
Shaka's successor, Dingane, did. First he decided that he and his

people should assume the white man's religion, the Christian faith. The Basuto would not then be considered barbarians and would not be attacked on that account. After making extensive inquiries among the traders who called at his mountain stronghold, he selected the Paris Evangelical Missionary Society from among the various missionary bodies active in Southern Africa. The French had no territorial ambitions in that part of the continent. He sent a special emissary named Adam Krotz to an outpost established by the Paris Society on the borders of Bechuanaland, and three missionaries lately arrived from France, Messrs. Arbousset, Casalais and Gosselin, responded to the appeal. Moshesh was delighted to receive them and paid Adam Krotz 100 head of cattle for his services. A close friendship between Moshesh and the Frenchmen soon developed, and the advice of the missionaries was of great value to the Basuto in the many difficult situations that developed during the ensuing years.

Though saintly and peace-loving, the Frenchmen had a practical turn of mind, and one of their earliest counsels to Moshesh was to buy guns and train his tribesmen how to use them. Patiently and methodically, he set about acquiring a motley collection of muzzle-loaders and even a few early carbines. Rifles vanished mysteriously from trekkers' wagons, from border farmhouses in the Cape Province, and even from military barracks. Gun-running became a profitable enterprise from the Cape and Natal, and most of the guns found their way into the mountains of Basutoland. Moshesh even managed to buy a small muzzle-loading cannon which he used to some effect in one of his skirmishes with the Boers who had settled in the Free State. He sent several 'captains' of his army into the Cape Province to learn the art of making gunpowder, and not only did the tribesmen make their own gunpowder but they succeeded in casting a small cannon.

The threat from the Zulus was removed early in Moshesh's reign, and he then had to deal with the far more serious danger to his independence from the whites. He managed to beat off several attacks from the Boers in the Free State, but realised that unless he could obtain allies he would be overwhelmed in the end. So he applied for protection from the British Queen. After long and difficult negotiations, this was granted in 1848, but was withdrawn six years later, when he was attacked from the Free State and very nearly defeated. The British again changed their minds in 1868 and Basutoland was declared British territory. Moshesh died two years later, in many ways the wisest and greatest African leader of the nineteenth century. Ten years after the death of Moshesh the

Government of the Cape attempted to disarm the Basuto, who immediately went to war. The campaign was carried on in a desultory fashion by the British who suffered a number of reverses, and after three years a peace treaty was signed allowing the Basuto to keep their arms. Basutoland was detached from the Cape and became a protectorate under the Crown. For a period after the death of Moshesh there was trouble between his sons with regard to the succession. In 1898 Lerotholi was appointed Paramount Chief and he and his descendants ruled from that time onwards.

From the Basuto we must return to the van of the Nguni trek southwards and consider what became of the tribes that pressed on between the rugged barrier of the Drakensberg and the Indian Ocean, entering Pondoland, East Griqualand and the Transkei. This country is far more mountainous and broken than are Zululand and Natal where Shaka formed his kingdom. Rivers run in deep, bush-clad gorges, and as often as not mists hang about the tops of the ranges. The advancing Nguni met more numerous and more vigorous bands of Hottentots and Bushmen and progress against these people was slow. Advance parties of Ngunis probably reached the Great Fish River towards the end of the fifteenth century and there the migration seems to have halted. It may even have pulled back in the face of some catastrophic drought, or even an outbreak of East Coast fever among cattle, or rinderpest. At all events, it took about 250 years for the Ngunis to establish themselves in Pondoland and the Transkei right to the Fish River. During their southward migration the Ngunis absorbed some Hottentots and even Bushmen who gave to the Xhosa language many of its clicks.

Round about 1750 these southward-migrating Ngunis and the northward-moving whites from the Cape met in that strip of countryside that lies between the Fish River and Algoa Bay. In those days the Cape Colony was under the control of the Dutch East India Company and was slowly expanding in an easterly direction. Parties of Boers were thrusting along the Swartberg, the Kouga Mountains and the Groot Winterhoekberge towards Algoa Bay, so that in this region was a confused mass of Xhosas, Hottentots, whites and a few troops of Bushmen. Sometimes they fought and killed one another and sometimes an uneasy accommodation was reached. For example, there were times when Bushmen served as hunters and rainmakers to the Xhosas. Hottentots were servants to both the Xhosas and the Boers, herding cattle and cultivating the fields.

Open conflict on a general scale broke out for the first time between the whites and the Xhosas in 1779, and the main cause of this clash is interesting. The Boers always followed a system of individual land-ownership, staking out their own farms and herding their cattle, as far as possible, within their own boundaries. The Africans, on the other hand, had always grazed their cattle on a tribal, communal basis, moving their herds backwards and forwards wherever the best veld was to be found. They refused to acknowledge the existence of boundaries and frequently sent herds of stock into some farm marked out by a Boer as his own. This resulted in stock-thefts, raiding, counter-raiding and a great deal of friction leading to the war of 1779. Meanwhile in the background three major influences were at work. The whites were pressing northwards and eastwards, the Xhosas were being squeezed down from behind in the opposite direction, and the authorities in the Cape Province were desperately trying to stabilise the frontier and prevent it from shifting eastwards. For nearly a century there were wars and forays, and different policies were followed by succeeding governors. Treaties were signed with various chiefs, neutral zones were proclaimed, settlement projects were attempted, and the frontier was moved up and down the map.

No African leaders emerged from among the Xhosas comparable with Shaka or Moshesh. Chiefs such as Gaika, Sandele and Ndlambe were of small stature. But one person must be mentioned, who was responsible for an incident so strange and tragic as to stand out among the most dramatic episodes of South African history. This person was Nonquase, a Xhosa Joan of Arc who was guided by voices and led her nation almost to commit suicide. Nonquase was a quiet, unobtrusive maid born in one of a cluster of grass huts surrounded by a stockade of thorn branches on a hillside near a running stream. As she sat dreaming beside this stream the departed spirits of her tribe came to talk to her, their voices sounding above the burble of the water as it tumbled merrily over the stones. The messages might have proved no more consequential than those so often received at a spiritualistic séance had it not been for an uncle named Mhlakaza, a forceful, scheming and ambitious man who saw an opportunity of furthering his own importance within the tribe. It was Mhlakaza who persuaded the chief to come and talk to his niece, who interpreted the allegorical messages from the tribal ancestors, and who called a great 'indaba' – a gathering of tribesmen – to hear the spirits speaking through the lips of Nonquase. First the maid correctly forecast rain, ordering the tribe to get ready to plough. Then in succession she correctly forecast the death of a headman, an outbreak of disease among the stock, a hail-

storm, and sundry other occurrences. Soon she was famous throughout the land, and uncle Mhlakaza basked in the favour he enjoyed.
But not for long.

In the spring of 1856, a few days before the first rains of the
season fell, the ancestral spirits came to Nonquase and ordered that
the tribe should do no ploughing, plant no crops, and should kill
and eat their cattle. On 18 February 1857, they declared, the sun
would rise up, blood-red; great herds of cattle would troop out of
the west, the underground storehouses would be filled with grain,
and lightning striking from the skies in a continual barrage would
drive the white people into the sea. Incredibly, the order was
obeyed. The tribe worked itself into a kind of trance, and feasting
and dancing continued far into the night, until by February of
that fateful year all the grain had been eaten and most of the stock
destroyed. It was estimated at the time that 70,000 Xhosas died
of starvation. Certainly, from that time onwards the tribe ceased
to be a border problem for the government at the Cape. Nonquase
herself had the grace to die of starvation, but uncle Mhlakaza
mysteriously disappeared, and rumour had it that he was, in fact,
a secret agent of the great Basuto chief Moshesh who wished to
destroy the power of the Xhosas in case they should threaten his
domain – a romantic and most improbable tale.

It is interesting to record that the Nguni trek southwards did
eventually reach the most southerly point of the African continent.
This happened just before and during the last world war, and what
brought it about was a sociological development of great importance to South Africa. Industries began to boom in the Cape Peninsula as part of the industrial revolution that took place between
1935 and 1945 after South Africa had abandoned the gold-standard
and brought her currency into line with British sterling. These new
industries sucked up the coloured workers who had previously
formed the main labouring classes in the Cape Peninsula, and a
labour vacuum was created at the bottom of the scale into which
Xhosas from the Transkei streamed. Shanty-towns mushroomed on
the Cape Flats and later the African townships of Langa and
Nyanga were built. The Government of Dr. Verwoerd has now
decreed that Africans must evacuate the Cape Peninsula, and a line
known as the 'Eiselen Line' has been drawn across the map from
about Mossel Bay northwards, which is to be the boundary shutting
Africans off from the rest of the Cape. But nobody really believes
that such a shift in population will ever take place. The Africans in
the Cape Peninsula are far too valuable as a source of labour.

Chapter 8

Trek North

I F THE season has been kind and the summer rains have fallen on the Amatola forests and the bush-clad flanks of the Katberg, a long tongue of brown water will thrust out from the mouth of the Great Fish River into the green-blue expanse of the Indian Ocean. One February morning in 1488 a small vessel with high poop and bulging sails came tacking up the coast against the Mozambique current, and when it ran into the brown flood-water the captain gave the order to heave-to. There, rocking on the heavy swells, he held a conference with his sullen, mutinous crew. They would proceed no further. So the captain gave the order to put about and the stout little ship soon faded into the haze of distance down towards Algoa Bay. Thus did the mariner Bartholomew Diaz, the first man to round the Cape from west to east, reach the mouth of the Great Fish River at about the same time that the Bantu did in their long trek southwards from the Great Lakes. Though neither was aware of it, this meeting lent a dramatic touch to the history of South Africa. It was almost as though Diaz put a spell upon the river, forbidding the migrating Africans to cross it, for they remained on the northern side of it for something like 250 years until the van of the migration of whites first reached them, trekking up from the Cape.

The Portuguese were seeking a sea-route round Africa to the east. First that romantic, lovable character Prince Henry the Navigator, then his nephew King John II, sent expedition after expedition down the coast of Africa. In 1485 Diego Cam reached the mouth of the Congo. Then, as we have related, Bartholomew Diaz rounded the Cape and reached the Great Fish River. Ten years later Vasco da Gama, following hard behind him, sailed past the Fish River to reach India, thus opening up one of the most important sea-routes in the world. For over 150 years no attempt was made by the white voyagers and traders who sailed round the coasts to settle in Africa. All the land from the Great Fish River down to Cape Point was inhabited by nomadic tribes of cattle-owning Hottentots and small groups of more primitive Bushmen lurking in the deepest kloofs and mountain caves. Game was plentiful, and in between the forests and scrub bush the veld was lush.

In 1510, just a decade after da Gama reached India, another Portuguese captain, Francisco de Almeida, landed with some companions on the shores of Table Bay in the hope of exchanging some rolls of cloth for cattle. But the party was suddenly attacked by a mob of Hottentots and all were killed. From then on the dangerous and inhospitable coasts were given a wide berth. Then in 1620 two sea captains, Shillinge and Fitzherbert, hoisted the British flag on Signal Hill, overlooking Table Bay, but no notice was taken of their action. A century and a half after Bartholomew Diaz and the first Bantu arrived at the mouth of the Great Fish River, the Dutch East India Company sent Johan van Riebeeck with a company of 125 persons in three ships to establish a victualling station at the foot of Table Mountain, for ships sailing to the east. This was in 1652. During the century and a quarter that followed, the station grew first into a settlement round the foot of Table Mountain, then into a patchwork of farms and villages spilling across the Cape Flats to occupy the strip of fertile, undulating land between the Hottentots' Holland and the sea. And as the population grew with further arrivals and its own natural increase, and there were demands for more land, the burghers settled along the wide strip of land between the Langeberg and the sea as far as Mossel Bay and George. Turning inland, they followed the Swartberg and the Winterberg to open up the districts of Beaufort West, Graaff Reinet and Uitenhage.

The next significant date in our brief survey is 1778 when the Dutch Governor at the Cape, van Plettenberg, made a tour of the new eastern outposts of the Colony and proclaimed the Great Fish River to be the boundary. From this time onwards the two migratory movements in southern Africa – the whites trekking northwards and eastwards and the Bantu driving downwards into the Cape Province – pressed up against each other and fought across the Fish River. They fought, and in many places they intermingled, forming the beginning of the multiracial pattern of the Republic as it is today.

An important point must now be made. The impression, so widely held, that the Africans had title to the land through prior occupation, and that the whites drove them out of it by conquest, is wrong. The Africans, as we know them today, are mainly the Bantu who came down from the north. Before either the Bantu moved in from the north or the white men pushed up from the south, the land was occupied by Hottentots and Bushmen, who were the original title-holders, if we may be permitted to use the term. As the Bantu advanced they wiped out the Bushmen and Hottentots, save for a few whom they assimilated. The whites, on the other hand, made no deliberate attempt to wipe out either the Bushmen or the Hottentots. The Bushmen were unassimilable. They stole stock when they got a chance to do so and fired their poisoned arrows at any intruder they could ambush. They were shot in retaliation. But generally they did not wait to be shot, retreating into their caves and kloofs and to the uninhabited fringes of the Kalahari desert. Many of them were wiped out by smallpox and other diseases introduced by the white man. The Hottentots fared a little better. Some were killed in armed clashes with the white man and a great many died of the white man's diseases. There were also droughts that took their toll. In 1867 a virulent epidemic of influenza from the east wrought havoc among the Hottentots, while in 1713 and 1755 severe outbreaks of smallpox spread through the Hottentots right up to the Fish River. Another degenerating factor was the extensive traffic in liquor. The whites themselves were of mixed character, drawn from several countries. They totalled about 1,500 by the year 1700, of which some 1,200 were Dutch, 200 French and about 100 were of German origin. By 1778, when Governor van Plettenberg declared the Great Fish River to be the north-eastern boundary of the Colony, the white population had grown to 15,000, partly through immigration and partly as a result of natural increase. Some 5,000 lived in Cape Town and the rest were spread throughout the Colony, on farms and in villages like Paarl, Worcester, Tulbagh, Stellenbosch, Swellendam, Mossel Bay, Uitenhage and Graaff Reinet. The population of coloureds – the progeny of whites and non-whites – totalled around 2,000 and there were some 16,000 slaves. The economy of the Colony depended upon stock-raising, wine-farming, wheat-growing and trade, both with passing ships and with Africans beyond the borders. Farms varied in size from small-holdings in the Cape Peninsula to ranches up to 5,000 acres in extent in the eastern areas.

A year after the declaration of the frontier the downward-moving Bantu and the upward-thrusting colonists came into violent collision. Strong bands of Xhosas raided across the Great Fish River into the thinly-settled regions stretching from Algoa Bay inland to Graaff Reinet. Farms were looted, some whites were killed, and large numbers of cattle were driven off. The burghers organised themselves into commandos and drove the Xhosas back across the Fish River, recovering 5,000 head of stolen stock. But within a few years the Xhosas came raiding again, and the pattern of sporadic attacks and counter-attacks continued for the next 70 years until

the power of the Xhosas was finally broken with the strange mass-
suicide event provoked by the voice-hearing maiden Nonquase and
her uncle.

Many changes took place in the colony during this period. There
were the decline and fall of the Dutch East India Company, the
short occupation of Table Bay by a French fleet, and the replacement of the French by a British occupation force. For a short while
the Cape was returned to the Dutch; then in 1806 the British were
back again and they remained in control of the Cape Colony for
more than a century. Meanwhile in 1795 the burghers in the
frontier district of Graaff Reinet revolted against the Dutch officials
and tried to set up a small republic of their own. A few months
later the burghers of Swellendam decided to follow this example,
but they had hardly driven out the Dutch officials before the
French fleet arrived in Table Bay. They did a brisk trade with the
French, and when the English came they agreed to accept the over-
riding authority of the British commander in Cape Town. When
the Cape was handed back to the Dutch, both Swellendam and
Graaff Reinet dutifully returned to the fold. The Dutch government
sent a vigorous and enlightened man, Commissioner de Mist, to
straighten out the affairs of the colony, but the second British occupation of 1906 took place before he could put any lasting reforms
into effect.

The British administration began fairly well. Troops were stationed along the Fish River to prevent the Xhosas from raiding into
the colony, and a number of administrative and economic reforms
were introduced. Then a series of events took place that once again
threw the border regions into turmoil and eventually caused the
Great Trek of burghers into the hinterland which began in 1835,
and was to prove of far-reaching significance to Southern Africa.
The first of these events was a clash between the burghers and the
missionaries who had established themselves in the border area and
even beyond the Great Fish River during the end of the eighteenth
century and beginning of the nineteenth century. These missionaries
had come from Holland, Denmark, France and England in a great
European movement to convert the heathens of the world to Christianity, and they founded mission-stations with churches, schools and
hospitals among the Hottentots and the Bantu.

From the outset the burghers regarded their activities with mis-
trust. The burghers lived on patriarchal lines, with their slaves and
their servants, their cattle and horses. Each farm homestead was
like a little hamlet, clustered near a spring or stream of water.
Almost invariably there was a small dam to hold the water, and

perhaps a willow-tree, with half a dozen ducks running free. The farm-house was plainly but sturdily built, four or five rooms in a row with intercommunicating doors and deep windows looking on to a stone-paved *stoep*. The roof was thatched, whenever possible with *riet*, the thin reeds that grew so profusely in the *vleis* and marshes. The walls were of sun-dried mud bricks or stone, thick and plastered, and there were gables at each end of the house and sometimes an ornate gable in the centre where the door led into the *voorkamer*, the main living-room. Heavy yellow-wood beams carried a ceiling of wooden planks, if they could be obtained. But as often as not the ceiling was of reeds with a thick layer of earth upon them. The floors were flagged with stone or stamped hard and covered with a mixture of dung and clay which in time took on a fine polish. They were comfortable homes, warm in winter and cool in summer, with a character that has somehow gone out of the bungalows that have since taken their place.

Behind the farm-house, across a yard, were the kraals for the cattle, sheep, goats and pigs, and the storehouses, with sleeping quarters for the slaves and their families. If the farmer employed Hottentots or Bantu as servants in addition to slaves, they built themselves huts in the surrounding scrub. The burghers were religious, and they had a dour, Calvinistic faith based on a strict interpretation of the Bible, which was reverently kept by every family, and on the front pages were recorded the births, deaths and marriages of all the members of the family. Every evening as darkness fell and candles were lighted, the family and the slaves and servants gathered in the *voorkamer* and the burgher read from the Bible and said a prayer. The slaves and other servants were treated kindly and were well fed, clothed and nursed through their illnesses, so long as they observed the master-servant relationship and understood clearly that the white man was superior and commanded obedience and respect. Forgetfulness, or stupidity, or some petty theft, or an assault by one slave upon another, or even failure to turn up to work, or drunkenness, or fornication could be treated tolerantly and with a sense of humour, but woe betide the slave or servant who challenged the superiority of his white master. The one thing about which there could be no argument was that the white man was *baas*. The burghers were hospitable folk, giving a ready welcome to a stranger and inviting him to share the family meal and to sleep in a deep feather-bed in the guest-room if there was one, or to share the room used by the unmarried sons. Food was plentiful, provided the season was good, consisting of a great deal of meat – fresh, salted, dried and pickled – pumpkins, potatoes, rice when it could be obtained from the Cape, a delicious bread baked with a yeast fermented from whole-wheat, and other delicacies including *melk-tert* and *boer-beskuit* (rusks).

A farmer's most prized possessions were his trek-wagon, most beautifully made, with large, iron-bound wheels of hardwood, and his guns. The wagon was pulled by a team of twelve to eighteen oxen, and when the family trekked away to *nag-maal*, the Communion service held periodically at the nearest town, a canopy, sturdily constructed of canvas over a wooden frame, was fastened over the wagon to shelter the stores, bedding and supplies. The farmers' wives made their own candles, soap and preserves, and the farmer and his sons cast leaden shot and bullets for the guns.

While the burghers, generally speaking, were tolerant and kindly towards their slaves and servants, there were, of course, exceptions. And there were servants who clashed with their masters, or resented punishment, or were wrongly flogged or over-worked. Inevitably complaints were carried to the missionaries, who as often as not passed on the complaints to the authorities, and charges were brought against the farmers. The burghers regarded the missionaries with deep distrust, mainly because they preached the heretical doctrine of equality between whites and non-whites, or at least the burghers believed that they did. Every complaint against a white was regarded as a challenge to the doctrine of *baasskap*, the belief that the white man was superior and must remain boss. The atmosphere in the frontier areas became heavy with rumour and suspicion. The missionaries were openly charged with inciting the Hottentots and slaves against their masters, and there was bitter resentment because the authorities appeared to sympathise with the missionaries.

Following a series of complaints lodged by a Dutch missionary named Van der Kemp, a Circuit Court on a visit to the border regions was ordered to carry out an investigation, and a dozen farmers were summoned to appear before the Court. The whole question became a *cause célèbre* and feelings ran high among the burghers. Most of the charges were dismissed by the Court, and Van der Kemp and his associates were severely reprimanded, but the bitterness remained and deepened during the years that followed.

Then occurred an incident, relatively unimportant in itself yet destined to play a significant role in South African history. In later years the story of this incident, sentimentally embellished, was to be repeated from pulpit and political platform, and it became an important symbolic saga like the tale of Horatio at the Bridge and the Charge of the Light Brigade. It had all the overtones calculated

to arouse the emotions of the average Afrikaner nurtured from birth
on a mental diet of white supremacy. The facts, briefly, were these :
two white officers and a dozen Hottentot soldiers went to arrest a
burgher named Bezuidenhout who for two years had refused to
obey a summons to come to court on a charge of ill-treating a
coloured servant. Bezuidenhout opened fire on the party, who
returned his fire and killed him. Bezuidenhout's brother swore
vengeance and managed to persuade a score or so of farmers to
join him in an ill-organised and poorly-supported revolt which was
easily suppressed by the authorities. The ringleaders were tried,
condemned to death and five of them were hanged at a place called
Slagter's Nek.

Whether or not Bezuidenhout did in fact ill-treat a coloured
servant, or whether he should have ignored a legal summons, or
whether his brother was wise to stir up a revolt on such a doubtful
issue, have simply not been considered in telling this unhappy story
over the years. What mattered were Bezuidenhout sacrificing his
life on the altar of white supremacy, the 'unforgivable' act of sending Hottentots to arrest a white man, the assumption that missionaries were at the bottom of the tragedy, and the savage act of
hanging five white men who had merely tried to uphold the white
man's appointed role of civilising darkest Africa. Some years ago a
beam of wood, said to have been the beam from which the rebels
were hanged, was discovered on a farm in the neighbourhood of
Slagter's Nek, and is today exhibited with the awe and sanctimony
often accorded in Europe to a religious relic. As for the authorities
of the day, they ought to have made allowances for the psychological factors that lay behind the abortive revolt and though
common for such an offence at the time, hanging was certainly a
harsh sentence to have carried out.

At all events, the talk in the border regions now turned to the
possibility of escaping from a regime that seemed only too ready to
listen to tales from 'Kafirs' (Africans) and missionaries. It was a
regime, moreover, that seemed to hold dangerous notions about
rights for barbarians, and failed to uphold the doctrine of white
supremacy. The Afrikaner is a fearless huntsman with a great love
of solitude and a remarkable capacity for fending for himself.
Hunting-parties had foraged far afield, crossing the Orange River
and exploring the high plateau of the Transvaal as far as the
Limpopo River. They told of fertile land, well-watered, healthy,
and ideally suited to the ranching of stock. They reported that one
of Shaka's generals, Msilikazi, had broken away from Zululand
with a large band of followers and had swept across the Transvaal

and Free State highveld, killing all the scattered tribes he encountered and leaving vast areas of countryside uninhabited.

Three other developments increased the urge among the burghers of the frontier areas to trek north in search of new lands where they could escape from a regime which they regarded as being unsympathetic to their traditional way of life. One was a decision to anglicise the colony. In 1822 a proclamation substituted English for Dutch as the official language, and the judicial system was remodelled with 'magistrates' taking the place of *landdrosts* and *heemraden*. The Burgher Senate at Cape Town was abolished and British coinage replaced the Dutch rix-dollar then in use. Though Dutch had been the official language used by most literate people, a popular dialect derived mainly from Dutch but including some Malay, French and English words, was beginning to be employed, especially among the coloureds and slaves. Known as *die taal*, it was the forerunner of Afrikaans, today one of the two official languages of the South African Republic and spoken by the majority of whites.

The second development was the freeing of the slaves, who numbered about 35,000 in 1820, when the white population of the colony was reckoned at approximately 47,000. The emancipation of the slaves at the Cape followed logically on the passage in Britain of the Abolition Act of 1807. In the Cape Colony, as we have already pointed out, slavery was on the whole free from the cruelty and abuses of other lands and was conducted as humanely as it is possible to operate so inhuman a system. There was little opposition at the Cape to the principle of abolishing slaves, but great indignation was aroused by the inept manner in which the British authorities carried out the operation. The slaves at the Cape were valued at £3,000,000, but after a long haggle the British Government decided to pay only £1,250,000. Only part of each claim was paid in cash and the rest was paid in 3½ per cent stock. Worst of all from the point of view of the burghers, payment was made only in London and not at the Cape, and this inevitably led to a racket in which fortunes were made by agents who collected the slave-titles from the burghers, went to London to obtain the money, and as often as not failed to return to South Africa. Even when a burgher did eventually get his money, he was lucky if he received a quarter of what the slaves had cost him. Incidentally, most of the freed slaves remained on to work with their masters, which is a fair indication how well they had been treated.

The third event was the landing of the 5,000 British immigrants at Algoa Bay in 1820 for settlement along the Great Fish River border. There was no friction between the new British settlers and and burghers, who did all they could to help them, but the coming of the British immigrants was a clear sign that this was to be a British colony, with the English language, British institutions and the British 'liberalistic' outlook towards the Hottentots and 'Kafirs'. What happened to the British immigrants is an epic that will be told in a later chapter. With two or three individual exceptions, the British settlers did not take part in the Great Trek. Their arrival had other significant implications for South Africa that will be discussed in due course.

The actual incident that triggered off the Trek was the war of 1834 when thousands of Xhosas swept across the Fish River border, burning and pillaging. The burghers immediately organised themselves into commandos and went to the aid of the British garrisons in the border zone. Riding with long stirrups in heavy 'dish' saddles, the burghers were superb and fearless horsemen, with an intimate knowledge of the bush country and a shrewd instinct as to what the Xhosa impis were likely to do. Though outnumbered by ten to one, they attacked the Xhosas with such vigour and skill that the Africans were quickly driven back across the Great Fish River and the war was soon over. The British Governor, Sir Benjamin d'Urban, was deeply impressed and loud in his official praises of the burghers, many of whom had suffered the pillage of their homes and loss of their cattle and sheep. Sir Benjamin promised them compensation in the form of additional land. His plan was to push the frontier back to the Kei River, to drive the Xhosas out of the territory between the Great Fish and the Kei Rivers, and to settle whites and friendly Africans there.

But when news of the scheme leaked out, a vigorous outcry was raised by the missionaries. They pointed out that one of the causes of the Xhosa attack was shortage of land. The Xhosas were being squeezed from the rear, their numbers and cattle were increasing, and they did not have enough pasture for their stock. It would be a cruel injustice to deprive them of their land, and it would only aggravate their economic problems. The missionaries had powerful friends in high places in Britain who persuaded the Colonial Secretary, Lord Glenelg, that the d'Urban plan would be morally wrong, and it was vetoed. This, for the burghers who had come so promptly to the aid of the British garrisons and who now saw no likelihood of compensation for their efforts and their losses, was the last straw. They decided to trek north.

Thus in 1834 three parties were sent out to reconnoitre, one to South-West Africa, another to the Zoutpansberg in the Northern

Transvaal and the third through the Free State to Natal. The reports brought back from Natal and the Transvaal were favourable and in the following year two groups of trekkers set out for the north with their wagons, their cattle, and as much food and equipment as they could carry. The main body of trekkers left in 1836. The first two groups were savagely attacked by the Zulu general Msilikazi, who almost wiped out one of them. The other group struggled on to the Northern Transvaal where many trekkers contracted malaria. Some of those who survived eventually found their way down to the Portuguese settlement of Lourenço Marques on the shores of Delagoa Bay.

The main group which set out in 1836 drove Msilikazi out of the Transvaal across the Limpopo River into Rhodesia. There he settled down in a region inhabited by his Nguni forbears three hundred years previously. He quickly destroyed the scattered tribes he found there and founded the Matabele nation in a vast expanse of country around the Matoppos and what is now the town of Bulawayo. Meanwhile the migrating burghers, known as the voortrekkers, settled in the Free State, in parts of the Transvaal and in the midlands of Natal. A small group of English had already settled at Durban, on the Natal coast, but the British Government had refused repeated requests to annex the territory. The trekkers who crossed the Drakensberg into Natal, under the leadership of Peter Retief, tried to negotiate a cession of territory from Dingane, the Zulu king, and some sixty of them, including Retief, were murdered at the royal Zulu *kraal*, as related in the previous chapter. After defeating Dingane, the trekkers did eventually establish a republic in Natal with its capital in the picturesque, mountain-ringed city of Pietermaritzburg, but it only lasted for five years. The British Government changed its mind and decided to annex Natal, and after a short struggle the burghers submitted. Most of them left their farms in disgust and returned over the Drakensberg to settle in the Free State and the Transvaal.

On the high plateau of the Free State and the Transvaal two main organised communities were then developed, one around Winburg in the Free State and the other around Potchefstroom in the Transvaal. Watching these developments, the British Government could not make up its mind whether to insist that the burghers were still British subjects, and to annex their newly-won territories, or to allow them to organise their own independent republics. Meanwhile a community of coloureds known as Griquas had settled across the Orange River in what is now the district of Phillipolis, and the British had a treaty with the Griqua chief,

Adam Kok. A British outpost was established at Bloemfontein, now the capital of the Free State, and an official was put in charge with a vaguely-defined authority over the territory between the Vaal and Orange Rivers, including the area occupied by the Griquas. In 1848 all this territory was formally annexed by the British Government, and the burghers in the Free State immediately rose up in arms. The British sent a force which defeated them, and the Orange River Sovereignty was then proclaimed. Four years later when the Sovereignty was in difficulties with Moshesh in nearby Basutoland, and when the Xhosas down on the Cape eastern border were again giving trouble, the British Government again changed its mind. The independence of the Free State was recognised and the British withdrew from Bloemfontein. A Treaty was also signed with the burghers of the Transvaal, recognising their right to run their own affairs.

Left on their own, the trekkers who had settled north of the Orange River first split into groups, then merged to form two republics, one in the Transvaal and the other in the Free State. By 1867, when diamonds were discovered at Hopetown, near the junction of the Vet and Vaal Rivers, the main northward trek of whites into the hinterland may be said to have been completed. Of course, as the population grew in the Cape Colony, and gold was found in the Transvaal, there was a steady drift to the north. But these later migrants were not trekkers in the same spirit and with the same motives that drove those burghers from the frontier region to move with their wagons, their horses and stock far into the hinterland. By 1867 the northward trek of whites from the Cape had been accomplished.

Chapter 9

Afrikaner Nationalism

A SQUAT FIGURE in bronze, standing high upon a massive granite
pedestal, dominates the central square of Pretoria, administrative capital and third largest city of South Africa. Broad
shoulders hunched forward; strong, stubborn chin sunk in a straggly
beard; eyelids pouched round small eyes set wide apart in a heavy,
unsmiling face, Oom* Paul Kruger broods with a kind of serene
impassivity over the green lawns, the jacaranda trees, the street and
the Palace of Justice over on the far side of the square.

Stephanus Johannes Paulus Kruger, four times President of the
Transvaal Republic and one of the most remarkable men to dominate the South African scene during the latter half of the nineteenth
century, may be described as the father of Afrikaner Nationalism.
He it was who gave a special ideological meaning and purpose to
the Great Trek. He, more than any other individual, welded the
scattered burgher communities who had moved into the hinterland
into an organic whole, and gave them cohesion, strength, and self-
confidence. He inspired a new and distinctive Afrikaans patriotism,
narrow, tough, highly resourceful and unrelenting. Oom Paul
Kruger created the image for Afrikanerdom, and to understand him
is to understand the Afrikaner. He rose to eminence and authority
because he was completely in tune with the thoughts, hopes and
aspirations of the burghers among whom he lived and worked. He
embodied everything for which they stood, and his bluntness, rough
exterior and resourcefulness were symbolic of his day.

Paul Kruger's humble origin as a younger son in a Boer family,
his physical strength and endurance, his courage, demonstrated over
and over again under conditions the trekkers could understand, his
prowess as a hunter, his Calvinism, his loud, strong voice, a certain
unpredictability about what he might say next, and above all his
'slimness' all made him a natural leader. This word 'slim' is peculiar to the Afrikaans language, and there is no exact English trans-
lation. It is 'cunning' without the primitive undertone to that

* ' Oom ', literally translated ' Uncle '. A term of endearment and respect
often applied to older men among the leaders of the community.

87

word. It is cunning combined with wisdom, rather like the lore of Solomon in contrast with the Sermon on the Mount. There was, in fact, a Solomonic quality about many of the sayings attributed to Paul Kruger. The fact that he enjoyed almost no formal education of any kind and could only write with difficulty was an asset to his career, not the reverse. It put him on the same plane as his fellow burghers. Had he been highly educated and scholarly he would have been suspect, as men like W. J. Leyds and Jan Christian Smuts always were.

Born in the Colesberg area of the Northern Cape, Paul Kruger was the fourth son of a struggling sheep-farmer. At the age of ten he crossed the Orange River with his parents and their wagon and stock in the first party of trekkers to set out in search of new homes in the hinterland. He helped load guns when the burghers were attacked by the former Zulu general Msilikazi, and he was with the commando that eventually drove Msilikazi across the Limpopo to found the Matabele nation as related in the last chapter. His family settled near the present town of Rustenburg, on the far side of the Magaliesberg mountains, and in due course he married and went farming himself.

At this stage it is appropriate to mention an incident that occurred shortly after Kruger's marriage and when he was farming, an event that had an important influence on his life and helped to create the aura that surrounded him, especially in his later years. Kruger belonged to the *Dopper* sect of the Dutch Reformed Church, the puritans of the Afrikaner community who adhered strictly to the doctrines of Calvin and had rigid notions of personal conduct. In his youth and early manhood he was inclined to treat religious matters flippantly, but then something happened to bring him up with a jerk, like a Boer pony wrenched back on its haunches with the curb.

'One night', wrote his biographer, Manfred Nathan, 'he gave his wife some chapters to read in the Bible. Then he suddenly left the house and did not reappear for three days. He went into the mountains near his farm Waterkloof. There he strove with the Lord, as did Jacob of old. At length his wife and friends became anxious. Some men went to look for him and climbed the hills. They heard somebody singing, but took no particular notice, and returned. Then it struck them that it might have been Kruger. They went out again and found him in miserable condition, what with hunger, thirst and fatigue, for he had fasted all the time.'

This story was widely related on the stoeps of the farmhouses in later years when he was President, and certainly helped to build the image of Oom Paul the patriarch, destined to lead his people out of bondage. After his 'conversion' Kruger always kept a Bible handy and made a practice of reading passages from it each day. In his presidential office and at his home in Pretoria a Bible lay on the table at which he worked, and he would thump its cover with the palm of his hand to emphasise a point he wished to drive home. Sometimes when he replied to a deputation of burghers in flowing, Biblical phrases, his words seemed to them to come out of the pages of the Great Book. At the same time Kruger never tried to force his beliefs upon anyone and was tolerant towards other religions.

At about the time of his 'conversion', Kruger began to take a lead in the public affairs of his community at Rustenburg. Before long he was elected commandant of the local commando, which was frequently called out to fight some African tribe or other. There were then four self-run but loosely-associated communities, one at Potchefstroom, another in the north in the Zoutpansberg, a third in the north-east at Lydenburg, and the fourth at Rustenburg. There was a single commandant-general for Rustenburg and Potchefstroom, A. W. J. Pretorius, and Kruger became his friend and trusted lieutenant. He went with Pretorius as a Boer delegate to the Sand River conference with the British in 1852 which gave the burghers of the Transvaal the right to manage their own affairs. This was Kruger's first experience of diplomacy, and afterwards Pretorius was loud in his praises of the role played by Kruger in the negotiations.

In the years that followed Kruger set himself the task, which he believed to be divinely inspired, of creating an independent Afrikaner nation. He saw himself as a new Moses and his fellow burghers as the Afrikaner volk whose ordained role it was to civilise and to rule the land of milk and honey which lay between the Orange River and the curving escarpment of the Drakensberg in the north and the east. His first task was to unite the quarrelling communities of burghers, beginning with the four settlements in the Transvaal. Then he must try to join the Transvaal with the Free State. The African tribes spread in a horseshoe round the western, northern and eastern regions of the Transvaal would have to be subdued, since they kept attacking the burgher communities and stealing their stock. Lastly, and most perplexing of all, he had to deal with the British, and this called for rare judgment and determination, since the British never seemed to know for long what they wanted, either with the burghers or the African tribes.

By 1860 it had been agreed to merge the four communities of the

Transvaal in a single republic, but about five years of civil strife occurred before this became a reality. In 1863 Kruger became commandant-general of the Republic, and during the succeeding years, until the Transvaal was annexed by the British in 1877, he was occupied mainly with campaigns against African chiefs in the Zoutpansberg, a sortie against Moshesh in Basutoland, a campaign against the Zulus, a war against Secocoeniland over towards the Portuguese border, a boundary commission to decide the boundary between the Republic and Portuguese East Africa, and various political disputes among the burghers, some of them of a turbulent kind. The British pretext for annexing the Republic was that it was weak and unable to subdue the African tribes, but Manfred Nathan describes the annexation as 'an act of sheer brigandage. It violated international law. . . . It had not even the merit of plausibility.' In 1881 the burghers revolted against the British and Kruger played a leading role, both in the fighting and in the negotiations that followed. The Boers heavily defeated a British force sent against them from Natal and the British decided to restore the independence of the Republic. Two years later Kruger was elected President.

In his seventeen years of office he achieved a great many things. Gold was discovered in the Transvaal, and as mines were opened up first at Barberton then on the Witwatersrand, wealth came to the Republic. While welcoming the flourishing state of his treasury, Kruger was always unhappy about the source of his newly-found revenue and on several occasions warned that gold and mammon might prove the downfall of the Afrikaner volk. Rich seams of coal were uncovered and industries were started. Railways were built, linking the Republic with Lourenço Marques, Natal, the Free State and the Cape. All these developments attracted an influx of fortune-seekers and immigrants from overseas, most of them English-speaking. These 'uitlanders' created new political problems for Kruger and the burghers, leading eventually to the Anglo-Boer war.

Kruger was determined to create a separate Afrikaner nation, with its own religion, language, culture, traditions and special way-of-life. He was inflexibly opposed to the idea that the Afrikaner should merge into a wider nationhood embracing all sections, as had come about in the United States of America. He regarded such a course as a betrayal of the spirit of the great trek into the hinter-land and a denial of everything for which he had striven throughout his eventful life. It was God's will, he believed, that the Afrikaner should be master, here in the land to which he had been providen-tially guided, for so it had been revealed to him during his three-day fast in the Magaliesberg. This conviction is shown by his opening words, spoken with deep emotion, when the parliaments of the Transvaal and the Free State met jointly on 2 October 1899, to discuss the outbreak of the Anglo-Boer war : 'To tell you what is in my mind : you know how the Lord transplanted the people to this country, and led it here amid miracles; so that we should have to say : "Lord, I no longer believe in thee," if things came to such a pass with us that now, when thousands of enemies are assailing us, we voluntarily surrendered the Land which He, and not we our-selves, gave us. Let us trust in God and together offer up our prayers to the Lord. He is waiting for our prayers and He will be with us. The decision rests with Him, and He will decide, not on lies but on the ground of truth.'

And that the President likened his own divinely-inspired role to that of Moses, who led the Israelites out of Egypt, was indicated by the closing passages of the same revealing speech : 'One short word more. Moses was a man of God, and the Lord spoke with him; but at a time of great stress and combat, his friends had to stay up his hands, for he was but a weak mortal. Aaron had to support him in the faith. So let us too remember our generals and fighting-generals in our prayers, and unceasingly offer our prayers to God. Let us support them in their faith, and let us not forget to strengthen with prayers the men who have to conduct the Government.'

Ostensibly the Anglo-Boer war was fought about such questions as the franchise for the *uitlander* community in the Transvaal, the manner of administering the Republic, relations with African tribes, and rival territorial claims. But the real, hidden issue was the clash between British imperialism and Afrikaner nationalism. Kruger's concept of a chosen people destined to rule the sub-continent was supported by a great many Afrikaners down south as well as in the Republics, and on their side the British, who were busy building a great empire, began to regard Afrikaner nationalism as a threat to their position in southern Africa. Professor Etienne Marais made a detailed examination of the papers relating to the Anglo-Boer war when the British archives were opened to the end of the nineteenth century, and his book on the fall of the Republic is perhaps the best and certainly the most authoritative on the subject. Professor Marais writes that the British High Commissioner, Sir Alfred Milner, 'came to the conclusion that the independence of the South African Republic was incompatible with the interests of Britain because the republic was the prime cause of the growth of Afrikaner nationalism throughout South Africa. Afrikaner nationalism was the real enemy. What was this Afrikaner nationalism of the late 1890s? Its portrait as painted by Milner looks remarkably like the visage it wears today when it has grown to full stature as a result of the Anglo-Boer war and an effort extending over half a century.'

Milner feared the narrow, exclusive character of the Republic. He believed that the English, who had migrated into the Transvaal following the discovery of gold, would be 'afrikanerised' if Kruger's plan of extending the franchise only gradually and cautiously were put into effect. On the other hand, as he wrote in one of his dispatches, if the English were admitted 'wholesale' to franchise rights, they would 'burst the existing mould'. Another Englishman who was convinced that Kruger aimed at Afrikaner hegemony in the whole of southern Africa was the Colonial Secretary, Joseph Chamberlain. In a memorandum to the British Cabinet he wrote that Kruger was seeking a 'united states of South Africa' to be dominated by the Afrikaans section.

Looking back from this historic perspective it would seem that there was a good deal of substance for Chamberlain's view. Kruger himself, as will be shown later, never wanted a small, isolated Transvaal, and always had in mind a wider 'confederation'. Moreover, in the years just before the Anglo-Boer war he had some brilliant men around him such as Jan Christian Smuts, who without doubt had grasped a new and most significant factor. This factor was also seen by Lord Selborne who wrote to Chamberlain after a visit to South Africa as follows : 'In a generation the Republic will by its wealth and population dominate South Africa. South African politics must revolve around the Transvaal, which will be the only possible market for the agricultural produce or the manufactures of the Cape Colony and Natal. The commercial attraction of the Transvaal will be so great that a union of the South African states with it will be absolutely necessary for their prosperous existence. The only question in my opinion is whether that union will be inside or outside the British Empire.'

The British could see that the key to the situation in South Africa lay with the Transvaal, which possessed such a vast treasure-house of mineral resources. They argued, correctly as events proved, that whoever ruled the Transvaal would in the end come to dominate the sub-continent, and they feared what they regarded as the narrow, chauvinistic character of Kruger's brand of nationalism. Where they made a tragic mistake was in believing that this nationalism could be eradicated by force of arms, and replaced by a broad, pro-British South-Africanism through immigration and anglicisation. They miscalculated when they thought that military intervention would be a rapid, relatively painless operation. Instead, it turned out to be a long and costly affair with psychologically-damaging aspects such as the burning of Boer homesteads and herding their women and children into concentration camps where many died from disease. The British also underestimated the depth and tenacity of the nationalistic sentiments that had been implanted by Kruger in the north, and by another outstanding Afrikaans leader, Onze Jan Hofmeyr, in the Cape Province.

We can see today how much wiser Milner and Chamberlain would have been had they set themselves firmly against armed intervention and had they sought to reach a friendly understanding with Kruger, as they could easily have done despite the activities of Rhodes and his friends and the sabre-rattling of jingoistic elements on the Witwatersrand and in Britain. Had the twin-goals of British policy been co-operation and confederation instead of coercion and subjugation the whole picture in South Africa, including even Southern Rhodesia, would have been vastly different, and in the long run far more advantageous for Britain and the Commonwealth.

The question may be asked whether Kruger would ever have agreed to closer association with the other states, and on what terms. In 1880 when the Transvaal regained its independence after the short British annexation, Kruger offered to enter into 'confederation' with the other colonies and states of South Africa, but unhappily the significance of this proposal was missed by the British at the time. Four years previously the idea of forming a confederation of Southern African States had been taken up by the Earl of Carnarvon, then British Secretary of State for the Colonies, who unfortunately handled it ineptly and it came to nothing. It was rushed before the Cape Parliament without proper preparation or explanation and rejected by that body. Its details were not thought out and no attempt was made to mobilise responsible opinion in favour of the project. Kruger, of course, was fully aware of Carnarvon's plan for federation, and had his offer been grasped and energetically followed up, the scheme might have been saved, even after the reverse it suffered in the Cape. Had the 'confederation' idea been revived fifteen years later, when difficulties were being experienced with the *uitlanders*, there is no reason to believe that Kruger would not have been sympathetic if the British had come to him in a spirit of genuine co-operation. Such a 'confederation' would, in time, have included the Protectorates and Southern Rhodesia and would have been free from the legacy of suspicion and bitterness caused by the Anglo-Boer war. There are a great many responsible observers who believe that a federation rather than a union would have been a far better structure for

South Africa, and that under a federal system the apartheid policy that has led to South Africa's exit from the Commonwealth and her isolation in the world could never have evolved.

Be that as it may, Britain went to war with Paul Kruger's republic to crush the narrow concept of Afrikaner nationalism which she feared would threaten the process of Empire-building upon which she was engaged and which might undermine her strategic hold on Southern Africa. She wanted to be sure that the gold and other resources of the Transvaal would remain under her own control and not fall within the grasp of some other predatory power. Though the Boers fought with a skill, courage, and stubbornness that took the world by surprise, their eventual defeat was inevitable. When the first phase of the war was over and the guerilla campaign was beginning, Kruger himself left on a mission to seek aid overseas and he died a lonely exile in Switzerland.

After the war Milner was appointed British High Commissioner in South Africa. His aim was to restore the economy of the Transvaal and Free State as quickly as possible, to develop the gold industry of the Transvaal, and launch schemes of massive immigration into the Free State and Transvaal in order to balance the Afrikaans section of the population numerically. As soon as the 'balancing' process had been completed the plan was to establish responsible governments in the two former republics, then to merge the four states in a South Africa that would have been thoroughly anglicised and would be well and truly within the British Empire. However, for various reasons Milner's plan did not succeed in the way he had hoped it would do. His land-settlement schemes attracted only a fraction of the British immigrants he had hoped for. The gold industry did not at first boom as had been anticipated and the growth of the Witwatersrand was slower than expected. There were significant political changes in Britain and the new Liberal Government there had different ideas about South Africa.

Full responsible government was given to the Transvaal in 1906 and to the Free State in the following year. Soon plans were set on foot to link all four states, and in 1910 the Union of South Africa was formed. Botha, Smuts and Hertzog, all Boer generals in the war, had entered the political arena, and the two former dominated the National Convention which worked out the constitution for Union. Botha and Smuts firmly rejected the idea of a federal form of government and insisted on a unitary system. They were northerners and they wanted the Transvaal, which would obviously make the biggest economic contribution to the new South African state, to have the largest say over all matters of common concern.

The National Convention was nearly wrecked by a dispute between the Transvaal and the Cape over the question of extending franchise rights to non-whites, and in the end a compromise was reached allowing the Cape to keep its franchise system which included coloureds and Africans. In later years the Transvaal had its way and the vote was taken away from the Africans in the Cape Province.

Botha and Smuts emerged as the two most powerful figures in the new Union of South Africa, and they followed a broad policy of South-Africanism which attempted to synthesise the cultures and traditions of the English and Afrikaans sections of the population. General Hertzog at first worked with them but in 1912 he broke away to form an Afrikaans Nationalist Party. Hertzog's goal did not differ, in its broad essentials, from that of Botha and Smuts, though the Nationalist Party he led assumed at times an image that disturbed him. Like Botha and Smuts, Hertzog aimed at a broad South-Africanism in which the Afrikaans and English cultures would be blended and in which both sides would enjoy equality. Where he differed from Botha and Smuts was in the approach to this goal of South-Africanism. They were leaning towards the English, he felt, and were not taking sufficiently positive steps to strengthen and assert the position of the Afrikaner. A great deal of leeway had to be made up in this regard, he urged. Before a harmonious fusion of both sides could take place the Afrikaner must first be raised to a position of equality. The Afrikaans language was in a far weaker position than English, and it must be raised up in the civil service, throughout the schools, in industry and trade. Culturally, economically, and in all ways the position of the Afrikaner must be strengthened. The Afrikaner was deeply attached to his republican ideal and South Africa must at least become a sovereign independent state, so that both the Afrikaner and the Englishman would develop pride in a common nationhood. He called this the 'twin-stream policy'. For the time being there would be two cultural streams in South Africa, Afrikaans and English, and when the Afrikaans stream was flowing strongly enough and the English stream had become sufficiently South African in outlook, the two could merge in the broad river of South-Africanism.

To Hertzog's banner flocked those 'hard-core' Afrikaners who had refused to accept defeat in the Anglo-Boer war and who cherished the Kruger concept of an exclusive Afrikanerdom, imbued with the ideals of the Great Trek and the Republics. These radicals were the apostles of *Krugerisme*, which was destined to be a significant influence in the political development of South Africa.

Krugerisme aimed at *baasskap*, the dominance of the Afrikaner within a restored Transvaal Republic to be run in the image of Paul Kruger, and if possible the supremacy of Afrikanerdom throughout Southern Africa. There was no question of a fusion of the two streams into a broad South-Africanism in which both sides would be equal.

At first it suited the Krugerites to support Hertzog and work within the Nationalist Party. But after he had attained power and had begun to insist on equality between the two streams, they became restive. Their concern grew when he declared himself satisfied with the sovereign independence of South Africa *within the Commonwealth* as achieved through the Statute of Westminster. They began to group within the Party, and to press for a more radical form of republicanism, and a rift appeared between them and Hertzog, which will be described in a later chapter of this book.

Meanwhile, in 1914, the first world war broke out. Botha and Smuts saw in the war an opportunity for South Africa to take an important step towards maturity and nationhood. They were anxious to demonstrate South Africa's ability to render help to the British Empire on a basis of equality. They immediately took over full responsibility for the defence of the southern half of the continent, thus releasing Imperial forces for services elsewhere. They organised an expeditionary force to capture German West Africa, and when this had been accomplished Smuts went up with his forces to take German East Africa. South Africa also sent forces to France and other theatres of war.

The Krugerites saw in the outbreak of war an opportunity to regain the independence of the two former republics. A rebellion broke out, led by a former Anglo-Boer war general, and it was Botha's painful task to subdue it. Hertzog found himself in a difficult position. A constitutionalist by conviction, he was opposed to rebellion and he did not support the doctrine of Afrikaner *baasskap* implicit in the revolt. He stood aloof until the crisis had passed. His followers made the most of the bitterness caused by the rebellion and of the discontents that inevitably grew as the war dragged on. When the war ended Hertzog led a delegation to the Peace Conference at Versailles to demand independence for the Free State and the Transvaal. The mission failed, as it was bound to do, but as a political propaganda sortie it was a great success.

Then Botha died and Smuts took over as Premier. Smuts never had the warmth and the ability to mix freely, the 'common touch' of Louis Botha. His philosophy of holism, his love of books and preoccupation with botany, his international outlook and the honours showered upon him overseas, his intellectualism and impatience with stupidity, all made the Boer from the *platteland* feel uncomfortable in his company. His Afrikaans following dwindled as Hertzog's Nationalist movement gained strength, and Smuts was forced to link up with the English-speaking Unionist Party. He was immediately taunted by the Nationalists with having allowed himself to become 'anglicised' and he lost further ground. Next came a post-war economic slump and there were serious industrial disturbances on the Witwatersrand which the Nationalists exploited to their own political advantage. Forming an allegiance with the Labour Party, which at that time had over 20 seats in a Parliament of 150, Hertzog succeeded in defeating Smuts at a general election in 1924. Hertzog's first task was to strengthen the position of the Afrikaner in the civil service, defence force, police and state-owned railways, then to draw Afrikaners into commerce and industry. The Afrikaans language and culture were promoted by all means possible, and Afrikaans newspapers and journals supporting the Nationalist movement were founded.

Hertzog then tackled the question of South Africa's international status. He was determined that the Union should become a sovereign independent country free from outside control of any kind. When he found that Britain was entirely sympathetic he decided to retain an association with her and with the other countries of the Empire provided that this could be done on a basis of equality. He began consultations through diplomatic channels and at Imperial Conferences, which ended in the creation of the British Commonwealth and the adoption of the Statute of Westminster in 1931. This provided that no act of the British Parliament could thereafter apply to South Africa. Thus the goal of independence for which Hertzog, Botha and Smuts had fought in the Anglo-Boer war had been attained and Hertzog declared himself to be satisfied. 'There is no single reason', he said, 'why South Africans should not meet in statesmanship and politics in a spirit of one consolidated South African nation.'

Chapter 10

'Black Peril'

T HE LITTLE town of Smithfield lies in a hollow in the high plateau of the Orange Free State, some ninety miles due south of the old republican capital of Bloemfontein. When the first of the Voortrekkers arrived there more than a century ago, this was lush country, teeming with game, but today the veld on all sides is scarred with erosion. There is a strange listlessness about the undulating landscape which is neither grassland nor karoo. Once the grass grew up to stroke a horse's belly but now a shimmer of heat dances on the rocky outcrops when the season is dry.

Nobody can remember how Smithfield got its English name. The townsfolk in the dreary, dusty dorp, and the sheep-farmers all around are almost wholly Afrikaans. They just call it 'Smitfield', which has the merit of a bilingual compromise. Smithfield may be nondescript, like a hundred other villages, but it claims the distinction of being better-known than most platteland towns in South Africa. This is because for something like twenty years it was the centre of the parliamentary constituency of General the Rt. Hon. J. B. M. Hertzog, one of the heroes of the Anglo-Boer war, founder of the Nationalist Party, and three times Premier of South Africa. General Hertzog had a romantic, sentimental attachment to the rural community that launched him on his political career and stuck to him so faithfully for all those fateful years, and he made a practice of delivering his most important speeches from the platform of the Smithfield Town Hall. It was from there that he proclaimed the first manifesto of the Nationalist Party; from there that he revealed the broad outlines of his 'Native policy', that he declared his intention to seek a new form of Dominion status for South Africa, and that he announced important new legislation.

It was from the platform of the Smithfield Town Hall that General Hertzog made the declaration on 18 April 1927, that came to be known as the 'Black Manifesto'. It was a declaration that changed the course of politics in South Africa.

General Hertzog first became Premier in 1924 at the head of a pact between his own Nationalist Party and the small Labour Party led by Colonel F. H. P. Creswell. The Labour Party was an off-shoot of the Labour movement in Britain and was predominantly English-speaking. It had been formed by artisans who came from overseas to work in the mines, on the railways and in the workshops. Its greatest strength was in the Transvaal where it drew most of its support from the mining community. Organised on traditional socialistic lines, the Party had leftist affiliations in Europe, and at first blush an alliance with the rigidly conservative, isolationist Nationalist Party of South Africa appeared incongruous. However, there were practical reasons of self-interest why the two movements should come together at that time. The Labour Party was bitterly hostile to General Smuts, who was regarded as the mouthpiece of the 'bosses and capitalists'. With considerable severity he had sup-pressed a revolt started by white miners on the Witwatersrand in 1922. The white workers were an élite class in the industrial struc-ture, clinging stubbornly to a colour-bar, and they believed that General Hertzog would uphold the colour-bar more resolutely than General Smuts might do.

On their side the Nationalists realised that the rural support upon which they relied would not be sufficient for them to gain and hold power. They would have to break into the towns. They could do this, first by retaining the political allegiance of Afrikaners who moved from the farms into the towns, and secondly by making a special appeal to the white worker in the towns. They promised legislation to strengthen the trade-unions and they undertook to 'protect' the white worker against competition from blacks. General Hertzog also believed that if the Nationalist Party began by working with the Labour Party it could end by swallowing the white labour movement, which in any event could never be a true socialistic movement while it remained a white élite, clinging to a colour-bar. So in 1924 an electoral pact was formed between the Nationalist and Labour parties, and this coalition won the general election and put General Hertzog in power.

The man who was mainly responsible for bringing about the alliance between Nationalism and Labour was a shrewd and am-bitious politician with a gift of eloquence and an opportunistic eye, the likeable, Falstaffian Mr. Tielman Roos. Born and brought up in Cape Town, he qualified as a barrister at the age of 23 and went to Pretoria to practise at the Bar. Jovial and quick-witted, Roos was an excellent mixer and he soon formed a wide circle of friends. When General Hertzog broke away from the South African Party in 1912 Roos promptly joined him. A pragmatist in the rough-and-tumble of politics, which he thoroughly enjoyed, he once confessed in an unguarded moment in Parliament : 'I regard politics as a game.' Preaching secession and republican independence, he became leader of the Nationalist Party in the Transvaal and was elected to Parliament in 1915 to represent the diamond-digging area of Lichtenburg in the Western Transvaal.

Five years after Tielman Roos had engineered the pact with Labour, General Hertzog had to face the electorate once again. The Labour Party had split and one of the Labour ministers had been expelled from the Cabinet. The Nationalists had gained further support from among the Afrikaans section of the population, especially in the Cape Province where a vigorous Afrikaans newspaper, *Die Burger*, had been established, but there were doubts whether the Nationalist Party would be strong enough to win an overall majority in Parliament standing on its own. An economic recession was beginning to be felt in South Africa and many political observers believed that the pendulum was beginning to swing back again towards General Smuts. Among Nationalists it was clear that some new and potent electoral issue was needed to offset the troubles in the Nationalist Party and the political effects of the depression, and to counter any trend that might set in towards General Smuts.

Once again Tielman Roos came forward with a plan. The Nationalists needed an emotional slogan and Roos urged that they should go to the country on 'the Black Peril'. He knew that all whites were instinctively afraid of the blacks, and he had been experimenting with the racial issue during a tour of the *platteland*. The thing to do, he urged, was to charge Smuts with planning to grant political rights to blacks and the electorate would react emotionally and sharply against the South African Party. The Nationalists would emerge as the champions of *wit baasskap*, the doctrine of white-man-boss, and General Smuts with his 'liberalistic' supporters in the Cape would find it extremely difficult to counter such a campaign.

It would be easy enough, Roos argued, to convince the electorate. General Hertzog had proposed legislation to introduce the principle of 'segregation' with regard to rights for Africans, and an all-party select committee of Parliament had been set up to examine the whole question of white-black relations. The select committee was making slow progress and many Nationalists had begun to suspect that General Smuts and the South African Party were deliberately obstructing and delaying. Tielman Roos urged that Smuts and the Cape 'liberalists' should be openly charged with planning to extend the common-roll franchise enjoyed by Africans in the

Cape to Africans in the other provinces. At first General Hertzog was opposed to the idea of fighting the election on the issue of white-black relations. For all his autocratic tendencies he was a parliamentarian by conviction and a man of intellectual integrity. He saw the long-term danger of making a party political issue out of what was then known as 'the native question'. A *gogga* (Afrikaans word for 'bogy') might be conjured up which in the end would become too fierce to control. But Tielman Roos was strongly backed in the Cabinet and had the support of the Nationalists in the Transvaal and Natal. He cut the ground from under his leader by making a public speech at Ermelo in which he declared that no better battle-ground for the coming general election could be found than 'the native question'. It was, he said, of vital concern to the whites to know where they stood in relation to the blacks, and he for one would have no hesitation in saying where the Nationalist Party stood. At this stage Roos suddenly became ill and went off to Germany for special treatment. To what extent his departure at that precise moment may have been diplomatic has not been revealed. He had placed his leader, General Hertzog, in a difficult position, and for some weeks Hertzog hesitated what to do. Had he immediately repudiated Roos and declared that he had no intention of dragging race-relations into the party political arena, he would have rendered South Africa a signal service. But he would also have split the Nationalist Party on the eve of a crucial general election. Before he could declare himself, General Smuts made a speech deploring 'the decision of the Nationalists to drag the native question into the party political arena'. He reminded General Hertzog that a parliamentary select committee was considering the problem of rights for non-whites. 'We are still in conference with the Government over the native question', said General Smuts. 'We are still in the middle of our work. But the Nationalists now want to bring the native question into the heat of the general election. The Nationalist Party has only one hope for the general election, and that is to relight the fires of racial friction, to set white against white with the blacks as pawns. It will be an unhappy day for South Africa if they succeed in fighting the election on a cry of white South Africa. I say today that we (the South African Party) don't intend to make the native question a centre of election squabbles. We think that will be a fateful thing and a calamity regarding native policy.'

Whether this speech was the final factor that goaded General Hertzog into accepting the campaign issue proposed by Tielman Roos has never been cleared up. Nor can it be determined whether

or not General Hertzog would have allowed 'the native question'
to be the main Nationalist plank in the campaign had General
Smuts not spoken at all. All that can be said is that General Smuts
in those days had a curious effect upon General Hertzog, who flew
into a fury whenever Smuts spoke. It is the opinion of the author
of this book, who had many opportunities of observing the relationship between these two men at that time, and who came to know
General Hertzog fairly well in later years, that the speech made by
General Smuts was a factor that influenced Hertzog to throw the
fate of the Nationalist Party in the 1929 general election on the
issue of white-black relations.

After General Smuts had spoken the Nationalist Press flew to the
defence of Tielman Roos and a furious argument of *tu quoque*
arose. It was Smuts, not the Nationalists, who wanted to drag 'the
native question' into party politics, the Nationalists charged. Denying the accusation hotly, the English-language Press demanded that
General Hertzog should say where he stood, and in due course
General Hertzog let it be known that he would announce his own
standpoint and that of the Nationalist Party in a speech at Smithfield. When the night arrived, the small hall was packed to capacity.
There was great curiosity to learn what the Prime Minister would
say, and Nationalists and pressmen converged on Smithfield from
all parts of the country. Loud-speakers were not available in those
days and the practice was to open all the doors and windows so
that the crowd packed round the outside of the hall could hear.
General Hertzog invariably spoke for at least two hours in a halting,
involved style, with occasional passionate outbursts when attacking
his political opponents, especially General Smuts.

On this occasion he began by saying that in view of the doctrine
of franchise-equality for whites and blacks that was being preached
in certain quarters, a great deal of anxiety was felt by the electorate.
'In that doctrine', he continued, 'every true South African sees,
and rightly so, the existence of his people endangered and the end
of the white man in South Africa threatened. South Africans have
every reason to be concerned. The measure of support extended to
the doctrine of native equality by South African Party members and
leaders in Parliament fills us who still feel for South Africa with
feelings of anxiety and fear for the future. Franchise equality is a
fact in the Cape. Unless the native vote in the Cape is separated
from that of the whites, the native vote will be the cause of the
greatest tragedy in the history of South Africa. What General
Smuts and his supporters advocate is in harmony with what one
may expect from the protagonists of equal rights for black and

white. Only men to whom South Africa as a white man's country
has ceased to have any meaning can plead such a cause.

'To the son of South Africa who feels for South Africa as a white
man's land, General Smuts's speech must have come as a tremen-
dous shock. The anxiety and concern of the white man for his
future and his posterity has been very considerably accentuated by
that speech and by what was revealed afterwards during the discussions in the House of Assembly. The veil has thereby been sufficiently lifted to convince us that the leaders of the South African
Party, General Smuts included, follow a policy that must inevitably
result in the downfall of South Africa as a white man's land.'

General Hertzog went on to describe the situation that would
arise in South Africa if the South African Party were to win the
general election. 'There will be followed the policy that the interests
of the native will predominate over those of the white man, and
where there is conflict of interests between the native and the white
population, preference will be given to the interests of the natives.'

General Hertzog charged one of the leading English-language
newspapers, the *Cape Times*, with advocating 'Kafir supremacy'.
He then turned to Professor Toynbee who had recently written a
book suggesting that the day might come when South Africa might
decide to restrict its area to those parts of its territory which were
capable of being made into a 'white man's land'. In the light of
recent developments this suggestion was prophetic, but General
Hertzog rejected it with scorn. Territorial apartheid formed no part
of his 'solution' for the problem of white-black relations. His plan
was to have 'segregation' in the political, economic and social
spheres, but he rejected the idea of carving South Africa up into
separate 'black' and 'white' areas. Whether General Hertzog linked
Professor Toynbee's suggestion with the policy of 'Kafir supremacy'
attributed to General Smuts and the *Cape Times* was not clear
from his speech, but he dismissed the whole idea in ringing terms :
'This policy must not be allowed to triumph. It is the solemn duty
of all South Africans, both Dutch- and English-speaking, to prevent
this, and it is to prevent such a calamity that I have come here
tonight to appeal to the people, to every son and daughter of South
Africa in the coming general election, to support the Nationalist
Party in its attempt to make South Africa safe as a white man's land.'

Thus, within the hierarchy of the Nationalist Party, Tielman
Roos had won his point, and the election campaign raged bitterly on
the emotional issue of white-black relations. Slagter's Nek, Dingane's massacre of Piet Retief and the Boer party, the Battle of
Blood River, the heroic deeds of the Voortrekkers, the 'misdeeds'

of the missionaries, and how Smuts and the South African Party
planned to allow black men to push white men out of their jobs,
resounded from platform after platform. The South African Party
was thrown on the defensive, as Tielman Roos knew would happen,
and the Nationalists won the general election with a comfortable
majority.

Whether, in later years, General Hertzog regretted having made
his 'black manifesto' speech has not been revealed. He certainly
resented the manner in which he was forced to make it, and he
showed his displeasure immediately after the election. Tielman Roos
was dropped from the Cabinet and made a judge of the Supreme
Court. But the sedate and exacting life of the Bench could not
satisfy the Puckish, unpredictable Oom Tielman for long, and three
years later he resigned from his exalted position to precipitate one
of the biggest crises in South African political history. Meanwhile
the Nationalists had enough seats in Parliament to form a government on their own, had they wished to do so. But General Hertzog
decided to retain his alliance with such sections of the Labour
movement as were prepared to work with him. The Labour Party
was split in two and had lost more than half its previous strength
in Parliament. In fact, Labour never recovered from this political
reverse and within a quarter of a century it had disappeared entirely
from the South African political scene.

What in fact spelt the doom of Labour as a political force was
the decision of the Nationalist Party to make white-black relations
the major political issue in South Africa. The black man formed
the solid base of the labour force in South Africa. A socialist movement which excluded this solid base was a political anachronism. In
any event, the Nationalists were in a far better position to champion
an exclusive white élite dedicated to the colour-bar than a Labour
Party founded on British socialistic tradition. In the industrial boom
that began after South Africa abandoned the gold-standard in
1932, non-whites moved into industry in a massive way, despite
colour-bars and other legislative restrictions put upon them. The
1960 Industrial Census gave the following breakdown of wage-
earners in industry and commerce (excluding professional, technical,
administrative, executive and managerial positions): 838,000 whites,
411,000 coloureds, 108,000 Asians, and 2,352,000 Africans. Moreover, between 1932 and 1960 the composition of this white working-
class élite changed from predominantly English-speaking to predominantly Afrikaans-speaking. Inevitably, as the Labour Party
declined in the field of exclusively white politics, the Nationalists
took over.

It must be recorded, however, that the Labour Party died a glorious death. After years of indecision and dispute, the party tried to return to the traditional path of socialism in a moderate form, and to speak for the worker, no matter whether his skin was white, brown or black. In the 1953 general election the Labour Party had five members in the House of Assembly compared with seventeen when the pact was made with the Nationalists in 1924. These five fought the apartheid measures of the Nationalists with great courage and tenacity, especially the bills that sought to strengthen the indusrial colour-bar. In the 1958 general election all the Labour members lost their seats, such was the potency of the 'Black peril' appeal to the electorate.

General Hertzog was determined, after his victory in the first 'Black peril' general election in 1929, to put his plan for 'solving the native problem' on a basis of segregation into operation. The plan was to remove the Africans in the Cape Province from the common roll and to allow them to elect four whites on a separate roll to represent them in the House of Assembly. The Africans in the other three provinces of South Africa who had never voted on the common roll would be given representation in the Senate. The whole of South Africa would be divided into four constituencies in which a complicated system of voting would take place, partly by chiefs and partly through electoral bodies. The four new Senators to be elected by Africans would all have to be whites. There would also be created a special forum in which Africans would express their views, to be known as the Natives' Representative Council. It would be elected by the Africans, would hold regular sessions, and would be consulted by the Government on all matters affecting the African people. General Hertzog's difficulty was that before he could implement this plan he would require the support of two-thirds of the members of the House of Assembly and the Senate sitting together. Such a majority could only be obtained with the support of a substantial section of the South African Party which was clearly in no mood to co-operate after the acrimonious 'Black peril' election campaign.

The course of national affairs in South Africa then took an unexpected turn. An economic recession which had begun in the United States of America and spread to Britain and various other countries in Europe, began to slow down the South African economy. Prices of farm produce slumped in the world's markets, money became tight and farmers began to default in their mortgage interest payments. To make matters worse, large areas of South Africa suffered from a serious drought. Britain decided to abandon the gold-standard in September, 1931, but the South African Government declined to follow suit. The decision was mainly political, though it must be conceded that several well-known economists advised the Government to remain on the gold-standard. General Hertzog and his Finance Minister, Mr. N. C. Havenga, saw this as an opportunity to demonstrate South Africa's independence in the economic sphere and when a clamour arose in South Africa for gold payments to be suspended and the South African pound to be pegged to sterling, General Hertzog merely hardened his resolve to retain the gold-standard.

During the ensuing months, despite stringent financial restrictions, South Africa suffered a serious drain of capital. The Government took special steps to prevent foreclosures on farm bonds. Many financial institutions were hard hit and at least one bank might have closed its doors had the State not come to its assistance. As the economy ground almost to a standstill, figures of unemployment mounted steadily. South Africa was in the grip of the most severe slump she had known since the turn of the century.

At this stage Mr. Justice Tielman Roos saw an opportunity of re-entering the political arena in dramatic fashion. He suddenly resigned from the Bench to lead a movement demanding that the Government should abandon the gold-standard and that all whites should sink their political differences and co-operate in restoring the prosperity of the nation. There was a surge of popular support for Tielman Roos and in December, 1932, the Government was forced to suspend payments in gold.

Almost overnight the political situation became fluid. Tielman Roos opened negotiations with General Smuts for a political alliance, but Roos set his terms too high, demanding the Premiership and at least five of his own supporters in the cabinet. The negotiations dragged on for some weeks, then suddenly General Smuts and General Hertzog got together. After some hard bargaining between them, a fusion was announced in which General Smuts agreed to serve under his former antagonist. Tielman Roos, whose intervention had precipitated the crisis, was left in the political wilderness and he died in retirement shortly afterwards.

The most important part of the agreement between Hertzog and Smuts was an undertaking by Smuts to support Hertzog's plan for settling 'the native problem'. This was a radical and fateful departure from Smuts's previous standpoint and the question has often been asked why he was prepared to change his views. At the time when these events took place the author of this book was political correspondent of one of the leading South African newspapers and was closely in touch with what occurred. He offers the following explanation : General Smuts had been deeply disturbed by the 'Black peril' campaign of the 1929 general election. He believed that the most important political need in South Africa was 'to take the native question out of the party political arena'. He did not like General Hertzog's plan and he did not believe that white-black relations could be determined on a basis of segregation. But he thought that if the whole problem could be viewed dispassionately and without party political recrimination, a workable arrangement might evolve from the Hertzog plan. In particular, General Smuts considered the decision to set up the Natives' Representative Council important. This could, he thought, become a valuable 'training-ground in democratic procedures'. Once African leaders had proved to be politically mature it would become easier to draw them into the more important political institutions of the nation.

History has since shown that the Natives' Representative Council was the weakest and most futile part of the Hertzog plan. Furthermore the 1933 fusion agreement between General Hertzog and General Smuts failed 'to take the native question out of the party political arena'. There was one outstanding South African, also a member of the coalition government and a close personal friend of General Smuts, who at the time saw clearly how dismally the Hertzog plan would fail. The late Jan H. Hofmeyr opposed the Hertzog bills in Parliament. In a speech that was prophetic he declared that the so-called 'settlement of the native problem' then being proposed would prove to be no settlement at all. The machinery would break down, and the foundations would be laid for bitter racial conflict in the future. But only a handful of parliamentarians was prepared to support Hofmeyr, and General Hertzog secured the two-thirds majority he needed for Parliament to pass his bills.

Another important reason why Smuts turned to Hertzog rather than to Tielman Roos for an alliance was the state of English-Afrikaans relations. On his side Smuts was having trouble with his English following. The Flag Act replacing the Union Jack with a new South African flag, the Government's drive to strengthen Afrikaans in the public services, and various republican statements from Krugerites in the Nationalist Party, had provoked a good deal of resentment on the English side. An announcement by the Government that it was considering abolishing the Provincial Council system filled the English-speaking province of Natal with alarm and sparked off a movement for secession from the Union. In point of fact there was not much substance in this movement, as later events showed, but both Smuts and Hertzog took it seriously. Hertzog dropped the proposal to abolish the Provincial system and Smuts was left to pacify his Natal followers, which did not prove easy. Smuts knew that Hertzog also had his radicals to contend with. The Krugerites were putting on pressure and there was a danger that they might capture the Nationalist Party or at least drive it in a more radical direction. It seemed to Smuts that if he and Hertzog could come together the cause of the Afrikaans-English *samewerking* (working together) would enjoy an enormous boost. No doubt small groups of diehards would break away at each extremity but in the middle would be a great movement standing for the kind of broad 'South Africanism' for which both he and Hertzog stood. Hertzog's 'two streams' could then flow into each other. Moreover the movement of the centre would enjoy the support of most newspapers, the mining industry, financial, industrial and commercial interests.

On the other hand there was not really very much of political value that Tielman Roos could offer. Smuts shared Hertzog's feeling that in some ways he was a political opportunist. There were occasions when he had espoused the cause of *Krugerisme* in its extreme form. In loosening up the political situation and providing an opportunity for fresh alignments, he had rendered a service to the nation. A coalition with him would probably ensure a victory at the next election, but it would not be a great victory, and the triumph would not endure for long. Once the economic recession had passed the Nationalists would recover their hold on Afrikanerdom and the pressure for an independent republic would increase. The real prize, Smuts felt, was a pact with Hertzog, and he was prepared to make far-reaching concessions to achieve it.

Chapter 11

The Broederbond

T HE EMOTIONAL heart and driving centre of Calvinism in South
Africa is in the Voortrekker town of Potchefstroom, lying in a
hollow of the southern plains of the Transvaal. Through the
town meanders the River Mooi, with its banks shaded by weeping
willow trees, said to be the finest in all Southern Africa. Though not
indigenous to the land but brought in from China a century or so
ago to soften the arrogance of the highveld, the willow-tree has
become an essential part of the landscape and is woven into the
songs and camping-tales of the Afrikaner folk. The streets of
Potchefstroom are tree-lined and lush with gardens, and it is
strange that so much controversy and bitterness can have come out
of a place so fair. This is the centre of the most austere section of
the Afrikaans Church, the *Dopper* sect to which Paul Kruger
belonged. Here, too, is a university and a theological college
moulded in the dour, uncompromising image of the Voortrekkers.
From the *dominees* (clergy) and academicians of Potchefstroom
have spread many of the political thoughts and currents that have
given to Afrikaner Nationalism its hard and narrow character. It
was in Potchefstroom that the first meetings were held to merge the
dissident Trekker communities into the Transvaal Republic, and it
was here that Paul Kruger first learnt the arts and wiles of leadership. It was in Potchefstroom that rebellion broke out at the beginning of the first World War. It was here, too, that the secret Afrikaner Broederbond was founded and developed into one of the
most remarkable movements to come out of Africa. Denounced by
two Prime Ministers in succession, praised by one section of the
Press and condemned by another, widely-known and discussed
wherever South Africans foregather, the Broederbond has no acknowledged identity, no known office, telephone number or address.
Yet there have been times when it has wielded a wholly dispropor-
tionate influence behind the scenes.

It was started in about 1918 by a small group of Afrikaans intellectuals and churchmen under the name of Jong Suid-Afrika
(Young South Africa). Pledged to work secretly, the original aims

of the society were to further Afrikaans as a language and promote
the ideals and culture of the Voortrekkers. As the years passed, however, the movement changed its name, widened its aims and altered
its rules and procedures. It was organised on the cell system, with
from five to ten members in a cell. The cells were linked to divisional committees which in turn were governed by the Groot Raad,
or Central Executive, consisting of twelve persons and known as
'the Twelve Apostles'. Total membership of the Broederbond varied
from time to time between 3,000 and 5,000. A candidate for membership had to be Afrikaans-speaking, over 25 years of age, a member of one of the three Dutch Reformed Churches, and a man who
had either become prominent in his profession or community or
showed promise of doing so. A prospective candidate had to be
proposed by two Broeders in good standing, and if the name was
approved by the Executive Council, an elaborate series of checks
was carried out, sometimes lasting over a period of two years.
Should the candidate then be considered suitable for membership, he
was guardedly informed about the movement and invited to join it.

An Afrikaner well known to the author of this book who witnessed
an initiation ceremony under curious circumstances which need not
be related here, described the ritual as 'like a scene right out of the
Middle Ages, with dagger, cloaks and dim lights, and a fearful oath
of loyalty and secrecy taken on a Voortrekker Bible'. Further details
of the initiation ceremony were given in a special report compiled
for the information of General Smuts during World War II. The
report was based on documents obtained by the Security Police,
and among other things it described a ceremony held in a church
vestry. On a table lay a form shaped like a body, covered by a
black cloth on which the word *Verrad* (treason) had been painted
in large red letters. While a dagger was plunged into the form, the
master-of-ceremonies intoned : 'He who betrays the Bond will be
destroyed by the Bond. The Bond never forgives and never forgets.
Its vengeance is swift and sure. Never yet has a traitor escaped his
just punishment.' According to the same report, there were three
'degrees' of membership, as with the Masonic Order, and further
elaborate rituals took place when a member was promoted from one
degree to the next. Passwords, special hand-grips and other recognition signs were employed.

A secret circular sent to members in 1934 stated : 'Let us bear in
mind the fact that the main purpose is for Afrikanerdom to reach
its ultimate goal of domination in South Africa. Brothers, our solution for South Africa's troubles is that the Afrikaner Broederbond
must rule South Africa!' Ten years later, in December 1943, a

leading member of the Broederbond, Dr. H. F. Verwoerd, was reported to have declared at a secret meeting of Broeders in Bloemfontein : 'The Afrikaner Broederbond must gain control of everything it can lay its hands upon in every walk of life in South Africa. Members must help each other to gain promotion in the civil service or any other field of activity with a view to working themselves up into important administrative positions.' In 1963 the *Sunday Times* in Johannesburg published secret documents of the Broederbond that came into its possession, among them being a circular stating : 'The main task remains the separate existence of the Afrikaner nation, with its own language and culture. We must do everything in our power to persuade English-speaking people to co-operate with us on the basis of the principles of the Nationalist Party. We should be constantly on guard that this does not result in the Afrikaner becoming more anglicised as the English-speaking person is afrikanerised.'

The Broederbond began to make its political influence felt behind the scenes when the first Nationalist Government assumed power under General Hertzog in 1924. There is no information whether an attempt was ever made to recruit General Hertzog himself to the movement, but it is highly probable that he was 'tested' and found wanting. The Broederbond could support his drive to secure greater recognition for Afrikaans as a language, and the steps he took to provide opportunities for Afrikaners to advance in the public service and State undertakings. But it could never have accepted his insistence on equality for the language, culture, traditions and rights of the English-speaking section of the white population. Hertzog proclaimed a 'two-stream policy'. His aim was to strengthen and increase the Afrikaans cultural stream until it equalled the English stream, when he believed that the two streams would merge into the broad river of South Africanism. The Krugerites and the Broederbond rejected this thesis. Their objective, as reflected in the statements quoted above, was a single Afrikaans stream absorbing the English but remaining narrowly and strongly Afrikaans.

After five years in office General Hertzog declared himself satisfied with South Africa's newly-won 'sovereign independent status' with the British Commonwealth, as defined by the Statute of Westminster (page 97), and there were murmurs of revolt from the radical wing of his own Nationalist Party. A group of Nationalists formed a body known as the Republican Bond to campaign within the Party for a republic according to the ideals of Paul Kruger, outside the Commonwealth, and this move greatly annoyed General

Hertzog, who suspected that the Broederbond was behind it. At a Nationalist Party congress in 1930 he threw down the gauntlet by declaring : 'The time has come for us South Africans, Afrikaans or English, to recognise the fact that as long as we remain separate and try to reach our goals along different roads, we must expect that most of what we as a nation wish to attain will not be achieved. After what has been accomplished at the Imperial Conferences of 1926 and 1930 there remains no reason whatever why, in the field of politics and statecraft, Afrikaans and English South Africans should not feel and act in the spirit of a consolidated South African nation.'

The next important development was the Hertzog-Smuts political coalition of 1933 described on page 106. This could obviously not be accepted by the Broederbond, which immediately set about organising a new opposition movement pledged to the Kruger concept of an independent Afrikaans republic. Those Nationalists who joined this opposition came to be known as the 'gesuiwerdes' – the 'purified'. Their objective was to capture the administrative organisation of Hertzog's Nationalist Party and its Press and prevent these from being absorbed into the new coalition movement as Hertzog intended. They found a strong leader in the dour and uncompromising Dr. D. F. Malan, former *predikant* (minister of the Church), editor of *Die Burger* in Cape Town, and Minister of the Interior in Hertzog's cabinet. Whether or not Dr. Malan was one of the early members of the Broederbond has not been revealed. When he was Prime Minister he admitted being a Broeder and it is probable that he joined the movement when the Smuts-Hertzog fusion split the ranks of Afrikaners.

The Gesuiwerdes did not disclose their intentions immediately. In order to secure as many seats as possible in Parliament they postponed their break with the coalition movement until after the 1933 general election. They then went into opposition and a bitter struggle began between them and the fusionists for control of the branches, constituency committees and provincial executives of the old Nationalist Party. With the help of the Broederbond, Dr. Malan and his Gesuiwerdes emerged with the lion's share, including the influential Afrikaans newspapers in the Cape and Free State, and the spoils were more or less divided in the Free State and the Transvaal. So upset was General Hertzog by the role that he knew the Broederbond to have played behind the scenes that he publicly denounced the movement in a speech at Smithfield in 1935. It was the first time that most South Africans, including even well-informed pressmen, heard of this secret body.

After describing the composition of the Broederbond, General Hertzog declared that its main object was 'to ensure that Afrikaner- dom shall attain its final destiny of being *baas* (boss) in South Africa'. It had infiltrated the civil service, teaching profession, churches and cultural bodies where, in Hertzog's view, it was exercising a dire influence. The reply of the Broederbond was to send a deputation to see General Hertzog privately and to explain that the movement was purely cultural and concerned only with the growth of Afrikaans and the furtherance of Afrikaans cultural activities.

Between 1934 and 1938 the Gesuiwerdes worked unrelentingly to remodel and consolidate the drive for an independent republic in the image of Paul Kruger. There was ample evidence of a master plan behind this movement. It was designed, not as an ordinary democratic party, but as a *volksbeweging*, a people's movement, with each segment carefully organised and the whole co-ordinated with a definite aim in view. The fight on the political front was carried on by the Nationalist Party under Dr. Malan. The Afrikaans churches gave religious backing and even helped the Party by keeping in touch with Afrikaners who moved from the rural areas into the towns. Cultural activities were co-ordinated into a purpose- ful 'front' and a good deal of politics was disseminated under the name of 'culture'. Plans were methodically laid to form an econo- mic front, and the appeal to Afrikaner republican sentiment was used to found a number of financial, commercial and industrial concerns. A systematic and highly-successful drive was launched through the teaching profession to introduce the spirit of 'Christian Nationalism' into Afrikaans schools run by the Provincial Councils. Afrikaans and English children were segregated into separate schools. An organisation was set up, financed through Nationalist funds, to infiltrate the trade-unions. The task of holding this *volks- beweging* together, preventing splits, and ensuring that the whole movement rolled along in the right direction, fell to the Broeder- bond, which began a process of getting its members appointed to strategic posts in the civil service and the executive bodies of organi- sations which might be of use to the republican cause.

The Gesuiwerdes were still busily organising when the 1938 general election was held and their following in Parliament was reduced to 27 as against the 111 who supported the United Party of Hertzog and Smuts. No wonder the Gesuiwerde movement was not taken seriously. No wonder its potency was not understood by the English-speaking section, who were luxuriating in an unprece- dented economic boom and felt that they could leave politics to

'Smuts and his crowd'. Smuts, they complacently felt, could be counted upon to look after their interests and see that South Africa remained snugly in the Commonwealth. Despite the apathy of the English section and the unrelenting determination of the Gesui-werdes, it is just possible that the Krugerite movement might have begun to decline had not an event occurred that was destined to give republicanism an enormous boost and to change the course of history in South Africa. This was the outbreak of World War II.

The Parliament at Cape Town was in session at the time. There was an immediate crisis in the cabinet, General Hertzog favouring a policy of neutrality and General Smuts urging a declaration of war on Germany. It is important, now that the heat and emotional-ism of those days have passed, to try to understand Hertzog's point of view. Hertzog was a parliamentarian by conviction and he re-jected Nazism as a doctrine. Yet he felt that Germany had been unduly harshly treated by the Versailles Treaty at the end of the first World War. He was on close terms of friendship with the German Ambassador in South Africa who had persuaded him that the reports of harsh treatment of the Jews, of Hitler's designs on the rest of the world, and of the ruthless, authoritarian character of Hitlerism were hopelessly exaggerated. One of Hertzog's chief lieutenants, Oswald Pirow, was of German descent and a National Socialist in outlook, and his line with Hertzog was that Germany was the only really strong bulwark in Europe against communism which, Pirow maintained, had far-reaching designs to subvert the black people of Africa. Pirow had paid a formal call on Hitler, who was supposed to have shown him secret documents revealing com-munist plans to stir up unrest and revolt among non-whites in South Africa.

In any case the nature of Hitlerism and the designs of Germany on the rest of the world weighed less with Hertzog than another purely South African factor which he considered to be of supreme importance. Here, he felt, was a great opportunity to prove to the Afrikaans people the reality of South Africa's 'sovereign indepen-dence'. The English section might feel aggrieved, and some of them might even shout loudly in their indignation, but would not the bulk of them stand loyally by the spirit of South Africanism? The Afrikaner had been asked to make sentimental concessions in the past; would not the bulk of the English now make a great conces-sion to Afrikaans sentiment? If they did this it would destroy the Gesuiwerde movement for all time and the two streams would merge all the more quickly into the broad river of South Africanism. South Africa would honour her obligations to Britain and the

Commonwealth, who would have the naval base at Simonstown and the use of South Africa's ports and docks, and if South Africa were drawn into the war at a later stage, without a doubt it would be on the side of the Allies. When that happened the Afrikaans section would be fully behind the war effort. Hertzog was misled about the causes of the war, but his understanding of its ultimate political consequences for South Africa was greater than was realised in his day.

On 6 September 1939, the issue was put to Parliament, and by 80 votes to 67 the House decided for an immediate declaration of war. General Hertzog advised the Governor-General, Sir Patrick Duncan, to dissolve Parliament and hold a general election, but Sir Patrick declined and General Hertzog resigned. General Smuts formed a new government and set about organising the nation for war.

Meanwhile Hertzog's followers in the United Party got together with Dr. Malan's Gesuiwerdes and proposed a merger on the principles of the old Nationalist Party before the 1933 coalition. But the Gesuiwerdes had made radical advances along the road of Krugerism since then, and the proposal had no chance of acceptance from the outset. Before it could even be properly discussed the Broederbond organised a great rally of anti-war Afrikaners at Monumentkoppie, where the Voortrekker Monument stood on a commanding hill overlooking Pretoria. Before an excited audience of many thousands, Hertzog and Malan stood together and announced that the split in the ranks of Afrikanerdom was now closed. However, a month later the Gesuiwerdes suffered a shock when Hertzog declared at a public meeting on his old stamping-ground at Smithfield that it was his aim to build up the Afrikaans and English sections into a united people and that 'he declined to be placed in the category of those who wished to break all constitutional ties with Britain'. A few days later the Hertzogites and Malanites met in Pretoria to consider the terms of reunion, but difficulties immediately arose. After two days of futile haggling the proceedings were adjourned.

The Hertzogites then held a congress and formed themselves into a Volksparty. During the ensuing weeks various individuals and ad-hoc 'unity' committees tried to bring the two sides together, but nothing much happened until Parliament met in January 1940. An agreement was then reached between the caucuses of Malan's Nationalist Party and Hertzog's newly-formed Volksparty to work together in the House. This was followed by a joint declaration accepting the principle of a merger of the two parties with Hertzog as leader, the detailed policy to be worked out later.

Then in April Hitler invaded Norway and Denmark, and a month later he overran Holland, Belgium and France. Italy declared war on Britain and France and South Africa declared war on Italy. The Gesuiwerdes concluded that Hitler was winning the war and that this was the supreme opportunity to obtain an independent republic shaped according to their views. The Hertzogites could, if necessary, be brushed aside. Leading members of the Broederbond set about organising a great republican demonstration in Bloemfontein. Not a word about it had been said to Hertzog, who was furious but powerless to stop the rally which drew a wildly-enthusiastic crowd of about 50,000. Resolutions were carried that the time had come to declare a free, independent South African Republic; that the republic must be 'founded on the religion, history and traditions of the Boervolk', and that it must embody the principles of Christian Nationalism. Hertzog and Malan were requested to make a public demand for such a republic, and a committee-of-action was appointed to put the decisions of the rally into effect.

Hertzog flatly refused to receive the deputation. He had information that the Broederbond had decided to eliminate him from the political scene. He knew that a rumour was circulating widely that he had been secretly intriguing with General Smuts to forestall the Kruger republic by establishing 'an English-orientated republic together with Rhodesia' when Germany won the war, as she seemed about to do. The Gesuiwerde newspaper in the Transvaal, edited by Dr. H. F. Verwoerd, was running a series of thinly-veiled attacks on Hertzog, and there was a whispering campaign on the *platteland* (backveld) suggesting that he was old and ill and losing grip. Hertzog decided to call the joint parliamentary caucuses of his own Volksparty and Malan's Nasionaleparty together and to tender his resignation as leader. He complained bitterly of the attacks made upon him and of the fact that he had not been consulted about the Bloemfontein rally. But Malan felt that a public breach at that stage would damage the Gesuiwerde cause and he made a conciliatory speech, paying tribute to Hertzog's great services to Afrikanerdom. Others among his supporters joined in the eulogies and Hertzog agreed not to resign. However, this did not suit the Broederbond, who laid plans for a further and more determined attack on the old General whom they had never forgiven for exposing them in 1935.

Next development was the Free State Congress of the joint Malanite-Hertzogite party, called to consider a detailed programme of principles. Opening the proceedings, Hertzog declared that he had been subjected to constant intrigues and 'subterranean influences' and warned that he regarded the Congress as a test of support for his own leadership. A duel immediately developed between him and the leader of the Gesuiwerdes in the Free State, C. R. Swart. Swart's opposition was especially galling to Hertzog. Tall, energetic and impetuous, Swart owed a great deal to Hertzog, who had encouraged him to enter politics, had appointed him to the organising staff of the old Nationalist Party in the Free State and had helped him to get his first parliamentary nomination. Closely associated with the innermost councils of the Church in a lay capacity and a member of the Broederbond, Swart had broken with his chief in 1933 to the deep disappointment of the latter. Incidentally, in later years Swart became Minister of Justice in Dr. Malan's first Nationalist government after Smuts was defeated in 1948, and was elected first President of the Republic of South Africa.

Two sets of draft principles were set before the Free State congress, one drawn up by Hertzog and the other submitted by Swart. Hertzog's draft contained a clause guaranteeing full equality of rights for the English section of the population, but Swart's draft gave no such undertaking. In speaking to his own draft Hertzog declared that he was not prepared to associate himself with a policy which did not assure equality to the English. Swart's policy of Afrikaner baasskap, he said, 'would lead nationalism deep into the wilderness, where not the Party only but Afrikanerdom itself might perish'. The two rival drafts were then put to the congress and Swart's was carried by a large majority. Hertzog did not at first react. Giving the impression that he had accepted the majority decision, he waited until the congress began discussing Swart's draft, clause by clause. Where, asked Hertzog, was a clause protecting the English section? Swart fumbled vaguely with his papers. Getting no response to his query, Hertzog stood up and reached for his hat. With a curious reflex action and a great scraping of chairs but no other sound, all the members of the Congress got to their feet. In silence Hertzog announced his resignation from the Party and stalked slowly out of the hall. Retiring to his farm in the Transvaal, he led a lonely and isolated existence until he died two years later, in November 1942.

In many ways he was a great South African. Throughout his long and distinguished political career he stuck consistently to his principles. His fight to redress the unequal balance between the rights and privileges of the Afrikaner and those of the English was fully justified at the time, and once he felt that he had secured equality he was prepared to defend the rights of the English even if it meant his own elimination from the political scene. The concept of sovereign independence within the British Commonwealth is a monument to his work in the international sphere, and it is a tragic twist of historic events that South Africa is no longer in the Commonwealth today. Hertzog failed dismally in the field of white-black relations. His policy regarding World War II seemed outrageous to the English-speaking South Africans at the time, yet the irony is that he was thinking of the English too.

In the ranks of the anti-war opposition a confused period of feuding and dissent followed General Hertzog's exit from the political scene. Many but not all of Hertzog's own followers broke away from the 'reunited' Nationalist Party to form the Afrikaner Party led by N. C. Havenga. A body known as the Handhawersbond was formed to protect Afrikaners against 'persecution' from the Smuts government, to counter pro-war propaganda, and to help the Nationalist Party into power. Organised on para-military lines, it was generally regarded as a movement in sympathy with Hitler, and at one time it claimed a membership of 100,000. The Handhawers held a national conference and elected a commandant-general and seven 'staff-generals'. Shortly after the conference its offices were raided by the police and some of its leading members were interned. Thereafter it declined as rapidly as it had mushroomed into existence and it played no further role of any significance in the events that followed.

Another movement known as the New Order was launched by Oswald Pirow. Pirow had been Defence Minister in Hertzog's fusion government and, as explained earlier in this chapter, had interviewed Hitler before the war. The New Order openly sympathised with the Nazi cause and it enjoyed a far greater influence than the size of its following warranted, mainly because of the eulogistic treatment it received from Zeesen Radio, to which large numbers of anti-war Afrikaners regularly listened. Pirow seemed important to the Gesuiwerdes when Hitler's star was at its height, but his New Order rapidly declined when the Nazi retreats began. Pirow himself returned to practise at the Bar in Pretoria and he produced a controversial news-letter for many years after the war had ended. He died in 1960.

But all these factions – the Afrikaner Party, the Handhawersbond and the New Order – were of minor concern to Dr. Malan compared with the Ossewa-Brandwag, which taxed all his resources and political ingenuity to the full, and very nearly succeeded in ousting him from the leadership of the republican opposition. The

Ossewa-Brandwag ('Oxwagon-Guard') was started a year before the war as a result of celebrations held throughout South Africa to commemorate the centenary of the Great Trek. Smuts and Hertzog intended these celebrations to be fully national in character, with the emphasis on Afrikaans-English nation-building, the theme to be the merging of the two cultural streams. The Government made a generous contribution to the funds of the Voortrekker Memorial and drew up plans for an organisation to run the celebrations with the assistance of the State. But the Gesuiwerdes had different ideas. For them this was a unique opportunity for an emotional demonstration in favour of Krugerism. Leading members of the Broederbond got to work with great skill and vigour behind the scenes. Moving in with well-prepared plans and ideas, Broeders quickly took over key positions and formed new committees. Before many weeks the whole affair became a thinly-veiled propaganda exercise in favour of Afrikanerdom and the republican cause. Part of the celebration was a ceremonial trek with ox-wagons from the distant provinces, converging on Monument Koppie, near Pretoria, where a massive granite monument to the Trekkers was unveiled. There were emotional scenes as the ox-wagons lumbered through the countryside, escorted by men and women dressed in the clothing worn a century before. Speeches were made at every halting-place, and the speakers were nearly always staunch republicans who saw to it that the Kruger ideal of freedom was duly emphasised. When the symbolic trek was over it was decided to found an organisation to embody and perpetuate the ideals of the trek, and this was named the Ossewa-Brandwag, known far and wide as the O.B. Organised on a commando basis, its first chairman was the Rev. C. R. Kotze, and its first commandant-general was a Defence Force officer named Colonel J. C. C. Laas. The movement was an instant success, and membership grew by thousands throughout the countryside.

When war broke out a year later the O.B. had offices in Bloemfontein, with commandos in every town and village throughout South Africa. Members dressed themselves in Trekker clothes and gathered round camp-fires to roast *vleis* (meat) and *boer-wors* (farm-sausages), dance traditional folk-dances, play the Trekker game of *jukskei*, and sit patiently listening for hours on end to orations on the republican destiny of the Afrikaner. Then when the war came, a new role opened for the O.B. It was to become the 'action front' for anti-war Afrikanerdom. Conventional political procedures might prove inadequate in a time of crisis, it was argued, and in an emergency the O.B. would step in and take charge. Differences of opinion arose within the higher command and Col. Laas was replaced by an Afrikaner held in high regard, the Administrator of the Free State, Dr. J. F. J. van Rensburg. The fact that van Rensburg was prepared to step out of one of the highest offices in the land, senior in some respects to that of a cabinet minister, gave the O.B. a further impetus.

From the day that van Rensburg took command of the O.B. a clash between him and Dr. Malan became inevitable. Neither was prepared to accept that the other could be the leader of republican Afrikanerdom. But their first contacts were friendly. After some long-range exchanges they signed a document known as the Cradock Agreement in which each undertook not to meddle in the affairs of the other. The Party would do the work of Afrikanerdom in the political sphere and the O.B. would confine its activities to the non-political sphere. But the ink was scarcely dry on this document before trouble broke out. Many Afrikaners were members of both organisations. Dr. Malan found that O.B. groups were forming within the ranks of his party and he countered this by reorganising on a cell system, isolating O.B.s as far as possible within the cells and excluding O.B.s from executive positions. The O.B. passed a series of resolutions objecting strongly and threatening retaliation. The Broederbond intervened with a move to organise a Committee of National Unity and Dr. Malan was given the title of *Volksleier*. Meanwhile a draft constitution for a republic had been under consideration in the Nationalist Party, and a copy had been sent to the O.B. To Dr. Malan's intense annoyance the O.B. published the document for general information in July 1941. This led to an exchange of recriminations and it was not long before each side ordered its followers to resign from the other organisations.

Dr. Malan was now determined to smash van Rensburg and to break the power of the O.B. At first, as Hitler rolled on from one success to the next in the World War, van Rensburg's strength grew rapidly. The Government became alarmed, and on 25 October 1941, an order was issued prohibiting civil servants and the police from belonging to the O.B. Some days later a number of policemen were arrested in a dramatic raid on Police Headquarters in Johannesburg. Several individuals holding key positions in the O.B. were interned.

Dr. Malan then proposed the formation of a national 'shadow cabinet' to be drawn from the Party and the O.B. to stand in readiness to take over the country should the Allies collapse. Hitler was expected to invade Britain at any moment, and most Nationalists felt that a Nazi victory was imminent. There followed a series of exchanges between Malan and van Rensburg in which van

Rensburg was cleverly outwitted and the O.B. made to look 'un-Afrikaans' and 'imbued with foreign ideologies' that did not con-form to the ideals of Paul Kruger. Malan had the immense advantage of the backing of four crusading newspapers which could build him up as the father-figure of the Afrikanervolk and could portray van Rensburg as a soldier of fortune. At about this time a series of bomb attacks and sabotage exploits occurred, and through rumour and insinuation these were laid by the Nationalists at the door of the O.B. The final factor that gave Malan victory over his rival, however, was that he sensed the turning-point for Hitler more quickly than van Rensburg did and began a process of repudiating National-Socialism, leaving the O.B. to hold the baby.

The general election of 1943 came before the struggle between Malan and van Rensburg had been concluded, and the Nationalists took a heavy drubbing. Many Nationalists were on active service and did not vote at all. Their friends and relatives either abstained from voting or supported the war issue. Smuts secured 110 suppor-ters in Parliament and Malan only 43, while Havenga's Afrikaner Party failed to gain a single seat. The same pattern was repeated in the Provincial Council elections the following year, in which the Government won 118 seats throughout the country and Malan took 48.

The Broederbond had, by now, decided to abandon its efforts to bring the O.B. and the Nationalist Party together, and it threw its influence behind Malan in his methodical drive to eliminate the O.B. and consolidate the republican 'front' before the 1948 general election. Despite its poor showing in the 1943 general election, the Afrikaner Party continued to exist, propped up by its sole news-paper, *Die Vaderland* in Johannesburg. None of the other anti-war bodies any longer counted for much. In the closing weeks of 1944 van Rensburg made one last attempt to draw the Nationalists into a *Volksfront*, but Malan peremptorily rejected the idea. From that time onwards he was in supreme control of the anti-Smuts oppo-sition.

His next move was to launch an appeal for a republican *stryd-fond* (fighting-fund) which within a year had passed its target figure of £100,000. He then took a step which was to have far-reaching consequences. Remembering the success of the 'Black Manifesto' in the 1929 general election he decided to fight the 1948 general election on the issue of white-black relations. It would be another 'Black Manifesto' election. Some of his advisers were worried. There was a world-wide surge of liberalism following the war and the soldiers were returning full of liberal ideas. Would it not be safer to concentrate on the grievances of ex-soldiers, the demands for social security, and the usual post-war reaction against any government which had imposed rationing and controls? Malan said that he would do all that as well, but the main issue would be 'the danger of liberal concessions to the blacks'. He appointed two special committees. The first and most important under the chairmanship of his staunch supporter and trusted friend, Paul Sauer, would examine white-black relations and produce a programme for the 1948 general election, and the second would draw up a social and economic programme.

Paul Sauer's committee rejected the Hertzog 'settlement' of 1936, which contained the principle of extending representation to non-whites on separate voters' rolls, and opted for physical separation. Political rights would be separated on a territorial basis and in all other spheres where whites and blacks had to work together there would be separate railway coaches, separate buses, separate residential townships, separate benches to sit upon, and separate entrances to public buildings. Sauer coined the all-embracing slogan of 'apartheid', which proved to be a winner.

With the blessing of Malan and the Broederbond, another important step was taken. Funds were raised to finance a movement to infiltrate the trade-unions, beginning with the powerful Mineworkers' Union. The white workers would be promised protection against competition from blacks. Existing colour-bars would be retained and further colour-bars imposed and there would be a system of job-reservation on a racial basis. The movement was an outstanding success, gaining thousands of votes for the Nationalist Party.

Then a co-ordinated, well-planned propaganda campaign was directed against the United Party Government, with its main target the Deputy Prime Minister, Jan H. Hofmeyr. Hofmeyr was the acknowledged leader of liberal thought in South Africa, and everything he had said and done to insist on more adequate political representation for non-whites and better educational facilities for Africans was now used to build him up as a sinister force scheming to destroy the white man and to undermine the foundations of Afrikanerdom. Hofmeyr was linked with the missionaries, whose activities had been one of the factors that prompted the Great Trek. The Government was beginning to have difficulties with African leaders, who made it clear that Africans expected a greater say in the country's affairs in exchange for the loyal support they had given to the war effort. The Natives' Representative Council was becoming restive, demanding that some notice should be taken of its repeated requests for relief from the burdens of the pass-system and for the redress of other grievances. Hofmeyr and Smuts spoke guardedly of the need for reforms and for more adequate representation of non-whites in the councils of the land, and the Nationalist Press raised a great scare that the Government had 'liberalistic' plans to sell the white man down the river.

The establishment of war industries, soon converted to peaceful purposes, had drawn a great influx of Africans to the towns, where lack of housing resulted in slum conditions and squatting. There were riots and loss of life. Crime flourished and a wave of robberies plagued such centres as Johannesburg. The Nationalists charged the Government with weakness and neglect. What was urgently needed was a Nationalist regime which 'would know how to handle the blacks'.

Before the general election took place, one further service was rendered by the Broederbond to Dr. Malan. It helped him to form a pact with the small Afrikaner Party headed by Mr. N. C. Havenga. Malan felt that Havenga would be useful to him, despite his insignificant following, since he would bring over the remnants of the Hertzogites and would reassure important financial, mining and commercial interests who remembered him as a 'reliable and conservative' Finance Minister in the highly-successful fusion regime. The Malan-Havenga coalition won the 1948 general election by the narrow majority of eight seats in the House of Assembly, and the Gesuiwerdes were at last in power. 'This is a revolution, not a political reverse', said Jan Hofmeyr when the final figures of the election were brought to him. The years that followed proved him more than right.

In the election General Smuts lost his own seat to a member of the Broederbond, Mr. W. C. du Plessis. It was a dramatic sequel to the action of the Smuts government when it issued a proclamation towards the end of the war, prohibiting members of the civil service from being members of the Broederbond. Some 500 civil servants resigned from the Broederbond, but du Plessis, who was an official in the Department of External Affairs, refused to do so and was dismissed from the civil service. Three years later he took his revenge when he stood against General Smuts at Standerton in the 1948 general election and defeated him. Another seat was found for General Smuts in Parliament, but shortly afterwards his health broke down and he died in 1950. One of the first actions taken by Dr. Malan on becoming Premier was to repeal the regulation forbidding civil servants from belonging to the Broederbond.

During the sixteen years of Nationalist rule in South Africa the

Broederbond has inspired the establishment of several new movements designed to promote the ideal of an exclusive Afrikanerdom,
and has served as a co-ordinating influence behind the scenes. The
new bodies included an Afrikaans association to rival the Boy
Scouts, a student movement in opposition to the National Union
of S.A. Students, a rival organisation to the S.A. Institute of Race
Relations, and a rival body to the Association of Chambers of
Commerce. The Broederbond promoted Christian National Education in the schools and it served as a pressure group in favour of the
Bantustan concept of apartheid. Its influence, politically, was on the
side of extremism, and it helped to secure the shift of power within
the Nationalist Party from the Cape to the Transvaal, resulting in
the election as Leader and Premier, first of Mr. J. G. Strydom and
then of Dr. H. F. Verwoerd.

In 1964, following a Press campaign against the Broederbond
and a demand by the Opposition in Parliament that its activities
should be exposed by a Commission, Dr. Verwoerd appointed a
Commissioner to inquire into the activities of the Sons of England
Society, the Broederbond and the Freemasons. Dr. Verwoerd refused a request that the proceedings be held in public and that
cross-examination of witnesses be allowed, and the Parliamentary
Opposition then declared that it had no further interest in the
Commission. In a report tabled in Parliament in March 1965, the
Commissioner declared that he could find no indication of any
discussion of party-political matters or of any subversive activities,
or of anything that would render any one of these bodies guilty of
exercising undue influence on the Government or other public
authorities.

PART THREE

Chapter 12

Republicanism

'DIE OU PRESIDENT', Oom Paul Kruger, liked to sit of an evening on the broad stoep of his home in Pretoria and watch the sun go down like a runaway veld-fire behind the Magaliesberg Mountains, over towards his farm near Rustenburg. Sometimes he would have a member of the Executive sitting beside him, as he smoked his pipe and talked over some problem of State. Or two or three members of the *Volksraad* would be with him, or even a small group of burghers, for the President was a simple man, accessible to all. When the night closed in he would move into the large *voorkamer* (living-room) of the house, and soon there would be bustle and activity as officials, members of the *Volksraad* and other personages began to arrive, each one to be greeted by the President.

A lively account of such an evening, typical of so many, was written by one of the directors of the Netherlands-German Railway Construction Co., die Heer Middelberg, who often took part in the nightly discussions at the President's home. Oom Paul liked to run his republic on patriarchal lines, and as often as it could be managed the Executive Council and more important committees of the *Volksraad* met at his house to do their business. There he felt on his own terrain, and there his slow-moving, outspoken and much-respected wife, Tant' Sann, could bring in a trayful of coffee and *boer-beskuit* (rusks) whenever a tense moment arose.

'Two committees', wrote Middelberg, 'sat in a large room at two tables on which there burned two candles. . . . From one table to the other wandered "die ou President", the members of the Executive Council, many *Volksraad* members who had nothing better to do, and Verwey and myself. The two tables continually disturbed each other. . . .'

The Government consisted of the President, his Executive Committee, and the *Volksraad*, or legislature. In later years a second *Volksraad* was added in order to give the new settlers on the gold-fields some say in the affairs of state. A settler, or *uitlander* as he was known to the burghers, could vote for the second chamber after only four years' residence compared with ten years' residence required to vote for the senior chamber. The senior *Volksraad* consisted of 24 to 28 members elected by one- or two-member constituencies, half of them retiring every two years. The President was the focus of power and authority and was elected by ballot among the registered burghers every five years. The Executive, over which the President presided, consisted of the commandant-general of the armed forces, the State Secretary, the Superintendent of Native Affairs and two other burghers, all of whom were elected by the *Volksraad.*

Only the President could introduce bills to the *Volksraad,* which had power to reject, amend, or approve. Any citizen or body of citizens desiring a law to be passed or amended had the right to petition the President, who was bound to acknowledge the petition but could act on it or not as he thought fit. Oom Paul treated petitions with considerable respect and often sent for the organisers to discuss the matter involved as he sat smoking his pipe on the stoep of his house. In theory the senior *Volksraad* was 'the supreme authority in the land' but in practice Paul Kruger dominated the *Volksraad* and came to regard it primarily as a rubber-stamp for his actions and policies. This is borne out by the speech he delivered at his last inauguration as President in 1898 when he turned to the members of the *Volksraad* with these words: 'Honourable Sirs, I rely upon you as the body of the legislative power to support me in these my views.' And to the members of the Executive he said : 'I thank you sincerely for the support you have given me hitherto, for the support you have given me when necessary, in the deliberation of affairs, and for the support you have given me in their execution.'

Kruger was one of a committee of three who drafted the 1858 *grondwet* (constitution) of the Republic, and his rugged and independent personality was stamped on almost every page of the document. He had a deep suspicion of party politics, believing that they disrupted a community. His concept of the ideal 'democracy' was a religiously-inspired *volk* (people) with a God-fearing leader who consulted the elders, 'consultation' being mainly a process of passing on his decisions and instructions. He likened himself and the Afrikaner-volk to Moses and the Israelites, and he often said that he could find no justification for political parties in the Bible. In 1894, when there were signs that an opposition party might be organised in the *Volksraad,* Kruger had a law passed forbidding the appointment of election-committees. Any burgher was free to stand for the office of President or for the *Volksraad,* but he must stand

as an individual, without a committee or ticket or organised body
of canvassers. 'In fact it is true to say that party politics, in the
sense in which the expression is understood in Britain and the
Commonwealth, remained alien to the political life of the Republic
until the end', writes Professor J. S. Marais in his excellent *Fall
of Kruger's Republic*. An individual might be labelled 'conservative' or 'progressive', but there was no caucus, no formal grouping
or organisation of any kind.

The Republic could in many ways be regarded as a theocratic
state. Kruger, as we have already recorded, believed himself to be
divinely inspired. There was the story of his 'conversion' during the
three days he spent alone on the Magaliesberg. 'The Bible', writes
Manfred Nathan, his biographer, 'was his book from the beginning
to the end; but it was more than a book – it was his guide and
companion, ever influencing and directing him. He always had it
about him; when at home, a large-print version lay on the table at
which he sat, ready to his hand. . . . At times, when he was in a
temper, he would bang his fist upon the Bible. . . .' In one of his
most celebrated speeches before the *Volksraad* and with the judges,
diplomats and leading citizens of Pretoria present, Kruger had this
to say : 'In framing Article 8 of the *Grondwet* we had in mind how
God had led the people and how God's word was a guide by which
we must act. Article 8 says "The people demands the greatest possible social liberty, and expects this because it has kept its religious
faith and its engagements, and because it has submitted to law,
order and justice, and has maintained the same." Now observe
whither this Article points. It points to God's word. The people
demands the greatest possible social liberty : not a licentious or reck-
less liberty, but one based upon God's word. That is the principle
which this Article contains. . . . Moses led Israel out of Egypt and
was the law-giver and fixed the law by God's command; and what
does the law say? That you shall not do what seems right in your
eyes, but what God orders.'

The Republic had a State Church, the Dutch Reformed Church,
but the relationship between State and Church appears to have
been a vague and loose one. The D.R.C. was split into three sects,
Kruger himself belonging to the smallest and most rigidly-conserva-
tive branch popularly known as the *Doppers*. It was this sect
which had its cultural centre at Potchefstroom and to which, in
later years, many of the most influential members of the secret
Broederbond Society belonged. During the 1860–1865 period of
civil strife between rival Boer communities in the Transvaal, Kruger
was once accused of plotting to impose a 'Dopper Republic' on

the Transvaal, but the charge was clearly untrue. Paul Kruger was too shrewd to risk splitting Afrikanerdom on religious lines. On the contrary, his objective was to unite the Afrikaner volk in all spheres, and to create a distinct Afrikaner way-of-life. His plan was first to fuse the trekker communities of the Transvaal, then to unite the Transvaal and Free State, and finally to bring about a united Afrikanerdom in the sub-continent. Hence the importance of language, religion and culture as unifying forces. There could be no thought of dilution of the volk by drawing in the *uitlanders* and giving them equal rights. Paul Kruger was as insistent on the exclusive character of his Afrikanerdom as were the Israelites on their Judaic order. And from his point of view he was strategically right, as was proved by the Afrikaners who carried on his principles to achieve their South African Republic.

When the committee of three was drafting the principles of the first *grondwet*, Kruger insisted that the title of the new republic should be the 'South African Republic' and not the 'Transvaal Republic' as seemed more logical, since there was already a republic in the Free State. No, argued Kruger, Afrikaners would one day have to come together throughout South Africa, so why not offer them a home now? The significance of this title was not lost on the British, who insisted, when the independence of the Transvaal was restored after the 1881 war, that the state should be termed the 'Transvaal Republic'. Kruger took no notice despite a protest by the British resident in Pretoria, and went on calling it the 'South African Republic'.

As the years passed, Kruger's determination to strengthen and develop Afrikaner hegemony in Southern Africa became more positive and more urgent. It was stimulated by two factors. On the one hand Kruger was quick to realise that the wealth brought to the Transvaal by the gold industry would mean that before long the Witwatersrand would become the economic heart of South Africa and would thus dominate the sub-continent. On the other hand Kruger knew that the British, prodded by Rhodes and Milner, with the backing of Salisbury and Chamberlain, had their own plans for a South African Federation under the Union Jack. Thus it became a race between the Kruger concept of a united Afrikanerdom with the Transvaal and Free State at the core, and the Rhodes-Chamberlain plan for a united South Africa within the British Empire. The British had behind them all the enormous resources of their imperial domains, but in South Africa Kruger had the Transvaal with its vast wealth and its strategic position at the cross-roads between the hinterland and the sea. 'The determination to

forestall an independent united states of South Africa lies at the root
of British policy after the proving of the deep levels on the Rand',
writes Professor Marais. 'The longer the South African Republic
retained her independence the greater seemed the risk that the
British colonies would be attracted away from the Empire.... If
the republicans' will to independence was not mastered, what would
then be the ultimate outcome? Undoubtedly, declared Milner, an
independent Republic of South Africa.'

Kruger's efforts to combine with the Free State were thwarted by
the British, who brought heavy pressure to bear upon the Free State
Republic whenever the question was raised. The nearest Kruger got
to union was his 1897 treaty with the Free State in which the ideal
of a federal union between the two republics was proclaimed and
which provided for the establishment of a permanent advisory
council to make recommendations for the purpose of paving the
way to union.

Such, then, was the movement for a united Afrikanerdom led by
Paul Kruger. As in the Transvaal, it was to be a non-party regime,
with an exclusive Afrikaans *volksregering* (people's government), an
electoral 'élite', an all-powerful 'father figure' embodied in the
President, and a *volksraad* to consult and to endorse his actions. It
was a movement resting firmly on a religious foundation and officially acknowledging a state-Church which had no formal say in
government yet exercised great influence behind the scenes. 'What
was this Afrikaner nationalism of the late 1890s?' asks Professor
Marais, and proceeds to answer : 'Its portrait as painted by Milner
looks remarkably like the visage it wears today when it has grown
to full stature as the result of the Anglo-Boer war and an effort
extending over half a century.'

Let us now take a quick look at this 'effort extending over half a
century' which resulted in the South African Republic of 1961. And
let us never forget the image of Afrikanerdom – its exclusive character, its Calvinism, its belief in the divine mission of the Afrikaner to
rule South Africa according to his lights – to which the Krugerites
held with remarkable determination. The epic fight of the republicans in the Anglo-Boer war is familiar history and need not be
related here. After the war Afrikanerdom split into two sections,
one of which was prepared to accept the new spirit of liberalism
that arose in Britain in place of the imperial concept of Chamberlain and Milner. This section included Louis Botha, Jan Smuts,
Denys Reitz and J. M. B. Hertzog. They, too, were working for an
independent South African nationhood, but they believed that the
best way to achieve it was to combine the cultural and economic

achievements of both the English and Afrikaans sections of the population. They wanted to bury the unhappy past and make a fresh start on broader lines.

The other section of Afrikanerdom refused to accept defeat in the Anglo-Boer war, declined to broaden the Kruger concept of Afrikaner nationhood, and set itself to attain a Kruger republic through political, cultural and religious means. When Hertzog broke with Botha and Smuts this section rallied behind him. That Hertzog still stood basically for the wider Afrikaans-English South Africanism did not seem clear at the time. What mattered to the Krugerites was that he fought for language, cultural and economic rights for the Afrikaner and demanded sovereign-independence for South Africa. But when Hertzog declared that a balance between Afrikaans and English had been achieved and proclaimed himself satisfied with the sovereign independent status conferred by the Statute of Westminster, the Krugerites became restless. This broader South Africanism, with Afrikaans and English sharing cultures and merging their traditions, was not what Oom Paul had fought for in the 'freedom war'. They formed the Republican Bond and the secret Afrikaner Broederbond, both pledged to further the Kruger ideal. The doctrine of an exclusive, Calvinistic Afrikanerdom was preached from the pulpit and taught surreptitiously in the schools. It spread through the Afrikaans universities. It was the main theme of Afrikaans writing and cultural activity.

The story of Hertzog's reunion with Smuts, their split over the question of neutrality in World War II; the tortuous political struggle for Afrikaner leadership in those early years of the war, and the triumph of 'purified nationalism' in the 1948 general election, has already been told. It remains to record how the republic was finally achieved and how it came to break with the British Commonwealth. It was necessary to describe Kruger's republic and his concept of the role of Afrikanerdom in some detail, since this has always been the Broederbond ideal, and the present South African Republic may yet be made to conform more closely to this pattern than it does at present.

When he became Premier in 1948, Dr. Malan took no immediate steps to introduce a republic. He had been returned to power in alliance with Mr. N. C. Havenga's small Afrikaner Party, and Havenga was opposed to altering the constitutional position. When the republicans demanded action, Dr. Malan pointed to his association with Havenga and to the need for consolidation. In 1949 Dr. Malan went off to London to attend a Commonwealth conference and he surprised everybody with the spirit of co-operation and moderation he displayed. He warmly welcomed the admission of India to the Commonwealth. Then after Malan got back to South Africa came a move for Havenga's Afrikaner Party to be merged with the Nationalist Party, and the republican policy of the new fusion had to be defined. The republicans in the north pressed for a clear-cut declaration that the intention was to achieve an independent republic with a minimum of delay, but Havenga was against this. His friends were surprised that he was prepared to go as far as the following, which was eventually agreed upon : 'The Nationalist Party is convinced that a republican form of government, separated from the British Crown, is most suited to the traditions, circumstances and aspirations of the South African people and is the only effective guarantee that South Africa will never again be involved in Britain's wars.' There was added a rider that the constitutional change to a republic must be 'by a special and definite mandate from the white voters'.

Three years later, in November 1954, Dr. Malan resigned. He was eighty years of age and in poor health. He was troubled by the mounting pressure from extremists in his party for quicker results on apartheid and for immediate action for a republic. A group of Afrikaans churchmen and intellectuals was pressing for total territorial separation of the races, involving the allocation of more land to Africans and the expenditure of vast sums of money on the development of African reserves, but Malan was not prepared to face the political or economic consequences. He decided that Havenga should succeed him as Premier, so that extremists in the party might be kept in check for a while longer. In a speech announcing his retirement he praised Havenga, and he let it be known to his supporters in the Nationalist caucus that he wished Havenga to be elected Leader. But Havenga was unacceptable to the Broederbond and to the republican activists who remembered his close association with Hertzog, and they were not prepared to wait indefinitely for the republic. They decided that Dr. Malan's successor should be J. G. Strydom, the Nationalist leader in the north, who stood unequivocally for the Afrikaner *baasskap* and a Kruger-like republic. This would mean wresting control of the Nationalist Party from the southerners, with their influential newspaper *Die Burger* and the important and growing group of Afrikaans financial, insurance and commercial concerns in the Cape Province. A swift and well-organised 'Strydom-for-Premier' operation was carried out behind the scenes, and on the eve of the caucus meeting which had to make the choice, Havenga was presented with a list of names which showed him to be in a hopeless minority.

He then withdrew his name and retired from public life, dying in retirement some years later like his former chief General Hertzog.

Straight from the caucus meeting that elected him Leader of the Nationalist Party, Strydom went to a traditional *braaivleisaand* (barbecue), a gathering of his friends and supporters round a camp-fire with coffee and meat and *boerwors* (sausages) cooked in the embers. 'Nothing', he declared to the delighted gathering, 'can now stand in the way of achieving a republic.' But unknown to himself and his friends, Strydom was already a sick man. He suf-fered attacks of lassitude and soon developed a heart condition from which he died four years later. Problems of implementing apartheid were piling up and there were tough fights in Parliament. There were grave disturbances among non-whites, and a movement arose for a 'freedom charter'. African women demonstrated against having to carry passes and riots took place at many centres. Living costs rose faster than wages and there was much concern over poverty among Africans. Dr. Verwoerd, as Minister of Bantu Administration, was pressing on with his measures to prevent whites serving on welfare committees along with Africans, to tighten up the pass laws and movements of Africans into the urban areas and to control the presence of Africans at church services, schools, hos-pitals, clubs and places of entertainment in the so-called 'white' areas. Police claimed they had evidence of a widespread treason conspiracy, and in a dawn raid 156 persons were arrested. Strydom began to feel, like Malan, that the republic could wait while more urgent matters were attended to.

In 1956 he went to a Commonwealth conference in London, and all that he said on that occasion was that a republic would be best for the good relations of both sections of the white people and that it was the policy of his government to declare a republic when sufficient voters favoured such a step. He was careful to add : 'But, of course, that won't affect our relations with the Commonwealth.'

By 1958 when the next general election came round, Strydom was obviously very ill. He was prevailed upon to remain in office for the election, which the Nationalists won with an increased majority. They fought the campaign on their apartheid record and a promise of more stringent measures to come. Then after the elec-tion Strydom died. He was a likeable man, with an attractive personality, a direct manner, and a knack of making friends. With-out any special intellectual qualities, his rise in the Nationalist Party was due, largely, to his insistence, without compromise or modification, on two simple principles : Afrikaner *baasskap* (domi-nation) and an independent republic.

After Strydom's death the southerners in the Cape made an attempt to regain control of the Party by putting up Dr. T. E. Donges for election as Leader. They counted on the northerners being divided between the Free State leader, Mr. C. R. Swart, and the extremist Dr. H. F. Verwoerd. But they underestimated the strength of the right. Voting at the first count in the Nationalist caucus was 80 for Dr. Verwoerd, 52 for Dr. Donges and 41 for Swart. At the second count Dr. Verwoerd secured 98 and Dr. Donges 75. Dr. Verwoerd had promised the republicans that he would press on with apartheid and the republic. In his first public declaration after his election he undertook to devote all his energies to the establishment of a republic. 'In South Africa', he added exultingly, 'we are being carried forward as never before by an overwhelming current of inspired nationalism.'

He gave instructions that a bill should be drafted for a referendum, and this was introduced to Parliament in the 1960 session. Coloureds, Indians and Africans, who together totalled three-quarters of the population of South Africa, were excluded from the voting. Initially South-West Africa was to have voted in the referendum but later the territory was excluded. The Government was becoming concerned over the South-West Africa issue at UNO. Moving the Bill in Parliament Dr. Verwoerd was blunt about his intentions : 'If we do not win this time, the strife will become harder and, I fear, more bitter. Now we fight with gentle methods. If we lose, we must fight harder and with a more vigorous hand. If the Nationalist Party loses in the referendum, then perhaps other methods will have to be used until the objective is attained.'

Though pressed to say what kind of republican constitution he had in mind, Dr. Verwoerd refused to give any details when the Referendum Bill was before Parliament. Would it be the 1941 draft constitution he himself had helped to draw up, and which Dr. Malan repudiated in later years? Would it be modelled on Paul Kruger's republic? Dr. Verwoerd refused to be drawn. There were strong rumours that behind the scenes the republicans were arguing among themselves over the nature of the constitution.

On 9 April 1960, while attending the Witwatersrand Agricultural Show in Johannesburg, Dr. Verwoerd was shot twice in the head and face by a wealthy, eccentric English-speaking South African named David Pratt, who was later committed to an asylum. Dr. Verwoerd escaped death by a narrow margin and among Afrikaners there was a great wave of sympathy for him. They felt, somehow, that he had passed through the Valley on their behalf. A legend grew that his escape was divinely ordained, and thereafter his position as Leader of Afrikanerdom became so strong that nobody remained on the scene to challenge him.

On the eve of the referendum Dr. Verwoerd made a shrewd political move. The atmosphere was heavy with charges that he planned to impose an authoritative regime, on the lines of the 1941 draft constitution, and that the republic would be outside the Commonwealth. Nationalist organisers reported that the voting might go against the Government. So Dr. Verwoerd, in one of his first declarations on rising from his hospital bed, announced that the constitution he had in mind would be on parliamentary lines, similar to the existing one, and that the President would not be a party-political figure. To underwrite this promise he arranged that one of his senior ministers would sponsor a motion in the Transvaal congress of the Nationalist Party, calling for a 'Christian, anti-communist, democratic constitution based on the parliamentary system in accordance with the South Africa Act of 1910'. A thorough job of lobbying was done before the motion was introduced to Congress; it was received without enthusiasm and carried almost unanimously and in silence (September 1960).

Over 90 per cent of the registered white voters recorded their views in the referendum, held a month later, which resulted in the small majority of only 74,580 in favour of a republic. Total 'fors' were 1,633,772 and those against 1,559,192. There is little doubt that had the public realised that South Africa would be out of the Commonwealth within six months, the vote would have gone the other way. Moreover, in the light of what is now known about the Commonwealth Conference in May 1960, only four months before the republican referendum was held, it is difficult to understand how Dr. Verwoerd could have given any assurance at all about South Africa's future membership of the Commonwealth. It was clear to every statesman who attended the 1960 conference that South Africa's position hung on a thread. Even had she not become a republic she would have had great difficulty remaining in the Commonwealth unless she was willing to make concessions on apartheid, which clearly Dr. Verwoerd was not prepared to do. Had Dr. Verwoerd really wanted to remain in the Commonwealth he would not have forced the Republic in the critical atmosphere left by the 1960 conference in London. Dr. Malan and Mr. Strydom had been prepared to shelve the issue for less cogent reasons.

Dr. Verwoerd did not himself attend the 1960 meeting but instead sent his Foreign Minister, Mr. Eric Louw. An exponent of the *tu-quoque* technique, nobody was more likely to irritate the Commonwealth statesmen than Mr. Louw. It almost seemed that

Dr. Verwoerd was asking for trouble at the London conference in 1960, and South Africa certainly ran into plenty of it. The proceedings were taken up almost wholly with a series of strong attacks on apartheid, and South Africa was left in no uncertainty whatever that she would no longer be welcome in the Commonwealth if she persisted with her apartheid policies. Indeed, it was only the fact that everybody knew that the issue would have to be faced squarely a year later, if South Africa persisted in her intention to become a republic, that prevented a showdown over her Commonwealth membership in 1960. So strained was the atmosphere at that meeting that Ghana publicly withdrew an invitation previously issued to Mr. Louw to visit Ghana as the guest of the Government. Canada made it clear that South Africa's continued membership depended upon modifying her apartheid policies, and at least one country awaiting Commonwealth membership indicated that it would not join if South Africa remained a member. Dr. Verwoerd did not convey the full gravity of the Commonwealth situation to the public of South Africa before the referendum was held. Had he done so, the referendum campaign might have assumed quite a different character.

Meanwhile the British Prime Minister, Mr. Harold Macmillan, began an all-out diplomatic operation behind the scenes aimed at keeping South Africa within the Commonwealth. And to his credit let it be recorded that he very nearly succeeded in avoiding the crisis that occurred at the special Commonwealth Conference in 1961. In his private exchanges with Commonwealth premiers beforehand, and in his talks in London on the eve of the meeting, he had so far improved the atmosphere that the mood was to grant South Africa's formal request to remain a member of the Commonwealth in her new status as a republic. Even President Nkrumah of Ghana, on his arrival at London Airport, was prepared to say that he 'had no wish for a showdown with South Africa'. Tunkŭ Rahman of Malaya was unexpectedly conciliatory. Mr. Diefenbaker of Canada, one of South Africa's sharpest critics, indicated that he would not oppose South Africa remaining a member if only she would acknowledge that other Commonwealth countries had strong feelings against apartheid. The Premiers gave Dr. Verwoerd every opportunity of explaining his standpoint on apartheid, which he did at very great length.

Then came the tricky business of trying to draft a declaration that would satisfy the other Commonwealth countries, yet make it possible for South Africa to remain a member. Any thought of trying to persuade South Africa to modify her policies had by then been abandoned, and what the Premiers tried to do was merely to issue an agreed statement recording each side's point of view. Drafts were exchanged, amended, and again exchanged. As *The Times*, London, reported : 'Agreement was very near on a form of words to keep South Africa in, to express nevertheless what the other members felt about South Africa's racial policy, and to state what Dr. Verwoerd had replied.' No ultimatum was delivered by any one of the Commonwealth countries to the effect that it would leave the Commonwealth if South Africa remained in.

Then suddenly Dr. Verwoerd withdrew his request for continued membership. He said afterwards that he was 'shocked by the spirit of hostility and vindictiveness shown towards South Africa' and that it was clear to him 'following the lead given by the Afro-Asian nations' that South Africa was no longer welcome. The object of all the attacks on South Africa, he added for the benefit of his Nationalist supporters who regarded *baasskap* as almost a religion, was to force on the Republic 'full political and social equality of all races in one mixed society'.

From that moment onwards, almost as though a button had been pressed, a vigorous and well co-ordinated propaganda campaign was launched in South Africa to convey the impression that Dr. Verwoerd had gone to the greatest possible lengths to remain in the Commonwealth but that the 'Afro-Asian group' had ganged-up to make this impossible. The Nationalist Press, the radio, and the State Information Office were all pressed into the drive to portray Dr. Verwoerd as the innocent and unwilling victim of a *liberalisties* (neo-communist) plot to evict South Africa from the Commonwealth. When he arrived at Jan Smuts Airport, Johannesburg, the Prime Minister was given a hero's welcome from a crowd of over 50,000 republicans. 'Most voters', exulted the Nationalist newspaper he had edited for so many years, 'won't shed a single tear at South Africa's expulsion from the Commonwealth.'

But non-whites in South Africa were deeply concerned. 'All coloureds', declared Dr. R. E. van der Ross, most outstanding leader among them, 'regret the departure from the Commonwealth with which they feel deep emotional ties'. The English-language newspapers wrote bitter editorials, and anti-Government speakers in Parliament warned of the dire consequence to South Africa of the isolation she would suffer in the world. There were murmurings and threats of secession in Natal, but life went on as usual and there was scarcely even a ripple on the Stock Exchange.

Ten weeks later, on 31 May 1961, the Republic was formally inaugurated and Mr. C. R. Swart, who was once private secretary to

General Hertzog and stood against Dr. Verwoerd for election as
Leader of the Nationalist Party, was installed as President. It should
have been a day of great rejoicing among the republicans, but
there were few ceremonies excepting in Pretoria where the crowds
that did turn up at the Groote Kerk and the Voortrekker Memorial
were of only modest proportions. On previous occasions, such as
the centenary of the Great Trek and the coming together of
General Hertzog and Dr. Malan, the republicans had turned out
in their hundreds of thousands.

But somehow now that the republic had been formally achieved,
the glitter had gone off the prize for which the followers of Oom
Paul Kruger, the father-figure of Afrikanerdom, had worked so
hard and unrelentingly – sometimes even by such devious ways –
for more than sixty years. Was it, perhaps, that the Krugerites were
uneasy about the foundations upon which this republic rested, or
did they believe that the real republic of their dreams, the one-
party, presidential state in the Kruger image, had yet to be
achieved?

Chapter 13

Black Nationalism

THE RISE of African nationalism as a political force in South Africa is a comparatively recent development. There was, of course, the Zulu nationalism inspired by Shaka, and the Basuto nationalism created by Moshesh with the people he drew together among the cloud-capped peaks of the Drakensberg. But the movement to unite black men of all tribes and affiliations in a concerted demand for economic and political rights began only fifty years ago and was at times almost wiped out by the forces it encountered.

The starting-point may be set in the year 1912, ironically enough at about the same time that General Hertzog broke away from General Botha to found the Nationalist Party of the Afrikaans-speaking section of the white population. The first African nationalist leader, Dr. P. ka I. Seme, was, like General Hertzog, a lawyer and scholar who studied abroad and returned to his native land with a burning desire to uplift his own people. Dr. Seme was born in Swaziland and was connected with the royal family there. It is not recorded whether he ever met General Hertzog, but had he done so the interview would have been full of courtesies, for both men had warm, friendly personalities, with an old-world politeness that sometimes broke down on a public platform when the atmosphere became charged with emotionalism.

Dr. Seme and his friends were bitterly disappointed by the National Convention of 1909 which produced the constitution of the Union. They resented the colour-bar that excluded Africans from ever becoming members of Parliament, and they were alarmed by the fact that the franchise system of the Cape Colony, where Africans and whites voted on a common roll, was not extended to the northern provinces. They feared, with every justification, that the northern view among the whites, which insisted on the common-roll franchise being confined to whites, would in the end be imposed upon the south. They felt that such issues could not be left in the hands of the white section of the population but that Africans must organise and assert their rights. So in 1912 Dr. Seme wrote to a number of leading Africans in various parts of South Africa and the upshot was a meeting at Bloemfontein, in the Free State. At this meeting it was decided to launch a movement to be known as the African National Congress and to include Africans of all tribes from all parts of the Union. The Rev. J. L. Dube, principal and founder of the Ohlange Training Institution for Africans in Natal, was elected the first President of the A.N.C. and a surprisingly moderate list of aims and objects was drawn up.

The A.N.C. pledged itself to strive for the recognition of Africans as full citizens of South Africa on a basis of equality with whites. There was no thought of black domination, nor was it suggested that whites should be forced into a secondary place or driven out of the land. All that was demanded was that Africans should be free to advance as far and as quickly as they were capable of going. The A.N.C. stood for 'racial unity and mutual helpfulness, and for the advancement of the African people politically, economically, socially, educationally and industrially'. There was nothing revolutionary about the movement. It did not seek to overthrow the existing order or to challenge the system of government. On the contrary it was pledged to observe constitutional methods, and its plan of action called for nothing more alarming than 'deputations, petitions, and negotiation'.

Steps were taken to form branches throughout South Africa. But progress proved slow. The process of absorbing Africans into industry and developing urban communities was only just beginning. Most Africans still looked to the rural areas as their homes and only came into the towns to work on a migratory basis, returning to their reserves and rural kraals after a year or so. The mining industry was the largest single employer of African labour, and the mines operated strictly on a migratory basis, with the African workers housed in compounds away from the business centres of the towns. Most Africans retained their tribal affiliations and looked to their chiefs in the reserves and rural areas for whatever political action might be required. The idea of organising politically across tribal boundaries was something new, and the chiefs were certainly not interested in any form of nationalism that was wider than the particular ethnic groups to which they might belong.

However, Africans were beginning to take root with their families in the so-called 'white' towns, and it was clear that the days of the tribal system were numbered. After two or three years the A.N.C. managed to establish a skeleton organisation and to gather members and collect subscriptions. During all the fifty years of the A.N.C.'s existence it was never very easy at any given moment to say precisely how strong the movement was. In a time of crisis or excitement there would be a stampede to join, while thousands who had never signed any membership card at all would march through the townships wearing A.N.C. badges. When the treasury was empty, funds would often be collected in fractional amounts from door to door. Nevertheless the A.N.C. could rightly claim on many important occasions to speak truly for the African people. It nearly always had the masses behind it, even at times when the signed membership was small. Its organisational methods were generally haphazard and inefficient and there was always considerable doubt whether a summons for a meeting or an order for a demonstration would or would not meet with any appreciable response. Some of the A.N.C.'s most successful protests were whipped up on the spur of the moment with instructions passed from mouth to mouth and a spontaneous response if the people were in the mood to demonstrate.

One of the first measures passed by the Union Parliament after the A.N.C. was founded seemed to confirm the worst fears of its leaders. In 1913 a Land Act was placed on the Statute Book prohibiting Africans from acquiring land excepting in certain limited areas amounting to about 12 per cent of the whole country. This touched Africans on a particularly sensitive spot, since shortage of land had long been a major grievance. The A.N.C. sent a deputation to Britain led by Dr. Dube, in the hope of obtaining the sympathy and backing of the British Government in its opposition to the Act, but World War I broke out while the deputation was in London and nothing further could be done.

Three years later, in 1917, the South African Government of General Louis Botha proposed a Native Administration Bill which would have imposed limitations on the movement of Africans into urban areas. General Botha, though schooled in the northern tradition and a conservative by nature, was tolerant and sympathetic, and after receiving a deputation from the A.N.C. he agreed to shelve the measure. This was one of the rare successes achieved by the A.N.C. and it won considerable prestige for the Congress movement.

In 1918 a new organisation was founded among the African people which grew rapidly and for some years succeeded in dominating the non-white scene to the almost entire exclusion of the A.N.C. Known as the Industrial and Commercial Workers' Union, it was founded by a tall, vigorous and eloquent African named Clements Kadalie, who had migrated to South Africa from Nyasaland. Kadalie had enjoyed a fairly extensive education during which he had studied the history of the trade-union movement in

Europe. In Bloemfontein he met a prominent African leader named 'Msimang who had been involved in a strike of African workers, and the two men decided to pool their knowledge and launch the I.C.U. Hearing that there was a good deal of discontent among African dockworkers in Cape Town, Kadalie went there to start the first branch of the I.C.U., while 'Msimang remained to organise in the north.

It was not long before Kadalie had succeeded in persuading the 2,000 black stevedores in the Cape Town docks to strike. The strike began as a protest against the export of maize and other foodstuffs while Africans were starving in many parts of the country as a result of drought conditions. Then a demand was made for the daily wage of 5s. to be raised to 8s. 6d. The Government moved in police and troops and large numbers of African dockers were deported to their reserves. Within a fortnight the docks were working at full volume again and it looked as though the strike had been a failure. But the Government was not happy about the wages paid for dock labour and ordered an inquiry which resulted in a substantial rise to 8s. per day. This unexpected success brought great credit to the I.C.U. and thousands of Africans throughout South Africa joined the organisation. In the Cape Province the I.C.U. also admitted a number of coloureds as members.

Kadalie and 'Msimang spent the following year organising throughout the industrial and commercial centres of South Africa and in July 1920 they held a national conference in Bloemfontein under the chairmanship of 'Msimang. The conference passed resolutions condemning the system of recruiting migratory labour for the mines and demanding the repeal of the pass-laws. It was decided to organise among farm-labourers, and soon the Government was receiving angry protests from farmers who complained that agitators were working among their labourers. There followed a series of strikes and disturbances in various centres of South Africa, some organised by the I.C.U. and others inspired by the International Socialist League run by whites. This League was the forerunner of the communist movement in South Africa. There was an extensive strike of African mineworkers on the Witwatersrand, sparked off by high prices charged in the concession-stores which served most of the mines. The Government used police and troops to settle the disturbances, in which eight Africans were killed and eighty wounded. At Port Elizabeth the I.C.U. called a strike among commercial workers demanding a pay increase. The strike leader was arrested and a large and threatening crowd of Africans marched on the prison. Police opened fire, killing 24 and wounding over 100.

These incidents, followed by a series of lesser disturbances, gave wide publicity to the I.C.U. and drew much sympathy for the movement from Africans, who began to regard it as an important political spearhead. In 1927 Kadalie made an interesting and unexpected move. He applied for the I.C.U. to affiliate with the predominantly-white South African Trade Union Congress. Kadalie claimed a membership of 100,000 for the I.C.U. This figure startled the executive members of the Trade Union Congress who feared that Africans might come to dominate the entire trade-union movement. They also had misgivings about the political aims of the I.C.U. which had demanded repeal of the pass-laws and was agitating against the colour-bar. After a great deal of discussion a resolution was passed by the T.U.C. Executive 'that much propaganda was necessary among white workers before the request by the I.C.U. could be granted'. An arrangement was made for close liaison to be maintained between the I.C.U. and the Trade Union Congress and high officers of the Congress regularly attended and addressed meetings organised by the I.C.U.

Kadalie then made two moves that cost the I.C.U. dearly and were largely responsible for its ultimate decline and collapse. He decided to move the head office of the I.C.U. from Cape Town to Johannesburg, and immediately this had been done he ordered a purge of leftist officials and office-bearers. The move to Johannesburg was sound in theory since it seemed logical to have the headquarters at the centre of South Africa's major industrial complex with the greatest potential for developing trade-unionism among African workers. But the move deprived Kadalie of the services and advice and guidance of a number of Cape coloureds who had far greater experience and organisational ability than did he and his fellow Africans. Kadalie also had strong grounds for believing that communists were planning to take over control of the I.C.U., but the purge of leftists resulted in many able and experienced men leaving the movement. The result was that its administration became chaotic and sharp disagreements soon broke out between the different regional committees. Kadalie started a weekly periodical, *The Workers' Herald*, for which there was an obvious need, but it was so badly run that it became a heavy burden on I.C.U. funds. The movement became involved in costly litigation and was soon heavily in debt. In an effort to gain further paying members its scope was broadened to include Africans outside the industrial and commercial spheres and in the end, according to Dr. E. Roux, 'it came to lose its strictly industrial character and became a political mass-party of national emancipation'.

Kadalie then went to England in search of help. Mr. Creech
Jones helped him to draw up a new constitution and Mr. W. G.
Ballinger was sent out to South Africa to try to reorganise the
I.C.U. But the rot had gone too far. I.C.U. members in Natal,
under A. W. G. Champion, decided to break away and form a
movement of their own, and this process of secession was followed
in other centres. From then on the decline was rapid and by 1930
the I.C.U. had virtually disappeared from the scene. Incidentally,
Mr. Ballinger married a remarkably talented South African who in
later years was elected to Parliament as one of the first representatives of the Cape Africans to be returned under General Hertzog's
1936 legislation. Margaret Ballinger was also one of the most outstanding parliamentarians to appear on the South African political
scene and her departure from the House of Assembly when African
representation was abolished by Dr. Verwoerd in 1961 was a great
loss to public life. Mr. Ballinger himself sat in the Senate representing Africans until this form of representation was also abolished.

The African National Congress had continued to play a minor
and somewhat spasmodic role while the I.C.U. held the centre of
the African political stage. Two major forces governed the development of Africans, and the A.N.C. fell between them, uncertain
how to proceed. One was the force of African conservatism, with
the chiefs and the older generation of professional and educated
men and women, and the other was the rising class of workers in
the urban areas. The collapse of the I.C.U. cleared the way for the
A.N.C. to move into the industrial and commercial spheres, but it
was slow to exploit this opportunity. It had been greatly weakened
by internal rivalries and disputes and the surprising thing was that
it had managed to survive at all. When General Hertzog introduced
his important bills in 1936, two schools of thought arose in the
A.N.C. One wanted to oppose the measures outright and the other,
which in the end prevailed, favoured a policy of compromise and
co-operation. One of those who urged outright opposition was
Professor D. D. T. Jabavu, an African intellectual of high standing,
and he made an attempt to rally and consolidate African opinion
against the bills which deprived Africans in the Cape Province of
their common-roll franchise and introduced the system of separate
representation in Parliament. Dr. Jabavu organised a movement
known as the All-African Convention, and this gained a fairly
wide and representative following. The Convention sent a strong
protest to the Government, and followed it up with a deputation to
General Hertzog, which was courteously received by him. Its repre-
sentations were, however, firmly rejected. Moreover, once the bills

had become law, the Convention became inactive and steadily declined in prestige. By 1948 when the Nationalist Party under Dr. Malan assumed power, the Convention had ceased to be a force in African politics.

Meanwhile the A.N.C. decided to allow its members to serve on the Natives' Representative Council set up by the 1936 Hertzog Acts, and several of its leaders including Dr. A. B. Xuma, Professor Z. K. Matthews, Dr. J. S. Moroka, Selope Thema, Dr. J. Dube, Godlo, and Mosaka were at different times elected by popular vote to sit on the Council. From the outset the deliberations of this body were of a surprisingly high order, and its ultimate failure cannot be laid at the doors of the African people who did their best to make it a wise, responsible and dignified assembly. It might possibly have been developed into a consultative and administrative chamber of some value had steps been taken in time to widen the scope of its functions and to give it some powers. But World War II intervened and there were more urgent matters for the Government of General Smuts to deal with. African opinion rallied overwhelmingly behind the war effort. Africans were recruited for the auxiliary services of the armed forces and the response was excellent. Officially, non-whites did not form part of the combat services, but there were occasions in the field of battle when some of them were armed and they fought with great gallantry. Africans believed that they would be rewarded for their war effort by receiving political and economic concessions after the war, and the lack of positive moves in that direction caused a rising tide of bitterness as the years passed. This was an opportunity for the African National Congress to reassert its leadership, and it did so. The industrial revolution in South Africa, begun when the gold-standard was abandoned in 1932 (page 106) and greatly accelerated by the war, was now in full swing, causing urgent problems of urban slums and lawlessness among the African people.

In 1943 the A.N.C. put forward demands for housing in the urban areas, removal of restrictions on movement, abolition of the pass-laws and a more adequate say in the government of the nation. These demands were backed up with speeches and resolutions in the Natives' Representative Council, but the Government's response was vague. The demands were repeated more forcefully the following year, and when no notice was taken of them the Council decided, in 1946, to adjourn indefinitely as a protest. This act, which amounted to a declaration of non co-operation, impressed the Government with the need to review the question of white-black relations, and in 1947 General Smuts made a speech in which he admitted, significantly, that the Hertzog 'settlement' of 1936 had failed. 'Changes in the native way of life have made this legislation ineffective', he declared. He went on to propose that the functions of the Natives' Representative Council should be extended. The Council should exercise authority over the administration of the reserves. Its five official members who were whites would be replaced by Africans and the Council would become a wholly African organisation with an executive committee.

Africans were disappointed by these proposals, which they considered inadequate and savouring of apartheid. The African National Congress described them as 'vague and disappointing' and demanded direct representation by Africans on all legislative bodies. The cry for independence was beginning to echo throughout Africa. Down in the south, where Africans were more advanced than in any other part of the continent, the mood was for emancipation with a minimum of delay. There can be no doubt that had the United Party won the 1948 general election (page 123) instead of the Nationalists, it would have been hard put to come to terms with African nationalism. Even the mild concessions suggested by General Smuts gained supporters for the white Nationalists of Dr. Malan, who were exploiting the white South African's growing fears of black domination. When the Nationalists got into power they lost no time in declaring war on black nationalism. They linked it with communism and charged it with being sustained and encouraged with funds from Moscow.

Actually, the charge was misleading and unfair. But it had just enough substance, at times, to give it an air of plausibility. The communists did their best to infiltrate and control the A.N.C., especially after the Communist Party was declared illegal, and evidence was produced that at one period certain unexplained financial contributions, believed to have come from communist sources, were paid into A.N.C. funds. The upshot was a crisis within the A.N.C. and a break-away of radical leftist elements.

The objective of the African nationalists was simply to bring about the political and economic emancipation of the African. In its moderate form, to which the great majority of Africans undoubtedly subscribed when Dr. Malan first assumed power, it went no further than the demand for equal rights and opportunities for all races, and certainly did not contemplate domination by the blacks. This was the view expressed consistently by the A.N.C. right up to the time it was banned. In its radical form, represented towards the end by a new movement called the Pan-African Congress, black nationalism demanded Africa for the Africans. The white man could stay, if he wished to do so, but as an underling on the black man's terms. By 1965 a majority of Africans probably held this point of view, so much had opinion hardened on the African side.

In 1950 the Government introduced the Suppression of Communism Act which outlawed the Communist Party and provided powers for banning any organisation, person, gathering or publication deemed to be furthering the aims of communism. Some 600 individuals were proscribed under the Act, and, according to claims made by police witnesses at various trials and inquiries, the remaining active communists either infiltrated into existing organisations or established 'fellow-travelling' movements. The African National Congress was an obvious target for infiltration and for some years the inner councils of the movement were full of intrigues by the communists, provoking counter-moves to cancel out their influence. In the confused succession of events that followed, it is difficult to trace where communist influence played a part and where the motivating forces were purely nationalistic.

Serious rioting occurred at various points on the Witwatersrand at the end of 1949 and beginning of 1950. A commission of inquiry found that the underlying cause was resentment against the police following indiscriminate raiding for passes and liquor and that lack of housing and recreational facilities were contributory factors. The commission came to the conclusion that 'communist propaganda precipitated the riots'. In May 1950 the African National Congress and other non-white bodies organised a one-day sit-down strike as a 'freedom demonstration'. There were disturbances at six points on the Witwatersrand; police opened fire and the casualties were 18 Africans killed and 30 wounded. In 1951 the A.N.C. and the S.A. Indian Congress (page 39) decided to launch a defiance campaign against oppressive measures. A letter was sent to the Government demanding direct representation of Africans and Indians in the councils of the State and calling for the repeal of the pass-laws and various other restrictive measures, including the Group Areas Act which was bearing particularly heavily upon the Indian community. The Government in reply stated that it had no intention of repealing the long-existing laws differentiating between whites and blacks but was willing to encourage African initiative and administration within the African community. The campaign was launched the following year and within six months 8,000 volunteers had been imprisoned for contravening the pass-laws and for breaking apartheid regulations at railway stations and post offices.

There were riots in various centres towards the end of 1952. At

Port Elizabeth an attempt was made to burn a railway station, while administrative buildings were attacked in the African townships. Four whites and 7 Africans were killed. Police opened fire on a rioting mob in Johannesburg and 3 Africans were killed and 4 wounded. At Kimberley 13 Africans were killed and 78 injured when police dispersed a mob attempting to set fire to government buildings. Two whites and 8 Africans were killed in a clash at East London. Disturbances of a less serious kind took place in Cape Town, Klerksdorp and Durban. As a result, mainly, of opposition from African women who no longer wished to expose their men-folk to the risk of being shot or imprisoned, the defiance campaign was then called off.

The African National Congress issued an appeal to the African people to exercise restraint and to prevent further outbreaks of violence, and for about four years there was comparative peace. In the political field, however, great activity continued. On its side, the Government introduced a Public Safety Act with severe penal-ties. Banning orders were imposed on leading members of the A.N.C. and other non-white bodies. Police were given increased powers of search, and widespread raids were made upon homes and offices. Meetings were attended openly by the police. The pass system was extended to African women.

On their side, non-white bodies, led by the A.N.C., combined to draft a 'freedom charter'. In June 1955 some 3,000 delegates gathered in Johannesburg from all parts of South Africa to discuss this charter, and the police raided the meeting. The 'charter' stated that South Africa belonged to all the people who lived within its borders and that only a democratic state based on the will of all the people could secure to them their birthright, without distinction of colour, race, sex or belief.

In December 1956 the police arrested 156 persons on charges of high treason, many of them leading members of the A.N.C. Of those arrested, 91 were committed for trial after a preparatory examina-tion lasting for a year. The State withdrew the indictment, and new charges of conspiracy to overthrow the Government by violence and to substitute a communist state were brought against 30. These were acquitted and discharged in March 1961. In giving their verdict the judges found that 'it was impossible for the court to come to the conclusion that the A.N.C.'s policy was to overthrow the State by violence'.

Widespread demonstrations by African women against having to carry passes took place in 1957 and 1958. There were clashes and unrest in African reserves in the Western and Northern Transvaal.

Rioting broke out in Durban in 1959 and 1960 and on one of these occasions nine policemen were killed. In 1960, following months of unrest, serious clashes occurred between Africans and police in the Transkei and in one incident eleven Africans were killed. A state of emergency was proclaimed in many districts.

Meanwhile in 1958 the troubles that had been simmering between the moderates in the African National Congress led by Chief Albert Luthuli, Oliver Tambo, Duma Nokwe and others, and the activists led by Robert Sobukwe, came to a head. Sobukwe objected to the A.N.C. co-operating with other bodies, especially organisations including members of other races, and demanded positive, non-constitutional action. He and his friends stood for Africa for the Africans, and he wanted no truck with the whites. The Sobukwe faction tried at a national congress to take over the A.N.C. and when this failed they broke away and formed the radical Pan-African Congress.

Plans were laid by the Pan-Africanists for a series of demonstrations and strikes designed to reach a climax in 1963 when it was calculated the Government would fall and an 'African socialist state' would take its place. Africans were ordered to present themselves without passes at police stations all over South Africa and to invite arrest. An atmosphere of extreme tension quickly built up and there were demonstrations at police stations throughout the country. In most cases the crowds were dispersed by the police without incident but at Sharpeville 69 Africans were killed and 178 wounded when the police lost control and opened fire. Between 21 March and 19 April altogether 83 civilians, mostly Africans, and 3 policemen were killed and 365 civilians and 59 police injured in riots at various places throughout South Africa.

The Government declared a state of emergency and thousands of arrests were made. In Cape Town 30,000 Africans marched into the centre of the city but dispersed without incident. The Defence Force was mobilised, African townships were searched, and altogether 11,279 Africans were detained. Many African leaders escaped from South Africa and set up organisations in other parts of Africa and in Europe to carry on the movement for 'liberation' of the Africans. Both the A.N.C. and the P.A.C. were banned, and towards the end of 1960 some 40 African leaders met in Johannesburg to discuss ways of representing African opinion. Police raided the meeting. It resumed later and called for a national convention of all races. A secret 'action council' was appointed. This body attempted to organise a stay-at-home protest to coincide with the declaration of a republic on 31 May 1961, but the Government called out the Defence Force and carried out widespread raids with the result that the demonstration went off at only half-cock.

Next came an era of sabotage. Leaders of the A.N.C., meeting secretly in Bechuanaland, formed an activist body known as the 'Spear of the Nation' to conduct acts of sabotage, while the P.A.C. formed an underground movement known as *Poqo*. This latter body was stated by a commission of inquiry to have been responsible for riots at Paarl in the Cape Province in 1962. Between 1962 and the present time numerous acts of sabotage, including dynamiting electric pylons, blasting railway signal installations, explosions in government buildings and arson, have occurred. Convictions have been obtained in the courts and at the time of writing various trials were pending. Police raided the headquarters in Johannesburg of a subversive movement, seized a radio transmitting set and various documents and made a number of arrests.

The position when this book went to press, was that the African nationalistic movement in South Africa had been driven underground and was represented by no organisation recognised by the Government. It had assumed a radical character, and what leaders it still had who were not in prisons, or had not been banned, or were not fugitives abroad, no longer thought in terms of co-operation and negotiation.

Chapter 14

Communism

I N SOUTH AFRICA today, it is a crime to expound the doctrines of
Karl Marx. It is a crime to be a communist, and the definition of
communism is so wide that almost any form of agitation against
the policies of the Government can be brought under the draconian
provisions of the Suppression of Communism Act. The Act says that
communism is 'any doctrine or scheme which aims at bringing
about any political, industrial, social or economic change within
South Africa, by the promotion of disturbance or disorder, by
unlawful acts or omissions, or by means which include the promotion of disturbance or disorder'. But that is not all. The definition
of communism also includes 'any doctrine which aims at the encouragement of feelings of hostility between the European and
non-European races of South Africa'.

The effect of this last proviso has been far-reaching. It has hung
like the celebrated sword of Damocles over the heads of newspaper
editors, politicians and others who have wished to condemn Government policies and to warn against the mounting inter-racial ten-
sions. For it has not been difficult for Nationalist spokesmen to
argue that opposition to apartheid engenders 'feelings of hostility
between Europeans and non-Europeans'. The doctrine of apartheid
has even been accorded a kind of legal sanctity. Thus Mr. J. G.
Strydom, Prime Minister of South Africa before Dr. H. F. Verwoerd : 'Anyone who purposely tried to upset the Government's
plan to put into operation its apartheid policy, or who failed to do
his duty towards the realisation of that aim, would be guilty of
treason.' Since its adoption in 1950 the Suppression of Communism
Act has been used against members of the Liberal and Progressive
Parties, trade-unionists, African, coloured and Indian leaders who
were well known for their opposition to the communist ideology.
Their real offence, in the eyes of the Government, was that they
practised or advocated multiracialism, or opposed the colour-bar,
or denounced one or other of the numerous apartheid measures.
To a great many whites in South Africa the terms 'communism'
and 'liberalism' have become synonymous, as can be shown by

reading the Hansard reports of almost any debate in Parliament involving race-relations.

It was in the last years of Paul Kruger's republic in the Transvaal that the first movement in South Africa seeking to establish a socialistic regime was launched. A body known as the Labour Union was founded in Johannesburg in August 1892 by a Scottish fitter-and-turner and two English miners. Its meetings were held somewhat theatrically behind locked doors and its constitution contained a clause binding its members to secrecy. Its aim was to mobilise the working men of the Transvaal 'to exert their industrial and political strength in the struggle against capitalism'. The Labour Union survived for about five years and its membership reached a total of around 500. The Union succeeded in forming a Trades Council including several small craft societies and branches of British trade-unions which had been established on the gold-mines, and the first May Day celebration to be held in South Africa took place in Johannesburg in 1895. The Labour Union was then disrupted by a series of disputes between radical and more conservative sections of its membership and charges were laid of misappropriating funds. By 1899, when the Anglo-Boer war broke out, the Labour Union had ceased to operate.

After the war the craft societies were revived and a Trades and Labour Council was formed. Next development was a decision by the British Government, at the request of the mining industry of the Witwatersrand, to import Chinese labour for the mines. This gave the Trades and Labour Council an opportunity to organise a series of protest meetings, and the trade-union movement grew in strength. The first party of Chinese labourers arrived in June 1904, but two years later the question of 'Chinese slavery on the Rand mines' became a major issue at a British general election, and the Conservative Government of the day was defeated by the Liberal Party. The new British Government immediately stopped the importation of Chinese labour to the Transvaal and took steps to see that most of the Chinese already on the mines were returned to China when their contracts expired.

At about this time an agitation arose in the Transvaal for responsible government, and this was enthusiastically supported by the Trades and Labour Council which formed a political body to help in the campaign, known as the Labour Representation Committee. The Committee included delegates from trade-unions, craft societies, the small Socialist Labour Party, the even smaller Independent Labour Party, the German Vorwerdts Club, the Italian Socialist Group, the Jewish Socialist Society, and the Friends of Russian

Freedom. The most radical and active of these bodies was the Socialist Labour Party which distributed Marxist books and pamphlets and kept in touch with socialist groups overseas.

Responsible government was granted by the British Parliament to the Transvaal in 1906 and the first elections were held during the following year. The Labour Representation Committee then formed an electoral agreement with *Het Volk*, the Afrikaans political party led by General Botha and General Smuts. For General Smuts, history must have appeared to repeat itself ironically when Labour joined with General Hertzog's Nationalist Party to defeat him seventeen years later. The Labour-*Het Volk* coalition won the day in the 1907 Transvaal election, three Labour members being returned to the Transvaal Parliament.

Meanwhile a Labour Party was established in Bloemfontein, capital of the Orange Free State, which had become a railway centre of some importance. But the Labour movement grew only slowly in Bloemfontein, surrounded as it was by an Afrikaans-speaking community of farmers. Labour put up candidates at elections but did not succeed in winning any seats until 1914 when it secured representation in the Bloemfontein Town Council and the Free State Provincial Council. Labour was a little more successful in the Colony of Natal. A Party was established there immediately after the Anglo-Boer war, with branches in Durban, Maritzburg and Ladysmith, and it succeeded in electing three members to the Natal Parliament. A more radical political organisation known as the Social Democratic Federation, with branches in Durban and Cape Town, was formed at about the same time, but it does not appear to have gained much of a following. 'Marxist elements' were blamed for a general strike on the Natal Railways in 1908 which halted traffic for some days.

When the four colonies came together as the Union of South Africa in 1910 the various labour movements decided to merge in a single party, and this was achieved at a conference in Durban. The South African Labour Party, as the consolidated movement was called, put up candidates for the first Union Parliament, and four were elected out of the 121 members of the Assembly. Two years later the Labour Party won a further seat at a by-election on the Witwatersrand. One of the Labour M.P.s later became a leading member of the Communist Party in South Africa and sat on the Executive of the Communist International at Moscow. Another expressed radical views and was probably also a communist. The leader of the small Labour Party in Parliament, Colonel F. H. P. Creswell, was a right-wing socialist who stood for a 'white-labour policy' and the imposition of a colour-bar in industry. During those early years of the first Union Parliament, Col. Cresswell struck up a friendship with General Hertzog, and this undoubtedly helped to bring about the Nationalist-Labour political pact which defeated the Smuts government at the general election in 1924.

Between 1910 and the outbreak of World War I in 1914 an economic recession occurred in South Africa and was marked by a series of strikes on the Witwatersrand and elsewhere, several of which resulted in bloodshed. In 1913 police and militia clashed with strikers in Johannesburg and 21 persons were killed and 50 wounded when a company of dragoons fired on an angry mob in the streets. On this occasion the Red Flag was hoisted by the strikers. Some weeks later African mineworkers struck for higher wages and better working conditions and troops were employed to suppress the disturbance. The year 1914 opened with strikes on the Natal coal-fields and on the railways. Martial law was proclaimed by the Government, troops were called up and the strike leaders were arrested. Nine men prominent in the Labour movement were taken secretly to Durban and deported from South Africa by sea. There was an immediate uproar and the small Labour group in Parliament staged an all-night protest. A few weeks later, at a general election for the Provincial Council in the Transvaal, the Labour Party scored the most spectacular success in all its existence in South Africa, winning a small majority in the Council.

When South Africa entered World War I on the side of Britain and the Allies in 1914, the Labour Party caucus in Parliament decided to back the war effort of Botha and Smuts. However, at the Labour Party congress a few weeks later, a strong anti-war movement developed. To prevent a serious split, a compromise motion was adopted, allowing each individual member of the Party to decide his or her own personal attitude to the war. But as the war dragged on, serious undercurrents developed in the party and a crisis exploded at the annual congress during the following year. After a noisy and excited debate a motion in favour of the war was carried by 82 votes to 30 and the radical anti-war section then marched out of the conference-hall singing the *Red Flag*. They formed themselves into the International Socialist League, which later became the Communist Party of South Africa, affiliated to the Third International formed by a group of Swiss, Italian and Russian socialists led by Lenin. Though it was on the war issue that the Party split, there was, in fact, a deeper and more fundamental cleavage within the Labour movement. This concerned the colour-bar. The conservatives, who were in the majority, were for imposing

a colour-bar in order to protect the white worker against competition from the blacks. The radicals argued that non-whites would
inevitably become the largest section of workers in South Africa
and that it would be unrealistic and illogical for a movement professing to speak for the working-man to uphold a colour-bar and
exclude Africans. The fact that Col. Creswell was able to carry the
majority of the Labour Party with him on a colour-bar policy
opened the way for the pact with General Hertzog in 1924 (page
99). At the same time it is ironical to reflect that the problem of
white-black relations ultimately led to the downfall of the Labour
Party and its disappearance from the South African political scene.

The International Socialist League formed by the radicals who
split away from the Labour Party in 1915 launched a publication
called *The International* and set about infiltrating the trade-unions.
The I.S.L. was blamed for a rash of strikes towards the close of
1918 and beginning of 1919. It had branches on the Witwatersrand,
in Pretoria, Durban and Cape Town. In 1920 the Second Congress
of the Third International was held in Moscow and it put out 21
points for affiliation. Accordingly, early in 1921 the I.S.L. called
a conference of leftist groups in South Africa and it was decided
to form a Communist Party on the basis of the 21 points. The first
congress of the South African Communist Party was held in Cape
Town in July 1921 and W. H. Andrews became secretary and
acknowledged leader of the movement. Andrews had sat in the
Parliament at Cape Town from 1912 until 1915 as a left-wing
Labour member and was one of the founders of the I.S.L.

It is not easy to discover the precise role played by the communists in the 1922 revolt on the Witwatersrand. Many different
organisations and individuals appear to have had their fingers in
the pie. There were the Nationalists, led by Tielman Roos, who
were anxious to embarrass the Smuts Government. There were the
white miners who were determined to resist a move by the Chamber
of Mines to increase the ratio of blacks to whites in the labour force.
There was Creswell's Labour Party, out to defend the colour-bar,
and there were the financiers who thought that it might be a good
thing to force a show-down with the miners. According to a well-
authenticated account of the revolt, 'the formation of commandos
and the task of instituting organisation and discipline into them
was taken up by the communists'. The report of a judicial commission which inquired into the revolt and the imposition of martial
law stated that the functions of the Central Strike Committee were
usurped by two bodies: '(1) a group known as the Council of
Action; and (2) the Communist Party in Johannesburg'. A mani-

festo issued by the Communist Party at the time of the revolt declared that 'without necessarily identifying itself with every slogan heard in this strike, the Communist Party of South Africa gladly offers its assistance to the Strike Committee, convinced that essentially this is a fight against the rule of the capitalistic class'.

Martial law was declared and an armed clash occurred in which planes, artillery, machine-guns and a tank were used. Some 72 police and troops were killed and 400 injured, while about 40 strikers were killed and 200 wounded, with a further 50 civilians killed and 200 wounded. The strikers raided police stations and seized arms, and for about three days a series of heavy actions was fought in Johannesburg and several towns on the East Rand.

The Communist Party appears to have dwindled in strength and activity after the strike. An attempt was made by the communists to affiliate with the Labour Party but this was firmly rejected by Col. Creswell, who by then was secretly negotiating with Tielman Roos for a pact with the Nationalists. It was at about this time that W. H. Andrews was elected to the Executive of the Communist International at Moscow, and he travelled to Russia and spent a year there. The 1924 general election in South Africa in which the Nationalist-Labour pact defeated General Smuts took place shortly after Andrews returned. In this general election campaign the communists gave what little support they had to the Labour Party.

During the ensuing five years, little was heard of the communist movement in South Africa. Then in 1929, on the eve of the 'Black Manifesto' general election which the Nationalists won (page 104), campaigning on the issue of white-black relations, the situation in South Africa was discussed at another congress of the Communist International in Moscow. Considerable dissatisfaction was expressed at this congress over the fact that communism was making such slow progress in South Africa. It was decided that in future communist activity should be directed primarily at non-whites, and a resolution was passed calling for the establishment of a Native Republic in South Africa. This resolution was heavily exploited by the Nationalists against General Smuts who was accused of favouring policies that would enable the blacks to obtain a communist republic.

The resolution had even more disastrous consequences for the communists themselves. It alienated most of the white members of the Communist Party in South Africa, whose organisational and political experience was badly needed by the movement. Without these experienced whites, the leadership of the party became increasingly ineffective, and within a few months the movement ceased to have any noticeable impact. Indeed, had the Communist International in Moscow deliberately chosen to administer a near-lethal blow to its offshoot in South Africa, it could not have devised a better way of doing so. Clearly the men in Moscow had little understanding at that time of the situation in South Africa. An effort was made by the communists on the Witwatersrand to organise an African Federation of Trade Unions, but this failed. A purge was ordered from Moscow of some of the older remaining members of the Party on the Witwatersrand, and the only effect of this was to cripple the movement further.

Little was heard of communism in South Africa for about seven years. The centre of activity shifted to the Cape Peninsula, where the more sophisticated coloured workers and mixed unions offered better scope for agitation and organisation. In 1937 a weekly news-paper, *The Guardian*, was established in Cape Town to promote communism and almost immediately the movement began to revive there. This revival was helped by world events : by the growth of Hitlerism in Europe and the anti-Fascist sentiments aroused by the Spanish civil war. A fellow-travelling body known as the Friends of the Soviet Union was founded in South Africa to create interest in Russia and many South Africans who were not communists joined it. By the time World War II broke out in 1939 the Communist Party in South Africa had recovered and had become a fairly vigorous body, though its membership does not appear to have been large – probably not more than 1,000 signed members. However, it wielded far greater influence than its small membership might have suggested through the key executive positions held by communists in several trade-unions and various leftist societies.

The Communist Party opposed South Africa's decision to declare war on Germany and a rift was beginning to develop on this issue among the ranks of industrial workers when Hitler attacked Russia in 1941 and the ranks were closed behind the Smuts Government and the war effort. Russia was invited by the Government to open consulates in South Africa, which she did.

All the portents appeared favourable for a considerable growth in communist activity in South Africa during the immediate post-war period, but for various reasons this did not occur. There was a wave of sympathy for the Soviet war effort. The Russian consulates were active, and cultural links were developed with the Soviet. At the same time, Africans, coloureds and Indians were clamouring for political rights. The shanty-towns that had sprung up on the fringes of the major industrial towns caused considerable discontent. There were agitations against the colour-bar, the pass-laws and the restrictions placed on movement into the urban areas. The communists had a skilfully-edited newspaper and they were free to organise as they pleased. They certainly made progress, but the growth of the communist movement was insignificant beside some of the other forces at work. It was completely overshadowed by the rising tide of African nationalism, which on the whole rejected the doctrines of Karl Marx, and it was insignificant beside the growth and triumph of Afrikaans nationalism, which always stood on the extreme right wing. That communism did not sweep like a veld fire through the ranks of discontented non-whites can probably be explained by the fact that the image of Russia, which looked very much like a dictatorship of another kind, and the Marxian ideology had little appeal to the African, and only a limited appeal to some coloureds and Indians.

When the Nationalist Government introduced the Suppression of Communism Bill to Parliament in 1950 the Minister of Justice, Mr. C. R. Swart, was hard put to present a really convincing case and his speech was an essay in melodrama. Communists, he said, led a secret organisation among Africans which was plotting a coup to overthrow the existing regime. At a secret sign 'water supplies will be poisoned, power and light will be cut off, and many people will be murdered'. This speech came to be known as the 'poisoned-reservoirs' declaration and it was derisively quoted for years afterwards. Before the Suppression of Communism Act came into force the Communist Party dissolved itself by resolution. The Act provided for a list to be compiled of active communists, and 437 names ultimately appeared on the list – 129 whites and 308 non-whites. These included 35 white trade-unionists, 12 coloured trade-union officials, 7 Asians and 21 Africans holding executive positions in the trade-unions.

The Government's next step was to expel the only communist in Parliament, Mr. Sam Kahn, and the only communist in the Cape Provincial Council, Mr. Fred Carneson. Both Kahn and Carneson had been elected by Africans on separate voters' rolls, and when by-elections were held to fill the vacancies caused by their expulsion from Parliament and the Provincial Council, two other ex-communists were elected in their places. The Government immediately banned these two successful candidates, even before they could take their seats. It then set about purging the trade-unions by issuing banning orders against executive members and officials who had been listed as former communists. Action was also taken under the Suppression of Communism Act against *The Guardian*. Its offices were raided, various documents were seized.

and the journal was banned. Almost immediately a new journal called *Advance* appeared, and when this, in turn, was banned, a periodical called *New Age* appeared. *New Age* managed to carry on until 1962 when an amendment to the Suppression of Communism Act laid it down that no newspaper could register under more than one name. Furthermore, no new newspaper could be registered unless the proprietor made a deposit with the Minister of the Interior up to an amount of £10,000. *New Age* was then banned and no similar journal has since appeared. A paper called *Fighting Talk* was banned in March 1963. In the same year a journal called *Spark* was suppressed through the process of serving orders on members of its staff prohibiting them from entering premises where any publication was 'prepared, compiled, printed or published'.

In 1956 the Government presented a note to the Soviet Consul-General ordering the closure of all the Russian consulates and the departure of their staffs. This action followed complaints in the Nationalist Press that the Russians were mixing socially with non-whites. The climax was a party given in Pretoria by the Soviet Consul-General to celebrate Russia's National Day, when vodka and other alcoholic drinks were served to non-white guests. The law in South Africa at that time prohibited whites from supplying liquor to Africans excepting under certain restricted circumstances, though whether or not the Russians did actually break the law is open to argument. In a statement to Parliament explaining the Government's decision to close the consulates, the Foreign Minister, Mr. Eric Louw, complained that the Russians 'had cultivated subversive elements in South Africa, particularly among the Bantu and Indian populations', and that the consulates 'had served as a channel of communication between such elements and the authorities in Russia'. He took exception to a broadcast talk from Moscow which he described as 'an incitement of the Bantu and non-European population to resist the South African Government'. The Soviet Government issued a reply in which it declared that there was 'no foundation for the allegations with regard to subversive contacts' and that relations with all sections in South Africa had not gone 'beyond the ambit of social intercourse customary for such occasions'. Incidentally, in recent years both the British and American embassies have made a point of inviting prominent non-whites to official receptions, but beyond threatening to boycott such occasions, the Government has taken no action.

Since the banning of the Communist Party, the listing of its active members, the suppression of its newspapers, the restrictions placed on various bodies and individuals under the Suppression of

Communism Act, and the activities of the Special Branch of the police against anybody suspected of leftist activities, it is difficult to form any realistic assessment of the present extent of communist activity in South Africa. The position is complicated by the fact that the Government persists in equating liberalism with communism and frequently employs the Suppression of Communism Act against well-known opponents of communism who may be active in opposing the apartheid policy. Nationalist spokesmen assert that the communist movement has gone underground, and this may well be so. But there is little evidence to suggest that the agitation for emancipation of non-whites is directed by communists or financed from communist sources, or that it is Marxian in character. The movement against apartheid is, in fact, largely unorganised and without clear plan or direction. Among Africans, if there is any ideology behind it, the driving-force is nationalistic, with an indigenous flavour peculiar to Africa. The mood of bitterness and hostility towards the white man is certainly growing, and if the communists could come with plans and the means to wage a struggle for the emancipation of the non-white, they would no doubt win many recruits. But so would any other agency, such as the African Liberation Committee with its headquarters at Dar-es-Salaam.

Chapter 15

The Liberals

I N SOUTH AFRICA the word 'liberal' does not mean quite what it does in other parts of the English-speaking world. The Oxford Dictionary defines liberal as 'open to the reception of new ideas or proposals of reform; favourable to changes and reforms tending in the direction of democracy'. But in South Africa the word is used to describe anyone who tries to uphold the doctrine of racial equality. It has even acquired a sinister undertone, and the Afrikaans term 'liberalisties' implies communist leanings. It is a companion-word in the political dictionary to 'kaffer-boetie' which is used with contempt to describe any white man who is willing to fraternise with the Africans.

It was the British who first brought liberalism to South Africa. They took over the Cape Colony in 1806, and 14 years later they planted some 4,000 settlers in the Zuurveld region of the Eastern Province in order to stabilise the border against marauding Africans. The arrival of these settlers, their struggle to make good under totally unsuitable conditions, their eventual dispersal throughout the land, and the disproportionately great contribution they made to the cultural, economic and political development of South Africa is a saga that has not enjoyed the full recognition it deserves. The 1820 settlement scheme was planned for military reasons. The Cape of Good Hope was regarded by the British Government primarily as a naval and military base, and the directive given to the Governor was to secure the base and stabilise its hinterland at the lowest possible cost to the British taxpayer. The most troublesome spot was the north-eastern border along the Great Fish River where the expanding colony pressed up against the territories inhabited by the Xhosas. The Governor was faced with the alternative of establishing a chain of military garrisons along the border in sufficient strength to check the raids, or of settling people in the border areas in sufficient numbers to defend themselves. He chose the latter alternative and tried to recruit settlers from within the colony. But the Boers farming around Swellendam, Beaufort West, Graaff Reinet and Uitenhage were not tempted by the offers of land. They knew that the Zuurveld, with its uncertain rainfall, lack of water, and rolling, bush-clad hills, and the deep valleys where a few rivers flowed, was unsuitable for closer settlement. Not more than 100 could be tempted by the Government's offers of land, and most of them had abandoned their small and uneconomic holdings after a few disastrous seasons.

So the Governor, Lord Charles Somerset, decided to bring in settlers from Britain. His plan was not taken very seriously until it suddenly became necessary to recall some of the British troops stationed along the Fish River border and to send them to India. Then the plan was rushed through with great speed. Those who appreciate the years of agricultural research, the soil-analyses, climatic checks and marketing studies that precede any settlement attempted in modern times, can only be appalled by the manner in which the 1820 settlement project in the Zuurveld was carried out. The 4,000 immigrants were landed at Algoa Bay, transported by trek-wagon to their allotments in the untamed border-country, and literally dumped down with their baggage in the veld to begin life in an utterly strange land. 'There we were in the wilderness', wrote one of the settlers in later years. 'When the Dutch waggoners had gone we had no means of following, had we wished to do so. ... We must take root and grow, or die where we stood'. They had to hack poles out of the bush to construct huts in which to live. At first it rained excessively, as it sometimes does in those parts, then there were months of drought. The wheat-crops the settlers tried to grow were wiped out with rust, since this is not wheat-country, as the authorities ought to have known. Cattle were stolen by raiding Xhosas and a child herding stock was murdered. The wonder is that a number of settlers, after obtaining more land and learning through harsh experience how to tame the veld, actually did manage to make good. But the majority of them scattered throughout the colony, spreading their knowledge of commerce, the trades and professions. They built schools, a few of which have survived as outstanding educational institutions to this day. They brought in British ideas of democratic government and administration. About half of them were of farming stock and a third were skilled artisans and mechanics. The rest were traders and professional men, including sixteen medical doctors.

When the 4,000 British settlers arrived, there were already about 1,000 English-speaking people in the colony, including government officials, and most of these lived in and around Cape Town. The Cape-Dutch population numbered about 43,000 and there were approximately 30,000 Hottentots and 35,000 coloureds and slaves.

Between 1820 and 1840 approximately 5,000 Cape-Dutch left the colony in the Great Trek and a further 4,000 immigrants from Britain settled in various parts of the colony. The ratio of English to Cape-Dutch in 1840 was roughly one to four, but the influence of the 10,000 British soon became predominant. They established the English language, reorganised the whole structure of commerce, stimulated industries, and set the colony on a course of steady development. When they disapproved of the actions or policies of the Government they protested vigorously. They founded newspapers, and one of them, Thomas Pringle, won a notable fight with Governor Lord Charles Somerset for the freedom of the Press.

The establishment in the colony of a parliamentary form of government modelled on that at Westminster was due, mainly, to pressure from the English section of the population. Following petitions to the British Government and Parliament a Legislative Council was set up at the Cape in 1834. All its members were appointed, but free speech was permitted and the public was allowed to attend its meetings. An agitation soon developed for representative government and this led to the establishment of the first Cape Parliament in 1854, consisting of a legislative council and a legislative assembly, both elected. In the 56 years of its existence the Cape Parliament achieved a remarkably fine record of wise debate, sound legislation and dignified procedure. In his *Romance of a Colonial Parliament*, Ralph Kilpin wrote that 'by spontaneously striking the happy balance between its own privileges and the rights of the taxpaying public, the old Cape House was an instant success'. He went on to say : 'The watchword of the House was "fair-play", and any interference with personal liberty or departure from healthy administration and sound constitutional practice was ruthlessly attacked on the floor of the House.' Such prestige did this parliament achieve that responsible government was granted to the Cape within eighteen years. A Prime Minister and Cabinet took over from the Governor and his Council, and a remarkably fine civil service with a reputation for efficiency and incorruptibility was built up. It is of interest to note that more than half of those who sat in the two houses of the Cape Parliament between 1854 and 1910 were of English stock despite the fact that the English population was in a minority. All eight Premiers who held office between 1872 and 1910 were English. The English thus played a leading role in the political life of the colony, and relations between them and the Afrikaans section of the community were excellent. It was the Afrikaner Bond, led by Onze Jan Hofmeyr, which put Cecil Rhodes into power. The Afrikaner Bond supported Rhodes' Glen Grey Act of 1894 which provided for the 'Bunga' system of African territorial and district councils. One of the foremost liberals of the day was an Afrikaner, J. W. Sauer, who stood for a policy of 'equal rights for all civilised men'. English-speaking liberals who played a prominent role in the affairs of the colony included Thomas Upington, Gordon Sprigg, W. P. Schreiner, and John X. Merriman. Merriman was the last Prime Minister of the Cape Colony, and he should unquestionably have been called upon to form the first government of the Union of South Africa in 1910. But by then the British had decided to surrender their political leadership in South Africa to the Afrikaans section, and in this mood of political retreat Merriman was passed over in favour of Louis Botha, the former Boer general of the Anglo-Boer war, who was then Prime Minister of the Transvaal.

In the franchise for the old Cape Parliament there was no colour-bar. To get the vote it was necessary to be able to read and write and to own property, and this applied to everybody, irrespective of colour. At first the property-qualification was set at £25, but when the Transkei was annexed to the Cape in 1887 this was raised to £75. As early as 1885 it was accepted in the Cape that tribalism among the Africans was unsuited to a modern state and that it should be replaced with a system more in keeping with Western standards. Accordingly the Governor of the day, Sir George Grey, deprived the chiefs of many of their functions and powers, appointed magistrates in the African territories, and introduced a system of Colonial Law in place of Native Law and Custom. In later years, as recorded above, Cecil Rhodes introduced his Glen Grey Act which changed the system of land tenure for Africans and provided for elected councils. The most notable of these councils was the Transkeian General Council, or 'Bunga' as it was called by Africans, which developed into a minor parliament and played an increasingly useful part in the government and administration of the Transkei until it was abolished recently to make way for Dr. Verwoerd's first Bantustan.

In those halcyon years at the Cape, when the colony was steadily developing as a model state with democratic institutions, a flourishing culture, and a spirit of mutual understanding and co-operation between the various races, the British were also busy in Natal, the lush, picturesque territory on the east coast between Pondoland and Zululand. The first whites to settle in Natal were the Boer trekkers, who founded a republic there. But in 1845 the territory was taken over by the British and most of the Boers departed inland across the range of the Drakensberg. Natal became a British Crown Colony in 1856, with a legislative council modelled on that established at the Cape in 1834. British settlers were brought in and a port was built at Durban, today the busiest and best-equipped harbour in Southern Africa. A sugar industry was established, with extensive canefields and factories, and Indians were imported to supply the demand for labour, thus introducing a further racial element to the population of South Africa. Railways were built and commerce thrived. But the English in Natal were not as liberal in their attitude to non-whites as their compatriots were in the Cape Colony. They were in closer contact with the African in his primitive state, and there was no leavening of coloureds. In later years, when problems of white-black relations were at issue, Natal tended to side with the Transvaal and the Free State.

A man who was influential in Natal for about thirty years during its most formative period between 1845 and 1875 and who helped to formulate the 'northern outlook' on African affairs was Theophilus Shepstone, who was first sent to the territory with the title of 'British diplomatic agent to the native tribes'. The problem was to bring about some sort of order among the scattered groups of Bantu, many of them fugitives from the Zulus, who were squatting all over the territory in a considerable state of poverty and unrest. Shepstone was given full authority but very little money. A man of strong personality and considerable energy, he soon earned the respect and confidence of the Africans. His first move was to re-settle the Africans in reserves. He wished to station magistrates and administrative officers in the reserves, as was being done at the Cape, but no money was available to pay salaries. He then fell back on the expedient of restoring tribal control. Appointing chiefs and headmen, he built up a structure of tribal administration and control, restored tribal law and drew up a Code of Native Law. He even established a Native High Court to try cases under Native Law, an institution which survives to this day. Thus the anomaly arose of two different and diametrically-opposed policies being applied in neighbouring colonies. The Cape aimed at the gradual replacement of the tribal system with Western institutions more in keeping with a modern state, while Shepstone worked to strengthen the tribal system. He, in fact, was the first to apply the doctrine of differentiation and his ideas were copied in the Transvaal and the Free State. General Hertzog claimed that his so-called 'Native Settlement' of 1936 was based on the foundations laid by Shepstone while several Nationalist speakers supporting the Bantustan concept of Dr. Verwoerd have argued that it embraces several aspects of the 'Shepstone policy'. It is interesting to reflect that Shepstone might have followed quite a different course had the money been forthcoming to pay the salaries of the magistrates he originally wanted to station in his native reserves. By such relatively minor factors is the course of history sometimes changed.

The greatest of the early liberals, who has been described as 'the great-grandfather of liberal thought in South Africa', was the missionary Dr. John Philip. In his day he exercised a far-reaching influence on South African affairs and his stature will grow with the passing of the years. Born in Scotland and trained for service in the Church, Dr. Philip was sent to the Cape in 1819 by the London Missionary Society, just ahead of the first party of British settlers. Travelling about the colony a great deal, and occasionally making expeditions into the hinterland, he eventually made his headquarters at Hankey, near Port Elizabeth. He died in 1851. During the thirty years he lived and worked in South Africa, Dr. Philip wrote many letters and articles, inspired agitations, influenced important politicians and statesmen, built churches, schools and mission-stations. He was constantly at the centre of controversy affecting white-black relationships. By the Afrikaans trekkers he was bitterly denounced and he has been described as a trouble-maker who did much harm to Boer-British relationships. Yet one of South Africa's leading historians, Professor W. M. Macmillan, reached the conclusion, after an exhaustive inquiry, that 'all the available evidence finally contradicts the tradition that Dr. Philip had a meddlesome itch for intrigue and interference. At a great many points his intervention was important and effective.'

Dr. Philip's aims appear rational enough when we examine them today; indeed, most of them had been achieved before he died. The trouble was that, like many another reformer, he was in advance of his day. At a time when most of the white inhabitants of the colony frowned on education for coloureds and blacks he insisted on establishing schools for non-whites. He refused to accept the current belief that coloureds and blacks were inherently inferior to whites and incapable of rising above certain limited levels of skill and knowledge. He demanded equality before the law for every individual, irrespective of race or colour. In those days the coloureds in the Cape had to carry passes and were not free to move from one employer to another without permission. Dr. Philip demanded that the pass system be abolished and that coloureds should have the right to sell their labour freely in the best market. He urged that they should also have the right to buy land.

Dr. Philip was, of course, by no means the only missionary to work among the coloureds, Hottentots and Africans, and to campaign on their behalf. The first missionaries who came to South Africa were the Moravian Brethren who arrived before the close of the eighteenth century while the Dutch were still in charge of the Cape of Good Hope. After the Moravians came missionaries from Holland, Denmark, France, Switzerland and Britain. French missionaries did much for the development of Basutoland and their influence is still strong there. Church missions, including the Afrikaans churches, were primarily responsible for providing education for Africans up to the time that the present Nationalist Government introduced the Bantu Education Bill a few years ago. For at least a century, from about 1850 until 1950, an accepted pattern of friendly co-operation developed between the church missions and the various governments concerned, and the practice was for governments to encourage and subsidise the missionary schools. As a result, there is hardly an African or coloured man of standing today who does not owe his education to a Christian mission.

Though the Afrikaans churches have not opposed the various apartheid measures and have sought to find a spiritual justification for the principle of segregation, there have been individual Afrikaans churchmen who have spoken out courageously against some of the doctrines of apartheid and have even faced expulsion from their ministries and the loss of their livelihoods. One such was Dr. A. S. Geyser, who was deposed as a minister of the *Nederduitsch Hervormde Kerk*, and the Rev. C. F. Beyers Naudé who resigned from the position of Moderator of the Southern Transvaal synod of the *Nederduitse Gereformeerde Kerk* so as to free himself to challenge certain aspects of apartheid. There has been speculation in South Africa as to the extent of the 'revolt' against apartheid among Afrikaans churchmen, and it is difficult to form an estimate of its extent and significance. A well-informed opinion given recently to the writer of this book was that approximately 25 per cent of Afrikaans church leaders sympathised with the standpoint taken by the Rev. Beyers Naudé and Dr. Geyser, and that the percentage was likely to increase. But even if a strong section of the Afrikaans Church should declare itself against apartheid, there is no reason to assume that the congregations would follow. The contrary is more likely, if the experience of leading English-speaking churchmen can be taken as a guide. A notable exception on the English-speaking side has been the appointment in 1964 of an African, the Rev. Seth M. Mokitimi, as head of the Methodist Church. The Methodists have the largest following among Africans of all the various church denominations and it remains to be seen what effect the appointment of Mr. Mokitimi will have on the white following of the Methodist church.

It was, perhaps, inevitable that the liberal outlook of the Cape Colony, summed up in the slogan coined by Cecil Rhodes of 'equal rights for all civilised men', would one day clash with the conservative policy of the north. The confrontation took place at the National Convention of 1909 which led to the Union of South Africa in the following year. The northerners, backed by Natal, made it clear from the outset that they were not prepared under any circumstances to accept the Cape franchise, and it was only with difficulty that the Cape delegates managed to secure a compromise allowing them to keep their franchise system while the vote was given only to whites in the other three colonies excepting in Natal, where the few coloureds there were allowed to remain on the voters' roll. The big mistake made by the Cape was to accept a Union instead of insisting on a Federation. The Transvaal, with its great wealth and its position at the centre of communications, was bound to dominate the whole of South Africa, and the Cape's only hope of pursuing its own liberal tradition against the conservatism of the north was to retain the maximum possible degree of local government under very strong constitutional safeguards. But the Cape delegates failed to see this. Indeed, they failed to realise that their liberal policy with race relations was in serious danger.

Another significant change occurred in 1910, unobserved at the time. The English-speaking section, which until then had played so vigorous a role in the politics of the land, withdrew their political leadership almost as though they were moved by some hidden impulse. When Merriman was overlooked in favour of Louis Botha for first Premier of Union, it was almost a symbolic act, for the English turned away from politics to concentrate on commerce, mining, and industries, leaving Afrikaners to run the government and staff the police and civil service. When powerful English interests wanted a change, they preferred to work through Afrikaans politicians, behind the scenes. It was the English-controlled mining and financial interests, really, which brought about the political fusion of 1933, though this does not appear on the record. English-speaking South Africans who became outstanding in the professions, in commerce or industry, and who might well have made a contribution to Parliament, declined to enter politics. Those who did so were mostly 'small potatoes' as an Afrikaans observer once scornfully remarked. From 1910 onwards the English section produced no political leaders in South Africa to compare with Botha, Smuts, Hertzog, Hofmeyr, Malan, Strydom, Steytler, or Verwoerd. It was

an Afrikaner, Jan Hofmeyr, who was almost the only man of
consequence to put up a fight when the Cape lost its franchise
system for Africans in 1936.

Jan H. Hofmeyr was born and educated at the Cape, a pre-
cociously brilliant child who matriculated while still in short trousers
and wrote a biography of his uncle, Onze Jan Hofmeyr the leader
of the Afrikaner Bond, while filling in time before going overseas
to the University of Oxford. After graduating with high honours,
Hofmeyr taught for a while at Cape Town, was appointed Principal
of the new University of the Witwatersrand, then Administrator of
the Transvaal, ending his term as Administrator shortly after the
1929 'black manifesto' general election which returned General
Hertzog's Nationalist Party once again to power. Up to this time
Hofmeyr had expressed no clear-cut political views, and overtures
were made to him by both General Smuts and General Hertzog.
Actually Hofmeyr was, at the time, trying to sort out his own attitude to the problem of white-black relations, which he rightly saw
as the cardinal question in South Africa. Strongly conservative by
nature, he had a great fondness for people, and his intellect rebelled
against anything that appeared immoral or unjust. A strong practising Christian, he knew most of the Sermon on the Mount by heart,
and it required no great erudition to decide who, in South Africa,
were 'they which are persecuted for righteousness' sake'. He approved his uncle's action in supporting Rhodes with the Glen Grey
Act which sought to replace tribalism with a more civilised way of
life, yet he had no rooted objection to the idea of territorial segregation between whites and blacks, provided such a policy could be
applied fairly. As late as 1927 he could praise the Shepstone policy
of native administration, which was based on segregation. But then
he realised that it was too late for segregation. The whites could
never be persuaded to give up sufficient land and sufficient mineral
and industrial resources to make separation work. Segregation might
have been applied as a policy 80 years previously while Shepstone
was wrestling with the problem of establishing law and order in
Natal and before the whites had occupied all the economically-
important parts of South Africa. But by 1930 it was too late to
distribute the land and resources of South Africa on a fair basis.
Any move in that direction could only be a deception, and therefore
unfair.

It was this question of segregation which decided the issue for
Hofmeyr. Hertzog and the Nationalists stood for segregation, later
to be redefined in sharper terms as the policy of apartheid. Smuts
and the South African Party were uncommitted, and Hofmeyr

hoped they could be persuaded to explore a new approach to white-black relations in which the liberal policy of the Cape would be leavened with the new economic liberalism he hoped would arise in the north. So he joined Smuts and was returned to Parliament in a by-election shortly before the economic crisis of 1931–32 which led to the Hertzog-Smuts fusion in 1933 (page 106). The price Smuts paid for fusion was to agree to Hertzog's 'native settlement'. This deprived Africans in the Cape of their common-roll franchise and dealt a mortal blow to the liberal policy of the Cape. Hertzog did agree to make a distinction between Africans and coloureds and to regard the coloureds as the white man's responsibility, whose political and economic rights must remain secure. Hertzog stuck rigidly to this principle, but the 'purified' Nationalists who took over his policy of segregation and turned it into apartheid extended it to include the coloureds as well. Hofmeyr fought the 1936 Hertzog bills with all the eloquence he could command, speaking and voting in Parliament against the measures though he was a member of Hertzog's cabinet. His break with Hertzog took place two years later, some months before the outbreak of World War II. After the war crisis and Hertzog's defeat in Parliament, Smuts appointed Hofmeyr Minister of Finance and Deputy Premier in the war cabinet.

The Government was so closely preoccupied with the problems of organising the war effort, countering subversion and running the country, that little thought could be given to race relations for some years. Nevertheless Hofmeyr's influence was exerted in important directions. He raised state expenditure substantially on educational and other social services for non-whites. He was primarily responsible for the educational services introduced to the armed forces which did so much to inspire servicemen with a desire for social reform and improved race relationships. After the war Hofmeyr pressed Smuts to review the whole question of native policy, and it was agreed to make this the first priority after the 1948 general election. But the Nationalists won the election and Hofmeyr was blamed by many of his own colleagues and important sections of the English-language press for the defeat. He died a few months later, from a heart attack. For nearly twenty years he had been the acknowledged leader in South Africa of liberal thought. He had tried to revive the Cape liberal tradition, and he had believed that in the end this cause must prevail. But what he did not know was that time was against him. Events in the world at large, and especially in Africa, were moving more rapidly than anyone realised.

After Hofmeyr's death there was an infusion of progressives into the United Party. The work done by the Army Education Services was bearing fruit and a crop of young men including Harry Oppenheimer, son of Sir Ernest Oppenheimer, the diamond, gold and industrial millionaire, became active in the United Party and some of them were elected to Parliament. But the Party suffered from a split personality. The conservatives and the progressives who came together in the 1933 fusion had never quite settled down into one family with a clearly-defined outlook. The conservatives wanted a race-relations policy that was more 'humane' yet not too far removed in its essentials from the broad concept of apartheid; the progressives demanded a clear-cut alternative to apartheid. The struggle came to a head in 1959, precipitated – ironically enough – by conservative elements in the United Party from Natal. The issue was whether or not further land should be purchased for occupation by Africans, and twelve M.P.s broke away to form the Progressive Party under the leadership of Dr. Jan Steytler. Harry Oppenheimer, who had meanwhile inherited his father's financial empire and had withdrawn from Parliament, immediately identified himself with the new Progressive Party and has continued to support it ever since.

The Liberal Party was formed a few years before the split occurred in the United Party which resulted in the formation of the Progressive Party. The Liberals led by Alan Paton, author of *Cry the Beloved Country*, have attracted a far larger non-white membership than the Progressives have done, and as a consequence they have been harried by the political branch of the police and many of their office-bearers have been detained for questioning. Restrictions have been placed on their meetings and their offices have been raided. In the 1961 general election the progressives lost all but one representative in Parliament, while the Liberals have so far failed to win a single seat.

The public-opinion trend in South Africa since 1961 has been against any political party which has tried to work across the colour line. With every successive crisis and every anti-white outburst in the other states of Africa it has become increasingly difficult to persuade white voters in South Africa that a working partnership with blacks is possible. By 1965 the movement into the white political *laager* had almost become a stampede.

PART FOUR

Chapter 16

Neighbours

I N THE states around the Republic that are her neighbours there is a great ferment of African emancipation. The Government in Pretoria has watched anxiously while the British Protectorates have moved spectacularly towards self-government and independence, while a grave political crisis has developed in Southern Rhodesia, and while the Portuguese have drafted in troops to quell a subversive movement in Mozambique.

The Protectorates differ greatly from each other. Their climates vary, their political and economic problems are dissimilar, and the African people who inhabit them speak different languages. The most picturesque of the three states is Basutoland, lying in the very centre of the grassy highveld and surrounded by the Cape Province, the Free State and Natal. It is mountain country, in the most rugged part of the Drakensberg, the great range that forms the backbone of South Africa. In Basutoland are the abundant sources of the Orange River, which flows westwards across the wide plateau, then through the arid Karoo, then past the fringes of the Kalahari desert to the Atlantic. And the swiftly-flowing Caledon River, which gives a mighty boost to the Orange, also rises in Basutoland, as does the Tugela, which flows between the hills and through the valleys of Natal to spill its brown floodwaters into the Indian Ocean. Among the misty peaks of Basutoland live the most independent, closely-knit community in Southern Africa, the 700,000 Basuto. Their country is about a quarter the size of England, with an altitude varying from 6,000 feet in the valleys to 10,000 feet on the high escarpments.

With an annual budget of only £600,000, smaller than that of many a country town in South Africa, Basutoland is almost entirely dependent for its economic survival upon the goodwill of the Republic, which surrounds it on all sides. Nevertheless the Basutos are busy setting up an independent kingdom, with their own monarch and a constitutional structure modelled on that of Britain. The first King of Lesotho, as the new state is to be called, will be Motlotlehi Moshoeshoe II, born during the last World War, former student at Oxford, eloquent, intelligent, and of serious, responsible character. Directly descended from Moshesh, founder of the Basuto nation and greatest of all African leaders, Moshoeshoe aims to be a king in the tradition of the Danish Royal House, living simply and moving freely among his subjects.

After a fairly turbulent existence during which they had to fight first the marauding Zulus, then the Boer settlers in the Free State, then the government of the Cape Province, the Basuto were placed under the protection of the British Crown in 1884 and fell under the authority of the British High Commissioner for South Africa. The administration was carried out by Resident and District Commissioners working closely with the Paramount Chief and using the tribal structure of sub-chiefs and headmen. A tribal council was created which gradually evolved into a national council. After World War II demands were made for legislative powers and a greater degree of local authority, and in 1957 the National Council was invited to submit recommendations. Thereafter events moved swiftly.

The Council engaged a constitutional authority of world repute, Professor D. V. Cowen, to draw up a constitution, and this was accepted by the British Government with minor modifications. It provided for a Legislative Council of 80, half elected and half nominated, with power to make laws on all matters excepting defence and internal security; an executive council and a House of Chiefs. As soon as the new Council had assembled it appointed a constitutional commission headed by a South African lawyer, W. P. Stanford, who had sat in the Parliament at Cape Town as a representative of the Africans of the Cape. The commission produced a plan for a monarchy, complete with king, prime minister, cabinet, elected lower house and a senate consisting of 22 leading chiefs and 11 further members nominated by the king. The plan was approved by the British Government, and it was also agreed that Basutoland would be granted full independence following a joint resolution by both houses of the proposed new parliament, or if demanded by a plebiscite. Basutoland will then be free to apply for membership of the British Commonwealth. All these steps are to be completed by the end of 1965.

Meanwhile, in Bechuanaland, the British Protectorate lying along the north-western boundaries of the Republic, a similar movement for self-government has been proceeding. Bechuanaland's other borders are with South-West Africa on her western side and Southern Rhodesia on her north-eastern side. The ancestors of the Bechuana tribesmen – the Bamangwato, Batawana, Bakgatla and Bangwaketse – moved down from Central Africa with the first wave of migrating Bantu who drove the Hottentots and Bushmen before them and were settled in the northern and eastern Transvaal when, in turn, the Ngunis came down behind them. Fleeing from the Ngunis, a section of these earlier Bantu turned westwards, towards the desert, and they occupied the flat, arid, and somewhat featureless country between the swamplands at the sources of the Zambesi and the Kalahari Desert. The Ngunis, as we have already related, moved on in a south-easterly direction, between the Drakensberg and the sea, to found the Swazi, Zulu and Xhosa nations.

Bechuanaland is one of the largest territories in southern Africa, 275,000 square miles in extent, 25 times as big as Basutoland. But its population of 300,000 is less than half that of Basutoland. About one-third of the territory is low-lying bush country, hot and malarial, and the rest is desert and semi-desert, with wide extremes of temperature. It is fairly good ranching country – where the diseases can be controlled, and the soil responds to irrigation. A few modest mining ventures produce small quantities of manganese ore and asbestos. The territory is largely unexplored and undeveloped and is capable of carrying a much higher population. Its annual budget runs at approximately £1,500,000.

Apart from inter-tribal disputes and faction-fights, the Bechuana people lived fairly peacefully in their featureless domain until 1870, when parties of Boer trekkers began to invade their territory from the Transvaal. The chiefs appealed to Britain for protection, and after a good deal of hesitation and several skirmishes between British patrols and parties of Boer huntsmen, Bechuanaland was declared a British Protectorate in 1885. Cecil Rhodes was active in the Kimberley-Mafeking area at the time, and he took a great interest in the territory. His British South Africa Company was given a charter to prospect in Bechuanaland in 1889 and to administer the territory, but after a few years the British Government took over the task of administration, stationing a resident commissioner there. A railway line was built through Bechuanaland, linking the Cape Province with Southern Rhodesia, and some small areas were opened for settlement by whites.

In 1920 two advisory councils, one consisting of Africans and the other of whites, were appointed to advise the Resident Commissioner, and thirty years later these two bodies were merged into a joint advisory council. Then in 1960 Bechuanaland was given its first instalment of home-rule, consisting of a legislative council with powers to make laws in a limited field, an executive council and a special African council to advise on tribal affairs. But the Bechuanas had far more ambitious ideas. They demanded a parliament of their own, adjusted to suit the special requirements of the territory. Since there were four tribes and the royal house of the largest and most influential had been disrupted by the refusal of the British Government to appoint the heir, Seretse Khama, as Paramount Chief after his marriage to a white girl, Ruth Williams, the Bechuanas decided against a monarchy on the lines of the Basutoland plan. Instead, they decided to make Seretse Khama, who was a man of great ability and high prestige despite the controversy over his marriage, their Prime Minister. Seretse Khama formed the Bechuanaland Democratic Party and his candidates won a substantial majority in the Legislative Council in the 1963 elections. Backed by the chiefs and leading whites, Seretse and the Council put forward their draft for a new constitution, and this was approved by the British Government. It came into force in 1965, when the first general election was held.

There is a legislative assembly of 32, elected on a non-racial common roll, with a few additional members elected by the Assembly itself to represent special interests. The speaker is elected, and there are a Prime Minister, deputy-Prime Minister and five other ministers forming a cabinet. There is also a House of Chiefs to serve as an upper chamber and to look after tribal interests. A Queen's Commissioner represents the British Government, and he retains control over defence, external relations, internal security and finance. He presides at Cabinet meetings. In all matters, including his own reserved powers, he must act on the advice of the cabinet. There is a Bill of Rights which can be enforced by an independent judiciary. A select committee of the existing Legislative Council, which recently looked into white-black relations in the territory, pronounced that these were 'marked by courtesy and respect'. The committee called for multiracial schools, a uniform system of taxation, a common legal code for all races, legislation to prohibit race-discrimination in public places, and a ban on racially-restrictive covenants in titles to freehold land. The capital, which has hitherto been at Mafeking, inside South Africa, has been moved to Gaberones.

Lying strategically where the boundaries of Zululand, the Transvaal and Mozambique meet in a spur of the Drakensberg, Swaziland is the smallest, richest, and most unsettled of the three British protectorates. Some 6,700 square miles in area, the parts of it where the Transvaal escarpment thrusts into the west are grassy highveld, healthy and picturesque. The rest is mostly bush-clad lowveld. The territory is fertile, well-watered and rich in minerals. It has a population of 260,000 Africans and 10,000 whites, and an annual budget of around £2,500,000. It has coal, gold, tin, asbestos and iron-ore. A new railway linking the iron-mines in the north-west with the port of Lourenço Marques in Mozambique was opened in 1964. Sugar is being farmed extensively in the lowveld and some 200,000 acres of the higher ground are being planted with trees.

Swaziland lay in the path of the downward migrations of Bantu and Ngunis from the headwaters of the Zambesi, and it was crossed and re-crossed time and again. A little over a century ago a clan of Ngunis, under Chief Sobhuza, moved away from the Pongola Valley to settle in the mountain country of Swaziland. Paul Kruger would have liked Swaziland, together with a strip of northern Zululand, to give the Republic direct access to Kosi Bay, on the shores of the Indian Ocean where a good harbour could have been built, but the British were nervous about this. Chief Sobhuza played off Boer against Briton as best he could until in 1881 the inde-pendence of Swaziland was guaranteed by treaty between the Transvaal Republic and the British. But the Swazis proved incapable of dealing with a horde of prospectors, concession-hunters, liquor-sellers and adventurers, and they appealed for help to both the Boers and the British. A tripartite form of control was then agreed upon, with the British, the Boers and the Swazis all participating. Later the British withdrew from this arrangement, leaving the control of Swaziland to the Swazis and the Transvaal, on condition that no attempt would be made by the Republic to incorporate the territory. After the Anglo-Boer war Swaziland was administered by the Governor of the Transvaal until 1907 when it became a British Protectorate with a resident commissioner. A council was created in 1921 to advise the resident commissioner on matters of particular concern to whites in the territory. From about 1950 onwards Swazi-land enjoyed a considerable boom, and many South Africans bought land there and invested in property and business undertakings of various kinds. Soon an agitation arose for some measure of self-government, and in 1960 a constitutional committee was appointed to go into the matter, consisting of 10 whites, 15 Swazis and 5 offi-cials, with the Resident Commissioner as chairman. The committee recommended that Swaziland should be developed into a state in which all its inhabitants would enjoy equality of citizenship, regardless of race; that all traces of race-discrimination should be eliminated and that there should be a British Governor and that the special position of the Paramount Chief should be suitably recognised. There would be a legislative council consisting of 12 members elected by the Swazi National Council and 12 elected by whites and coloureds. There would also be an executive council of official and elected members.

The plan was rejected by the British Government and a period of confusion and dissent followed in Swaziland. A meeting of the Swazi National Council called by the Paramount Chief – the 'Ngwenyama' – broke up in disorder. An African nationalistic movement known as the Progressive Party was formed in opposition to the chiefs, and it demanded universal franchise. Early in 1963 a constitutional conference was held in London, attended by representatives of the Paramount Chief, the white Advisory Council, the Progressive Party, and several other political movements. The British Government put forward a plan for a Legislative Council of 32, ten to be elected by Africans 'by traditional methods', ten by whites on a white voters' roll, and eight persons to be elected on a multiracial roll. Four additional members would be nominated. The Paramount Chief's delegates offered an alternative scheme, somewhat similar to the Basutoland plan, with a king, a prime minister, cabinet, and a legislative assembly consisting of an equal number of whites and Africans. No agreement could be reached and the conference broke up. Four months later the British Government announced that it had decided to impose a constitution on its own responsibility. There would be an executive council consisting of the British Commissioner and four members, and a legislative assembly with 24 elected members. A speaker would be appointed and the four members of the Executive would sit in the assembly. Of the 24 ordinary members of the legislative assembly, eight would be elected by the Paramount Chief and his council. A non-racial voters' roll would be compiled, which would elect four whites and eight others of any race. Four more whites would be elected on a voters' roll consisting of whites only. This plan was strongly opposed by all sections in Swaziland, but the British Government declared that it would be implemented nonetheless.

In Swaziland a period of strikes and unrest followed, and British troops were flown in from Kenya to maintain order. Deputations went to London from the whites who protested against the franchise proposals debarring 7,000 South Africans out of the white population of 10,000 from voting, and from the Paramount Chief who objected to the powers given to the legislative council to control land and minerals. However, the British Government declined to reopen discussions on the constitution, and steps were taken to put it into effect. The Paramount Chief then decided to

form a political party of his own with which to fight the first
general election under the new constitution, and when the election
took place in June 1964, his candidates swept the board. The Paramount Chief also secured the support of all the whites elected to
the Assembly, so that from then onwards he completely dominated
the political scene in Swaziland. He made no secret of the fact that
his objective was to secure a constitutional monarchy similar to the
new constitution for Basutoland.

Between Swaziland's north-eastern border and the Indian Ocean
lies the Portuguese province of Mozambique (Moçambique or
Portuguese East Africa), stretching up the coast for more than
1,000 miles and 304,000 square miles in extent. It is fertile, tropical
country, flat in parts and hilly in others. There are extensive
forests of hardwoods, especially in the northern districts bordering
Rhodesia, while at Gorongoza, near the port of Beira, is the most
interesting game reserve in the world. Many parts of the territory
are malarious and unhealthy, and diseases such as east-coast fever,
nagana, and heart-water take heavy toll of cattle. Bilharzia is rife
among humans. However, with the application of scientific methods
to wipe out mosquitoes and tsetse-fly and to control ticks and other
parasites, large-scale development of agriculture is possible. The
Portuguese have recently opened up several settlements in the territory and sugar is being extensively grown under irrigation.

The full extent of mineral resources is not known. Substantial
deposits of coal exist in the Zambesi valley, near Tete, and are being
mined. Small quantities of gold have been found near Manica and
there have been reports of promising indications of oil. Until
recently there has been little industrial activity in the territory but
a drive to establish industries is at present taking place. Much of
Mozambique's revenue has in the past come from sales of timber
cut from the forests and from the earnings of the 100,000 African
labourers sent to the gold mines of the Witwatersrand in the neighbouring South African Republic. The harbour at Lourenço Marques, serving the Transvaal, Rhodesia and Swaziland, and the
harbour at Beira serving Rhodesia, Zambia, and Malawi, also
contribute substantially to the budget. The population consists of
6,600,000 Africans, of which only 100,000 were until recently
counted as 'civilised', some 50,000 whites, and about 25,000 half-
castes.

In the southern half of the territory, below the Zambesi River,
the Africans are of Bantu stock with a strong infusion of Nguni
blood, more especially in the area lying between Swaziland and
the hinterland of Delgoa Bay. The Ngunis probably arrived there

in the same migration that brought down the ancestors of the Xhosas, Zulus, and Swazis from around the headwaters of the Zambesi. In the northern half of Mozambique province, on the other side of the Zambesi, the Africans are of similar stock to the Nyasas. The first Portuguese settlement in Mozambique territory was at the ancient port of Sofala in 1505. There the trail began from the coast inland to Zimbabwe and the legendary kingdom of Monomatapa, and it was hoped to open up a valuable trade in ivory and gold. But Sofala proved to be unhealthy and difficult to defend, and the Portuguese moved to the island of Moçambique, off the coast, where they built a fort and maintained a garrison. The Dutch tried to capture the island during the seventeenth century, but they were driven off. From Moçambique Island the Portuguese sent expeditions from time to time to explore the African hinterland, but nothing much came of their efforts. One party moved inland from Sofala in search of gold and managed to reach the Rhodesian plateau. But they found several of the ancient mines abandoned and there was no sign of the civilisation with strange buildings and great wealth about which slave-raiders had spoken.

The Portuguese themselves required slaves for the development of their colony of Brazil and they conducted a fairly extensive slave trade from Mozambique until the traffic was abolished in 1878. Meanwhile settlements on the mainland had been established at Lourenço Marques, on the shores of Delgoa Bay, at Beira near Sofala, and elsewhere. In 1752 a governor was sent out from Portugal to look after the territory. During the years between 1840 and 1890 when the 'scramble for Africa' was taking place, the Portuguese made an attempt to link up Mozambique territory with their other colony of Angola, on the west side of Africa. The idea was to establish a corridor across Southern Rhodesia to the Zambesi, then in a north-westerly direction across Northern Rhodesia to the Angola border. An expedition was sent inland from Beira to explore the route and lay claim to the land, but Cecil Rhodes heard about it. He was at that time busy with his scheme to secure an all-British route up the centre of Africa from the Cape to Cairo, and he moved quickly to forestall the Portuguese. He made a treaty with the Matabele chief Lobengula, securing Mashonaland in Southern Rhodesia as a British sphere of interest, and he sent a column of pioneers to occupy the north-eastern area of Southern Rhodesia. The column clashed with the Portuguese who had gone to lay claim to the territory, and the Portuguese retired to Mozambique territory. A treaty was then signed between Britain and Portugal defining the borders of Mozambique and recognising the Rhodesias as a British sphere of interest, thus disposing of the Portuguese plan for a 'corridor'.

In his book of memoirs, the Transvaal President, Paul Kruger, related how Cecil Rhodes came to seek his support against the Portuguese. On a journey back to Cape Town from the hinterland, Rhodes called on the President in Pretoria, and offered to obtain the port of Lourenço Marques for the Republic. Kruger replied : 'How can we work together there? The harbour belongs to the Portuguese, and they won't hand it over.' 'Then we must simply take it,' said Rhodes. The President wrote in his memoirs that he reacted sharply to this proposition, and Rhodes went away. After that Rhodes made no further attempt to gain Kruger's support for his African designs.

Until about 1950, the province of Mozambique was administered directly from Portugal. There was at first a governor, then the territory was divided and two governors were appointed, one for the south and the other for the north, with a Governor-General in charge of both. Africans in the territory could become Portuguese citizens by passing a fairly stiff 'civilisation' test, and about 100,000 had qualified by the time the system was changed. No statutory colour-bars were imposed, but the Portuguese observed a fairly rigid class-system, drawing a sharp distinction between Africans who had 'evolved' and those who were regarded as primitive and who lived under tribal conditions. Administration of the African population was on the whole fair but severe, and heavy punishments were meted out for theft, assault and other infringements of the law. In 1951 Mozambique was proclaimed an overseas province of Portugal and was given seven representatives in the National Assembly in Lisbon. A council was created in the province to advise the Governor-General, and this consisted of five unofficial members elected by various corporate bodies, such as the Chambers of Commerce and Industries, and seven official members. Mozambique was divided into four provinces and nine districts, with a governor in charge of each province and an administrator in charge of each district.

A further change was announced in 1961 when full Portuguese citizenship was conferred on all the inhabitants of Portugal's overseas territories. The policy, it was proclaimed, would henceforth be one of multiracial integration. Democratic elections were introduced to several of the larger towns in Mozambique territory and workers in commerce and industry were given permission to negotiate wage agreements by collective bargaining. The number of deputies representing Mozambique in the National Assembly at Lisbon was increased to ten and provision was made for their election by direct suffrage. At the same time an ambitious scheme was announced to open up the territory through settlements and by encouraging industries.

Meanwhile in Angola, or Portuguese West Africa, on the other side of Africa, a nationalistic revolt broke out, and reports began to appear in the world Press of a similar agitation in the central and northern districts of Mozambique. An African nationalistic organisation was stated to have been formed, with headquarters across the border in Tanzan. The Portuguese drafted large numbers of troops into the territory and constructed airfields at strategic points along the borders. More recently a military drive appears to have been carried out in the northern area and a number of African refugees fled into Malawi and Tanzan. The Portuguese themselves gave no indications as to the extent and significance of these operations but the presence in the territory of some 25,000 troops suggested that there might be a threat of guerilla warfare on similar lines to the troubles that had occurred in Angola.

Of all South Africa's neighbours, Southern Rhodesia has reached the highest stage of development. With a population of 3,770,000 Africans, 224,000 whites and 20,000 coloureds and Asians, she has an annual budget of £28,000,000. She has the largest colliery in the world, at Wankie. There is a small but efficient steel industry, capable of development, and gold and other minerals are mined in various parts of the country. For most of the year the climate is congenial and healthy, though bilharzia, malaria, east-coast fever and other tropical diseases have to be fought, as in other parts of Central Africa. The big hydro-electric plant at Kariba, which Southern Rhodesia now shares with Zambia, will ensure an ample supply of power for several decades to come. In agriculture, Rhodesia is in some ways ahead of the Republic in the south. Her farming systems are modern and productive and she has practised soil-conservation more vigorously and effectively than South Africa has done. More than 95 per cent of African children are in schools run by local communities, and health services are among the best in Africa.

The modern history of Southern Rhodesia began in 1890 when Rhodes sent his pioneer column to block the passage of the Portuguese. Following a war with the Matabele, the Jameson raid into the Transvaal Republic, and the Anglo-Boer war, the process of settling Southern Rhodesia went ahead steadily. This was first carried out by the British South Africa Company, which held important concessions to prospect and exploit the natural resources of the territory. By 1922 Rhodesia had advanced sufficiently for a measure of home-rule to be introduced and a referendum was held to decide whether the territory should be joined to South Africa as a fifth province or whether it would be granted self-government as a separate state. By 8,774 votes to 5,989 the decision went in favour of a separate state. Southern Rhodesia was then given a parliament and a government consisting of a prime minister and cabinet. Its progress was steady and uneventful until 1953 when the Central African Federation was formed consisting of Southern Rhodesia, Northern Rhodesia and Nyasaland.

Unfortunately, however, the promoters of the Central African Federation did not grasp the important fact that no stable association could be brought about until the foundations of each state had been made secure. And in order to secure the foundations it was essential to work out a fair and enduring formula for white-black relationships. Africans throughout the continent were demanding full equality and a speedy end to colonial domination, and they bitterly opposed the federation plan in all three of the states concerned. Campaigns for secession and independence were waged in Nyasaland and Northern Rhodesia, and when they succeeded the Federation fell apart. Southern Rhodesia was back on her own again, as a self-governing state under the Crown.

Unhappily the cause of inter-racial co-operation, which had appeared so promising in Southern Rhodesia, suffered a shattering reverse with the failure of the Federation. In 1961 a two-to-one majority of whites in a referendum had agreed to a multiracial constitution which gave the franchise, on a qualified basis, to all races, and made it possible for Africans to become the majority in Parliament in due course. But within the short space of a year, public opinion among the whites swung sharply to the right, and the liberal government of Sir Edgar Whitehead, which had sponsored the constitution, was defeated at a general election. The new constitution had been opposed at the referendum by a party called the Rhodesian Front, and its leader, Mr. Winston Field, replaced Sir Edgar Whitehead as Premier. But Mr. Field was not considered sufficiently resolute in reversing the tide of liberalism, and in April, 1964, he was replaced by an extreme opponent of multiracialism, Mr. Ian Smith, who was given overwhelming support by the white electorate when his party won all 50 of the A-roll seats in a parliamentary general election a year later. Thus, emphatically, did the whites of Southern Rhodesia come to reject the principle of inter-racial government for which they had voted so large a majority in the referendum only four years previously.

What had brought about this radical change in public opinion? The major psychological causes were, without a doubt, the tragedy of the Congo; the anti-white trends in various emergent states in Africa; the extremist demands of African leaders in Rhodesia and the technique of intimidation often used by them to compel support; vacillation by the British Government of the day; apartheid propaganda from the Republic in the south, and the attacks on Southern Rhodesia at the United Nations and elsewhere, lending colour to the complaints of right-wing politicians in Rhodesia that the whites in Africa were the victims of 'an Afro-Asian plot' to drive them into the sea.

Rhodesia was not given full independence at the break-up of the Federation, as were the other two, less-developed states. Mr. Field, and Mr. Smith after him, demanded independence. The British Government insisted on Africans having a greater say in Rhodesian affairs, but the whites in Rhodesia were in no mood to make concessions. Mr. Smith threatened a 'unilateral declaration of independence' and the British Government, now led by Mr. Harold Wilson in place of Sir Alec Douglas-Home, warned that serious economic consequences would follow an unconstitutional move for independence.

Meanwhile a state of tension existed in Rhodesia. There were periodic disturbances and sporadic acts of sabotage. The two main African political parties were banned and some 1,800 Africans were held in various places of detention. A newspaper which sympathised with African aspirations had been shut down. It was a crisis, too, which had a bearing on political thought in South Africa, so closely linked historically and economically with Rhodesia. In 1961 the progressive elements in South Africa could point to the courageous experiment with multiracial government which the Rhodesians appeared to have launched, and could urge their compatriots to follow this example. Yet within a year the experiment had failed, and it was not long before the whites in both countries were stampeding into their respective *laagers*.

Chapter 17

World Relations

THE ROAD to Swaziland rolls over the high, dreary sourveld of the Eastern Transvaal, past the grove of mimosas that shelters the sad little village of Lochiel. Curving on down the escarpment, it enters a country of rounded hills, and it curls between two of them into the town of Mbabane. South Africans have travelled that road for half a century, by car, on horseback, by trek-wagon and on foot, without ever realising that an international boundary had been crossed, or even knowing where the border lay. Then suddenly, one mid-winter's day in 1963, a border-post appeared on the Mbabane road, and the barricades went up. Flags were hoisted and the police were there. All travellers, especially the Africans in their rattling old cars, or when they came on horseback, or with their bicycles or on foot, had to stop and show their papers. South Africans on the road to Swaziland realised with a shock that an era which everyone had taken for granted had come to an end.

The ending of this era brought not only barbed-wire fences and border formalities, but an important change in diplomatic policy as well. Ever since 1910 when special provision was made in the Act of Union for the Protectorates to be incorporated in South Africa, everyone had taken it for granted that sooner or later the territories would be joined to the Union. Successive prime ministers from Smuts in 1920, Hertzog in 1925 and 1935, Dr. Malan in 1949 and Strydom in 1956, had asked the British Government to make the transfer, until the 'Protectorates question' had become a standing diplomatic issue, almost like India's annual complaint against South Africa at the United Nations. Smuts was told that the time was not propitious. Hertzog was told that the British Government would like to consult the inhabitants of the Protectorates before a decision could be reached, and he agreed that this should be done. Then in 1935 the British Government said that both the inhabitants and the House of Commons would have to be consulted, and neither at that time was likely to give a favourable reply.

When Dr. Malan assumed power after General Smuts had been defeated in the 1948 general election, he decided to approach the

British Government from a different angle. It was obvious that the Africans in the Protectorates would be more firmly opposed to incorporation than ever before and that British public opinion was unhappy about apartheid. But his own followers were pressing for something to be done about the Protectorates, and his political opponents were taunting him with having undermined South Africa's position on this issue through his apartheid policies. So he decided that the request to Britain should come, not from the Government but from the South African Parliament. In 1954 he moved in the Assembly : 'This House resolves that the transfer to the Union of Basutoland and the Bechuanaland and Swaziland Protectorates, to be administered in terms of the schedule of the South African Act of 1909, or such other terms and conditions as may be agreed upon, should take place as soon as possible.' The reaction in London was swift and emphatic. Speaking in the Commons, Mr. Churchill said there could be no question of the British Government agreeing to a transfer at that time. The British pledge not to hand over the territories until the inhabitants had been consulted and until the Commons had been asked to express its views, still stood.

Dr. Malan retired from politics later that year and was succeeded by Mr. J. G. Strydom. While attending a Commonwealth Conference in London in 1956, Strydom discussed the question of the Protectorates with the British Premier, Sir Anthony Eden, who repeated what Churchill had said. After this the South African Government appears to have abandoned the idea of securing the Protectorates through the procedure laid down in the Act of Union. The South African Defence Minister, Mr. Erasmus, wanted to erect a network of radar stations, and he thought it better to formalise the right to fly over the Protectorates – something that had always been taken for granted hitherto. So in 1958 an agreement was signed with the British Government giving South African planes the right to fly over the Protectorates, to conduct search and rescue operations in the event of an air mishap, to inspect emergency airstrips in Bechuanaland, to build a road through a remote corner of Basutoland leading to a radar site on one of the peaks of the Drakensberg, to survey Swaziland for radar sites, and to map out an emergency route through Bechuanaland to South-West Africa.

In this same year Dr. Verwoerd succeeded Mr. Strydom as premier. Important developments were taking place that affected the question of the Protectorates. Basutoland was making plans for an independent monarchy, and Bechuanaland and Swaziland had been promised home-rule. Then, most significantly of all, Dr. Verwoerd decided that the time had come for South Africa to become a republic. This meant that the South Africa Act, passed by the British Parliament, would fall away, and with it the legal provisions for Britain to transfer the Protectorates to South Africa. A new and radical approach to the Protectorates problem would be required. Since the Africans in the Protectorates were aiming at independence, the time would come when they, and not Britain, would have the power to decide whether they wished to be linked to South Africa, and Dr. Verwoerd decided to make a direct appeal to them. He made a speech, late in 1963, in which he put the following offer : If the Protectorates would agree to develop under the wing of the South African Republic, land would be purchased to extend and consolidate their borders (a subject of special interest to Swaziland); industries would be opened up on their borders, funds would be provided for the development of their economies, and they would be encouraged to become fully self-governing ban-tustans. The bantustans could be linked in some way with one another and with the Republic. As for the whites in the Protector-ates, they would enjoy no rights there but would be given rights in the Republic instead. This pronouncement was officially ignored in both Britain and the Protectorates.

As the year 1964 wore on, there were clear indications that relationships between the South African Republic and Britain in regard to the Protectorates were becoming increasingly difficult. There had been incidents involving political refugees who fled from the Republic into the Protectorates. In Basutoland an African named Potlako Leballo claimed to be the leader of the banned Pan-African Congress. In Maseru he opened a campaign head-quarters, issued Press statements, and sent orders to agents in the Republic until the Basutoland police raided his office. There were complaints that refugees had been abducted by the South African police from Basutoland, Swaziland and Bechuanaland. Dr. Ver-woerd, in a public statement, said that if the Protectorates per-mitted political refugees to organise against South Africa, they must expect retaliation. A series of diplomatic notes was exchanged with the British Government which announced that a distinction would be made between 'ordinary political refugees' and persons who attempted to organise a revolution in South Africa from the Protectorates. It was British policy to prevent action in any territory under British control which was designed to foment violence in the Republic. South Africa then declared that all air-carriers licensed in the Republic must land at certain designated aerodromes in the

Republic and obtain clearance before proceeding to one of the Protectorates. Their licences would be taken away if they failed to comply with this order.

The Nationalist Government of the Republic has not abandoned the principle that the Protectorates must one day form part of South Africa. The Tomlinson Commission, which prepared a report for Dr. Verwoerd on how the Bantustans should be developed, declared : 'Although the Protectorates were artificially excluded from the Union in 1910, these territories remain the heartlands of the Bantu inside the territories as well as outside the territories, in the Union.' That view remains unchanged today. In Pretoria the Protectorates are regarded as essential to the success of the Bantustan concept, and every effort will be made to draw them into the scheme. But no further approaches for the transfer of the Protectorates are likely to be made to Britain. In future the Republican Government will aim its diplomacy directly at the Protectorates themselves, as each in turn secures home-rule and independence. Moreover, Dr. Verwoerd has some strong cards to play. One is the influence that South Africa can exert on the economics of all three territories. Another is his policy of not allowing rights to whites in the Bantustans. Dr. Verwoerd clearly believes that in time this will appeal to Africans in the Protectorates, especially to the Chiefs. A third inducement is the offer to enlarge the Protectorates by incorporating into them, as Bantustans, the adjoining African reserves.

So much for the question of the Protectorates. Relations between South Africa and Mozambique, which are governed by a treaty regulating the use of port facilities at Lourenço Marques by the Republic and the recruiting of labourers in Mozambique for the mines of South Africa, have long been on a friendly basis, and appear likely to remain so. There is a close working arrangement between the police and immigration authorities in both territories, and information regarding subversive elements is freely exchanged. Fugitives from one territory to the other are quickly arrested and sent back over the border. There were reports recently of negotiations for a defensive agreement, but the rumours were denied in Lisbon. However, towards the end of 1964 Dr. Verwoerd made a speech suggesting the formation of a Southern African 'common market' to include the Protectorates, Mozambique, and Southern Rhodesia.

The record of South Africa's relationships with the wider world, since the Nationalists secured power in 1948, has been one of increasing hostility and isolation. When Dr. Malan became Premier he took the External Affairs portfolio as Smuts and Hertzog had

done before him. But Malan had little understanding of world
affairs and needed advice and help. He decided to call in an experienced diplomat, Mr. Charles te Water, one-time President of the
League of Nations Assembly and a former South African High
Commissioner in London. Appointing te Water 'Special Ambassa-
dor-at-Large', Dr. Malan sent him off to visit as many countries as
possible. His instructions were to 'counter the misapprehensions
that have arisen with regard to the Government's racial and other
policies' and to recommend a diplomatic plan of campaign for
strengthening South Africa's position in the international sphere.
Te Water was a protégé of General Hertzog and had resigned the
post of South African High Commissioner in London at the outbreak of World War II. He enjoyed many friends among statesmen
overseas.

Te Water decided that it was essential for South Africa to work
out a pan-African policy in which she could take the lead, and that
this task should be given first priority. He accordingly set out on a
tour of nations in Europe with dependencies in Africa. He went to
Portugal, Belgium, France, Italy and Britain. He quickly discovered
that it would be impossible to sell the idea of apartheid to any of
these countries, and that the best that could be done with them was
to try to correct some of the exaggerated reports that were current
regarding the treatment of Africans in South Africa. Furthermore,
he found a strong movement to emancipate dependent peoples and
discard discrimination on a basis of colour. Te Water came back
to tell Dr. Malan that any thought of a frontal drive to persuade
other governments to accept or even tolerate the policy of apartheid
was out of the question. As long as it pursued apartheid the
Nationalist Government would be forced into a defensive role,
whether it liked it or not. South Africa's approach, especially to
the states in Africa, should be indirect. She should concentrate on
the states 'south of the Sahara'. Her role must be that of 'good
neighbour'. She must meticulously refrain from involving herself
in any question concerning white-black relations, and she should
concentrate on the economic, scientific and cultural spheres. Here
she had a great deal of value to offer. The Institute of Medical
Research in Johannesburg and the veterinary research laboratories
at Onderstepoort had acquired a wealth of scientific information
regarding human and animal diseases in Africa; research institutions had made important discoveries in agriculture; South Africa
led the world in her knowledge of mining, and advanced technical
work was being carried out in her laboratories. All this could be
made available to the other states in Africa. South Africa should

take the lead in organising pan-African scientific, veterinary, medical, agricultural and economic associations.

Te Water also felt that South Africa should raise the status of her diplomatic representatives abroad, should send missions to various states where she was not represented, should open up more consulates – especially in Africa – and should establish far more comprehensive information services. He saw an opportunity for a more positive diplomatic approach in the sphere of defence. South Africa had the strongest and best-equipped Defence Force in Africa and she should offer to serve as the key defensive bastion for the West in Africa south of the Sahara. At that time plans were being made to form NATO, and te Water suggested that South Africa should try to get herself included in that organisation.

Dr. Malan accepted most of te Water's proposals. In 1949 he announced that the status of South Africa's major diplomatic posts abroad would be raised. He declared that South Africa was waiting for an invitation to join NATO. He said that South Africa was firmly on the side of the West in the cold-war with the East, and that his government was sounding out nations with possessions in Africa with a view to a common approach on problems of mutual concern. Moves were initiated, through the United Nations organisation and by direct negotiation, to form various scientific and technical bodies, to exchange information and give assistance on a pan-African basis. South Africa was one of the first countries to send an air-crew for the Berlin air-lift in 1949. A year later, when the United Nations intervened in Korea, South Africa contributed a fighter-squadron to the United Nations forces. However, her request to be included in NATO was politely but firmly turned down. Already a chill breeze of hostility to South Africa was beginning to drift through the diplomatic corridors of the world.

If NATO was excluded, then the Nationalist Government was determined to take the lead in forming a defensive organisation for states in Africa south of the Sahara. This would be complementary to NATO and possibly even formally linked with it in some way. The Defence Minister, F. C. Erasmus, was instructed to organise such a body, and he sounded out the British Government in June 1951, while attending a Commonwealth Defence Conference in London. The British were not enthusiastic but agreed to discuss the idea further at a conference in Nairobi, and to invite South Africa, Belgium, Egypt, Ethiopia, France, Italy, Portugal and Southern Rhodesia to send delegates, with the United States present as an observer. Egypt declined the invitation but all the others responded favourably. South Africa sent a strong delegation, led by Erasmus and another member of the cabinet. However, no firm commitments were made with regard to a common defensive organisation, most of the delegates asking for time to consider the South African proposals.

A further conference on African defence was held in 1954, this time at Dakar. It was called primarily to consider plans for co-ordinating forces and supplies in the western regions of the continent, but South Africa again put her idea of a 'southern NATO', as before without arousing much interest. Five months later, while on a visit to London, Erasmus decided to make a plea in public for his 'southern NATO'. In the course of a speech he declared that urgent consideration should be given to the formation of an African defensive organisation among states south of the Sahara. He feared that the 'quit Africa movement', as he described the drive towards independence then proceeding throughout Africa, would create a vacuum into which the communists would move unless something definite was done to counter the danger.

In 1957 Erasmus again went to London for defence talks with the British Government. He managed to persuade the British to call a further conference 'to examine the idea of forming a Southern African alliance, on similar lines to NATO, for the defence of the sea routes round Africa', as a responsible report of the discussions put it. But nothing more came of the project and the conference was never held. What Erasmus had described as the 'quit Africa movement' was rapidly gaining momentum. When pressed by South Africa to say why they did not appear to be enthusiastic about a 'southern NATO' the British replied that in their view it would be better to try to bar the gateway to Africa in the Middle East than to meet aggression on the African continent itself. But it soon became apparent that the real reason for the reluctance, not only of Britain but of every other state, to enter into defensive alliance with South Africa was her apartheid policy. Erasmus had dis-banded the Native Military Corps and the Cape Corps of Coloureds. Government policy was to employ coloureds in the Defence Force only as cooks and camp staff and to give them neither arms nor training. Africans were not employed in the Defence Force in any capacity whatever. With all the other states in Africa these policies raised important difficulties. The first was how, in a joint campaign, the forces could be properly integrated if one of the leading participants insisted on a colour-bar. Another was the manpower limitation which South Africa imposed on her-self by insisting on using only whites in her Defence Force. In the event of conflict, would there not be a serious fifth-column in South

Africa? If the whites had to supply all the manpower for the fighting services, who would man the industries that would be needed to sustain the armed forces? These and many other practical questions arose, while, of course, there was the big objection everybody else had to the policy of apartheid.

Meanwhile within the Nationalist Party a school of thought arose, led by Eric Louw, which strongly disapproved of the te Water policy of 'indirect approach'. What was needed, this section argued, was a direct, aggressive approach. Apartheid had proved to be a potent political slogan among the whites of South Africa, and was there any reason to suppose it would appeal any the less to whites in other parts of Africa? The two main factors to be exploited were the prevalent fear of communism and the fear among whites throughout Africa of being dominated by blacks. Contacts should be made with white leaders in Kenya, the Rhodesias and elsewhere, while the thing to do when South Africa was attacked at the United Nations was to hit back hard, charging the critics with practising race-discrimination in their own countries.

Te Water retired from the scene. In 1954 Dr. Malan gave up the leadership of the Nationalist Party and was replaced as Premier by Mr. J. G. Strydom. Eric Louw was then appointed Minister of External Affairs and he lost no time in applying his aggressive technique. The opportunity came almost immediately when South Africa found herself under heavy fire at the United Nations. A resolution was passed in the U.N. Assembly, with only six abstentions, expressing concern over South Africa's policy of race-discrimination and calling on South Africa to observe its obligations under the Charter. South Africa announced her withdrawal from the U.N. session in protest and recalled her permanent representative. Next South Africa withdrew from UNESCO following criticisms of apartheid expressed at a conference of that body in Montevideo.

Meanwhile, South Africa's relations with India, which had become strained during the last months of the Smuts regime, rapidly worsened. One of the first actions of the Nationalist Government after taking office in 1948 was to repeal a bill passed by the Smuts Government which gave a form of limited indirect representation to the Indian community in the Parliament at Cape Town. The new Nationalist Minister of the Interior, Dr. T. E. Donges, stated that the policy of the Government was to reduce the Indian population of South Africa through repatriation and that they were to have no political rights. Early in 1951, in reply to a request made by India, delegations from the Indian and Pakistan governments came to Cape Town to discuss with the South African Government how to break the deadlock that had arisen between South Africa and the other two countries. It was agreed that a high-level conference would be held between the three countries as soon as it could be arranged. Shortly afterwards Dr. Donges announced a Group Areas bill designed to enforce business and residential apartheid. It was clear that the Indian community would be particularly hard hit by this measure, and the Government of India appealed to South Africa to suspend action on the Group Areas Bill until it could be discussed at the proposed conference. South Africa refused to delay the bill and India and Pakistan immediately called off the conference.

India then raised the whole question of her relations with South Africa at the United Nations and a resolution was passed calling on South Africa, India and Pakistan to discuss their differences at a conference. South Africa announced that she had no intention of observing the terms of the resolution since it constituted an unwarranted interference in her own domestic affairs. India continued to raise the matter year after year at the United Nations, which repeatedly called upon the three countries to hold a conference. However, South Africa declined to waive her objection to U.N. interference in her domestic affairs. In 1957 India issued an order compelling all South Africans in India to register and warning that failure to do so rendered them liable to deportation.

South Africa resumed her seat at the United Nations Assembly in 1956 and Eric Louw attended in person. Speaking against a motion calling upon South Africa to reconsider her apartheid policies, Louw again declared that he was not prepared to tolerate interference by the United Nations with South Africa's domestic affairs. He then withdrew the South African delegation, leaving only 'token representation'. In 1959 the African National Congress in South Africa, supported by the South African Indian Congress, the Trade Union Congress and the Congress of Democrats, announced a boycott of goods produced by firms supporting the Nationalist Party. A number of bodies in England, including the Trade Union Council and the Labour and Liberal Parties, announced their support for the movement, and Eric Louw made a speech warning that South Africans might retaliate by refusing to buy British goods.

The incident at Sharpeville, when police opened fire on an African crowd demonstrating against the pass-laws and a large number were killed and injured, took place in March 1960. There were demonstrations and shootings in other parts of the country as well, and a state of emergency was declared. South Africa suffered a bad Press throughout the world and a number of countries took action against her. Ghana, Malaya, Nigeria, the Sudan, Iraq, Liberia, Algeria and Burma imposed boycotts on South African goods. A motion was carried in the British House of Commons deploring apartheid, while the Canadian Parliament expressed its disapproval. The United Nations Security Council called on South Africa to abandon apartheid and there were protests and demonstrations against South Africa in many countries.

Louw decided to attend the 1961 session of the U.N. Assembly in person. After a procedural wrangle and a number of heated speeches a motion was carried calling upon member nations to take individual action to apply economic sanctions against South Africa and to break off diplomatic relations with her. During the months that followed, almost all the states in Africa with the exception of Mozambique and Angola, administered by Portugal, closed their airports and harbours to South Africa. Hasty arrangements had to be made by the Republic to route South African aircraft flying to Europe via Loanda or Brazzaville, with the next stop at either Las Palmas or the Cape Verde Islands. Czechoslovakia and Yugoslavia closed their consulates in South Africa, and Canada, Israel and the Netherlands announced a ban on arms to South Africa. A similar total ban was announced by the British Government in 1964 when the Labour Party was returned to power.

An Organisation of African Unity was formed by the Casablanca Group and the Monrovia Group of African states at a joint conference in Addis Ababa in June 1963. It was decided at this meeting to train 'freedom fighters' to operate within those states of Africa 'still under white rule', including South Africa, and headquarters for this operation were established at Dar-es-Salaam. According to intelligence reports received in South Africa, however, very little in the way of training or organisation appeared to have been carried out by the end of 1964.

South Africa was excluded from the Olympic Games held in Tokyo in 1964. She was asked to withdraw from an international conference on tourism held in Rome, while at a regional conference for Africa of the World Health Organisation the majority of delegates walked out as a protest against South Africa's presence at the conference, and it had to be abandoned. Such was the pattern of international protest against South Africa in many sporting, cultural, and scientific bodies as this book went to press. The Republic was on the defensive in almost every capital of the world. The only positive diplomatic step that Dr. Verwoerd could take in the increasingly isolated position in which he found himself was to try to strengthen the defences of the white *laager* he had created by offering economic concessions to the states around him. Economic pressures had brought about Union in 1910 and economics might help to draw the neighbouring states around the Republic now. A customs agreement favouring both countries at the expense of overseas manufacturers was signed with Southern Rhodesia. Then Dr. Verwoerd called for the formation of a Southern African 'common market' to open up trade and commerce in the sub-continent. Nor was this merely an empty gesture, since the South African economy, despite the boycott movements overseas, was booming as it had never done before.

Chapter 18

South-West Africa

THRUSTING UP from the Antarctic, the cold Benguella current swings north-westwards at Cape Point to scour the coast of Africa as far as the mouth of the Congo. And where this current flows the winds are cool and little rain falls, so that the coastline is parched and there is neither life nor vegetation. Thus the long curve of the west coast of Africa from Cape Point to the Congo is bleak and arid, and along the shore is sandy, waterless desert all the way from the Orange River to beyond the Cunene. There is a segment of this coastal desert, stretching from Cape Cross to the Cunene, 300 miles long and some 70 miles wide, which is known as the Skeleton Coast. Atlantic rollers pound on half-submerged reefs and shifting sandbanks and the bones of many a shipwrecked mariner lie buried among the wind-swept dunes that mark the end of the tides and the beginning of the desert. No man who managed to struggle through the breakers and the quicksands to reach the shore could long survive in this wilderness. It was this strip of desert along the coast that kept the early voyagers and adventurers from Europe out of South-West Africa. Not until the year 1800 when a few huntsmen ventured up from the Cape Colony did the whites show any interest in the territory, and even then the bleakness of the inland plateau was a strong discouragement to the trekker in search of new pastures.

This plateau, rising from the coastal desert, extends northwards all the way up the central regions of South-West Africa. The rain that falls upon it averages about six inches per year in the south, increases to twelve inches in the central parts of the territory around Windhoek, and averages about twenty-two inches in the north. There are no rivers of any consequence and for most of the year the watercourses are dry. Water is obtained from wells and bore-holes or by digging in the sandy beds of the rivers. In the south the plateau resembles the South African Karoo, with its stony outcrops and scrub-bush. In the central region there is bush and grass, and clumps of acacias and kameeldoring trees are scattered over the plains, with fairly dense growth along the watercourses.

As the traveller lays a winding dust-trail over the gravel roads leading northwards towards the Okavango the veld becomes more
verdant and there are belts of mopane forest-land. Here and there
the plateau is crossed by ranges of low mountains, the tallest rising
to 8,500 feet above sea-level.

Despite its lack of water South-West Africa is a fairly prosperous
country. Diamonds are mined at the mouth of the Orange and at
several points along the coast, while lead, tin, tungsten, vanadium,
zinc, asbestos, copper and iron-ore are all extracted in varying
quantities. Gold has been discovered in several places but so far no
deposit or reef has proved of any great value. Four million karakul
sheep do well on the arid, karoo-type veld in the south, and pelts
from the lambs form a valuable export. About 1,500,000 head of
cattle are ranched, mostly in the central regions, and both stock
and dairy products are sent to the main markets in the neighbouring
Republic. The S.W. African budget, at £16,500,000 annually, returns a regular surplus.

There was a time, many thousands of years ago, when the Kalahari Desert extended right across the southern half of the territory
from the Atlantic to the plains of Mashonaland, cutting off
Southern Africa from Central Africa. The Bushmen were the first
people to evolve from the earlier hominids around the Kalahari,
and Hottentots evolved from the Bushmen. As the Kalahari desert
receded southwards from the Cunene and eastwards from the coast
in South-West Africa, Bushmen and Hottentots moved into the
region which had previously been desert. Then from the north came
men of Negroid origin who mixed with the Hottentots to form a
race known as the Berg Damara. Some centuries before the first
white man explored S.W. Africa a strong Hottentot clan living on
the central plateau overthrew the Berg Damara and employed
them as slaves and herdsmen. Meanwhile the great migration of
the Bantu from around the Great Lakes in Central Africa took
place southwards past the eastern confines of the Kalahari, and
westwards above the northern limits of the Kalahari. In the van of
the westward thrust above the Kalahari came the Ovambos, who
were a race of agriculturalists and who drove the Hottentots, Berg
Damaras and Bushmen before them, settling on the northern
plateau of S.W. Africa in an area marked by a line from the
Cunene River to the Etosha Pan and from Etosha to the sea. After
the Ovambos came the Hereros, a more vigorous, more warlike
tribe of pastoralists who settled in the hill country south-east of
Ovamboland. They, too, drove the Bushmen, the Hottentots and
the Damaras to the south and east, into the fringes of the desert.

Then from about the year 1800 onwards white men came probing up from the Cape Colony, first as huntsmen, then as traders. In the northern districts of the Cape Colony were groups of coloureds who had firearms, and a Hottentot clan living on the S.W. Africa plateau employed a company of coloureds in a war against the Hereros, who were defeated. The Government at the Cape decided to intervene and a special commissioner was sent up in 1876 to find out whether the tribes of S.W. Africa wished to come under British protection. In 1878 Britain decided to annex a small trading settlement that had grown up at Walvis Bay. Meanwhile a German trader named Luderitz had become interested in the territory and he persuaded the German Government to make a bid for South-West Africa. Negotiations were opened with the British, who agreed to allow the Germans to annex the territory with the exception of the small settlement at Walvis Bay. Seven years later the Germans founded a trading company to exploit S.W. Africa and a number of German settlers were established on the plateau. The town of Windhoek was founded among the hills in the central region and it was linked by railway to the port of Swakopmund, near Walvis Bay. Mining ventures, farming settlements and several more narrow-gauge railways were developed as the years passed.

In their dealings with the Africans and coloureds who had settled in the territory the Germans were severe and demanding. In 1893 a clan of coloureds led by Hendrik Witbooi became restive and the Germans attacked his village and killed 150 men, women and children. Ten years later the Hottentots in the Bondelswartz area rebelled and were quickly suppressed with considerable loss of life. In the following year the Hereros revolted and killed a number of German settlers. Retaliation was swift and ruthless and the Hereros were reduced from a tribe of about 80,000 to 15,000 starving refugees.

When the first World War broke out in 1914, forces from South Africa occupied the ports of Luderitz in the south and Swakopmund in the centre, and from these points a general military attack was made on the territory, which surrendered in July 1915. After the war South Africa was asked to assume the mandate for S.W. Africa in terms of Article 119 of the Treaty of Versailles, and responsibility for governing the territory was formally accepted by the Parliament of Cape Town in September 1919. In 1926, by an Act of the South African Parliament, S.W. Africa was given a form of home-rule consisting of a Legislative Assembly elected by whites only, an executive committee and an Administrator, and the Assembly was given powers to legislate over a wide range of local affairs. After the rise of Hitler in Germany a Nazi movement developed in S.W. Africa aimed at restoring the territory to Germany. The German community formed about 40 per cent of the white population and was organised into two political movements, the Deutsche Bund and the National Socialist German Labour Party allied to the Nazis in Germany. The N.S.G.L.P. was banned by the Administration in 1934 but it continued to operate as an underground movement, stirring up a good deal of unrest among the German community in the territory. In 1935 the South African Government decided to appoint a commission to investigate the situation in S.W. Africa and the Commission recommended that the territory should be administered as a fifth province of the Union of South Africa. While accepting that such a step would be 'within the terms of the mandate', the South African Government did not consider that it would improve the situation in S.W. Africa, and took no further steps.

Two years later there was another wave of unrest due to Nazi activities, and the South African Government sent in 300 armed police. It was then decided to absorb the local police force into the South African police, who thereafter took over the task of policing the territory. Shortly before the outbreak of World War II an attempt was made by the Nazis to land 157 German 'immigrants' in S.W. Africa, but they were turned back by the immigration authorities. A sharp protest came from Germany and the Administration replied by posting strong guards at radio, cable, and power stations. The Germans took no further action, however, and after a few days the crisis passed. When war was declared, police made a swoop on the Nazi element and many Germans were interned. The remainder of the German community gave no trouble and the territory remained quiet throughout the war.

The non-German section of the white community, mostly Afrikaans-speaking, were divided into two political groups. The larger, during and after the war, was the United Party associated with the United Party led by Smuts in South Africa, but not part of it. The other group was the Nationalist Party, which was a branch of Dr. Malan's Nationalist Party. At a general election for the S.W. Africa Assembly in 1945 the United Party won a clean sweep against the Nationalists. Shortly before the war ended the Assembly passed a resolution asking that the mandate be terminated and that S.W. Africa be incorporated in the Union, and General Smuts undertook to consider the constitutional position. At a meeting of the U.N. General Assembly in London in 1946, Smuts announced that he intended to consult the inhabitants of S.W. Africa regarding the future of the territory and the question was again put to the S.W. African Assembly, which passed a unanimous resolution asking for incorporation in the Union. Meetings were then called of the chiefs of all the African tribes and at each tribal gathering a memorandum was read explaining the issues upon which a verdict was desired. The chiefs were asked to say whether they wished the existing form of control to continue unchanged, whether they would like South Africa to submit an agreement to the United Nations for control under the U.N. Trusteeship system, or whether they thought the territory should be incorporated as a fifth province of the Union. According to an official report by the South African Government to the United Nations, all the tribes asked for incorporation into the Union with the exception of the Hereros, numbering about 25 per cent of the African population. The Hereros demanded that the territory should become independent.

Later that year General Smuts, in an address to the Trusteeship Committee of the United Nations, gave an account of the consultations that had taken place in S.W. Africa and asked the Committee to agree to incorporation of the territory in the Union. A dramatic moment occurred when the delegate from India, Sir Maharaj Singh, rose to attack the South African proposal. He had spent some years in South Africa as High Commissioner for India, Sir Maharaj explained. Africans in the Union were inadequately represented in Parliament and their rights and freedoms were restricted in many ways. Their condition in South Africa did not justify handing over the Africans of S.W. Africa to control by the Union. General Smuts' request was rejected by the Trusteeship Committee and later the U.N. Assembly adopted a resolution inviting South Africa to submit a trusteeship agreement to the United Nations for the control of S.W. Africa. General Smuts decided to consult the South African Parliament and in April 1947 he moved a motion urging that after consultations with the inhabitants of S.W. Africa, legislation should be introduced giving representation to the territory in the South African Parliament. Four M.P.s and two Senators were suggested. The motion was carried. Smuts then visited Windhoek and in an address to the S.W. African Assembly he denied that the United Nations and the Trusteeship Council were the heirs of the League of Nations and the Mandates Commission.

Next development was a strong attack on South Africa in the General Assembly of U.N., led by the United States delegate. Educational services for Africans in S.W. Africa were inadequate, it was charged, and Africans were not given sufficient opportunities to run their own affairs. Whites, who formed only 10 per cent of the

total population, owned 58 per cent of the land. The debate ended
with a resolution appointing a special committee to report on what
steps should be taken to remedy the situation in S.W. Africa.

At about this time General Smuts was defeated in the 1948
general election in South Africa, when the Nationalists took over.
The new Premier, Dr. D. F. Malan, paid a visit to S.W. Africa
where he announced that the territory would be given representation in the South African Parliament by six M.P.s and two Senators.
At the same time the S.W. African Assembly would be increased
from twelve to eighteen members. No non-whites would be given
votes. The U.N. Trusteeship Council was informed of these decisions when it met later in the year and the Council again passed
a motion calling upon South Africa to submit a trusteeship agreement for S.W. Africa. In reply, South Africa notified the Secretary-
General of U.N. that 'the Union Government has at no times
recognised any legal obligations to supply information to the Trusteeship Council on its administration of S.W. Africa' and that
henceforth no reports would be submitted.

When the Trusteeship Council met in December 1949, the Rev.
Michael Scott asked leave to make a statement on behalf of the
Hereros and 'various other native chiefs' in S.W. Africa, and after
a strong protest by the South African delegate, who charged that
Mr. Scott was busy undermining the loyalty and goodwill of the
natives in the territory, the request was granted. Mr. Scott attacked
the South African Government's policy of race-discrimination and
went on to complain that the whites of S.W. Africa, who comprised
only one-tenth of the population, were to send six representatives to
the Parliament at Cape Town while the Africans, who formed nine-
tenths of the population, were getting no representation at all. By
thirty votes to seven the Trusteeship Council passed a resolution
regretting that South Africa had not complied with the decision of
the U.N. Assembly that S.W. Africa should be placed under the
Trusteeship Council and requesting the International Court of
Justice at The Hague to express an opinion on the legal aspects of
the dispute.

After hearing evidence the International Court pronounced that
S.W. Africa was still under international mandate, that the machinery provided by the U.N. Charter for a mandated territory to be
brought under the Trusteeship system was applicable to S.W.
Africa, that South Africa was not competent to modify the international status of S.W. Africa without the consent of the United
Nations, and that South Africa was bound by her international obligations to submit annual reports on her administration of S.W.

Africa to the Trusteeship Council. However, the court also found that the U.N. Charter did not impose a legal obligation on South Africa to place the territory under the Trusteeship system.

In 1952 the Trusteeship Council invited the Herero tribe in S.W. Africa to send a delegation to appear before it, but the South African Government refused to issue the necessary passports. The Hereros then asked the Rev. Michael Scott to make a statement once again on their behalf, which he did. South Africa immediately withdrew her delegate from the United Nations as a protest, but returned two years later. Expressing appreciation of the return of the South African delegation, the General Assembly passed a resolution which went on to invite South Africa to co-operate with the Trusteeship Council and to submit annual reports on S.W. Africa. The Trusteeship Council was instructed to find out how far the various agencies of the United Nations might be of assistance in S.W. Africa. Two years later the Trusteeship Council was again addressed by the Rev. Michael Scott on behalf of the Herero tribe, and this time South Africa decided to close its offices in New York as a protest. South Africa was once again requested to submit reports on S.W. Africa and to place the territory under the Trusteeship system.

During 1957 the Secretary-General of the United Nations was instructed to explore ways and means of resolving the deadlock with South Africa, and at his suggestion a Good Offices Committee was appointed to discuss with South Africa 'a basis for an agreement which would continue to accord to the territory of S.W. Africa an international status'. The Committee was invited to visit Pretoria, and after consultations there with the South African Government a statement was issued suggesting that S.W. Africa might be partitioned, and that the northern half might be placed under the Trusteeship system, with the southern half annexed to South Africa as a fifth province. However, the U.N. General Assembly rejected the principle of partition and requested the Good Offices Committee to reopen discussions with the South African Government on the basis of the territory undivided. Meanwhile South Africa had decided to boycott the proceedings at the United Nations as a protest against a further appearance of the Rev. Michael Scott before the Trusteeship Council on behalf of the Herero tribe.

On 10 December 1957, serious rioting occurred at the African location in Windhoek. Africans had refused to move to a new township and had boycotted the municipal beer-hall as a protest. Fighting broke out between Africans and pickets at the beer-hall and police were called in to stop the trouble. Africans turned on the police and municipal officials, the beer-hall and a number of police and municipal vehicles were burnt, the gaol was stormed and the African prisoners were released. Troops in armoured cars were called out to suppress the riot and 11 rioters were killed and 50 wounded. Nine African states lodged protests at the United Nations and a letter was sent from U.N. to South Africa expressing grave concern. South Africa immediately appointed a judicial commission to inquire into the riots, and this body found that the police were justified in acting as they did. The Commission added that the trouble had been stirred up by the Hereros 'at the instigation of their champions in New York'. Chief Hosea Kutako, head of the Herero tribe, issued a statement describing the Commission's report as 'misleading'.

At a conference of African states held six months later at Addis Ababa it was decided that Ethiopia and Liberia, who were both members of the old League of Nations, would take proceedings in the International Court of Justice against South Africa under Article 7 of the mandate granted to South Africa by the League in 1920. This Article provided that where a dispute between a mandatory power and another member of the League of Nations could not be settled by negotiation it should be submitted to the International Court. Ethiopia and Liberia declared that a dispute existed with South Africa over the administration of S.W. Africa and they asked the Court to order South Africa to cease applying apartheid in the territory in violation of Article 2 of the Mandate and Article 22 of the League of Nations Covenant. South Africa objected that the Court did not have jurisdiction to try the case, but in December 1962 the Court held by eight votes to seven that South Africa's obligation to submit to the jurisdiction of the International Court still remained despite the disappearance of the League of Nations. The Court then proceeded to hear evidence and argument on the case brought by Ethiopia and Liberia and was expected to give judgment by the end of 1965.

Meanwhile a curious incident occurred, popularly known in South Africa as the 'Carpio affair'. It began in 1960 with a resolution by the U.N. Assembly calling on the members of a special committee appointed to deal with the S.W. Africa dispute, to visit the territory and conduct investigations on the spot. On the score that there was a case before the International Court and that the whole question was accordingly *sub judice*, South Africa refused to allow the committee to visit S.W. Africa. In March 1961 the U.N. General Assembly expressed concern that South Africa had withheld consent and called on nations friendly to South Africa to exert pressure on her to adjust her conduct so as to conform to the U.N. Charter. The special committee on S.W. Africa then renewed its application to visit the territory. South Africa again refused to give consent but added that a person of high international standing would be allowed to visit S.W. Africa. The special U.N. committee then decided that if it could not visit S.W. Africa the next best thing would be to visit Ghana and Bechuanaland where a number of political refugees from S.W. Africa had sought asylum. Statements could be heard from these refugees. Ghana gave permission for the committee to go there, which it did, but the British Government announced that it would only allow the committee to go to Bechuanaland on condition that the members of the committee undertook to make no attempt to enter S.W. Africa from Bechuanaland. The committee declined to accept this condition. Instead, it went to Southern Rhodesia and Tanganyika where several political refugees from S.W. Africa were interviewed. The committee presented a report to the U.N. in October 1961, recommending immediate termination of the S.W. Africa mandate. The report called for a United Nations 'presence' to be established in the territory, for universal suffrage to be applied, and for a new constitution to be drafted in consultation with all sections in S.W. Africa, to be followed by a popular referendum.

By 90 votes to one the General Assembly of the U.N. then appointed a seven man 'action' committee to follow up the report. Dr. Victorio Carpio was appointed chairman and Dr. Martinez de Alva vice-chairman, and the committee was instructed to visit S.W. Africa and, if possible with the co-operation of South Africa, to achieve the evacuation of South African military forces from the territory, the release of political prisoners and the repeal of all apartheid laws, and to make preparations for a general election. The South African Government declared that it could not allow the committee to visit S.W. Africa but invited Dr. Carpio and Dr. de Alva to come to Pretoria for talks. The invitation was accepted and after discussions in Pretoria in which Dr. Verwoerd himself took part, Dr. Carpio and Dr. de Alva were taken by the South African Government on a tour of S.W. Africa, followed by a visit to the first of the new South African 'Bantustans', the Transkei.

While the two U.N. representatives were in South Africa various statements of a contradictory character attributed to Dr. Carpio were published in the Press. One remark in particular attracted a good deal of attention : 'I would like to see apartheid succeed as it is contrary to what I had thought.' During the last few days of the visit Dr. Carpio fell ill and was confined to bed in his hotel in

Pretoria, and while he was in bed a joint communiqué was issued in the name of Dr. Carpio, Dr. de Alva and the South African Government in which it was stated that the U.N. delegation 'had found no evidence that there was a threat to international peace and security within S.W. Africa, or signs of militarism, or that the indigenous population was being exterminated'. South Africa, the statement added, had agreed that the economic and social development of non-whites in the territory should be speeded up and that U.N. experts would be associated with a five-year development plan. Dr. Carpio later repudiated the communiqué and declared that he had taken no part in its drafting and had refused to support it when a draft was brought to him as he lay ill in bed. Heated exchanges followed between Dr. Carpio and Dr. de Alva. The action committee finally produced a report recommending that the General Assembly of U.N. should take firm and decisive action aimed at wresting control of S.W. Africa from South Africa, but the committee had fallen under a cloud of recrimination and little interest was aroused by its report.

A month after the report was issued, Dr. Verwoerd appointed a commission headed by the Administrator of the Transvaal, Mr. F. H. Odendaal, to draw up a five-year development plan for S.W. Africa. Next move at the U.N. was to transfer the question of S.W. Africa to the special committee in charge of 'implementing independence to colonial countries'. A resolution in the General Assembly requested South Africa to allow a U.N. 'presence' to be established in S.W. Africa. South Africa was asked not to assemble armed forces in the territory or to remove any inhabitants from their homes or locations to other homes or locations. The discussions in the General Assembly were marked, on this occasion, by condemnatory speeches from nations which had hitherto refrained from attacking South Africa at U.N. For example, the British delegate charged the Nationalist Government of South Africa with having 'deliberately denied basic human rights to the people of S.W. Africa'.

The commission on S.W. Africa appointed by Dr. Verwoerd issued its report in January 1964. It recommended that the 'Bantustan' policy of apartheid being applied to South Africa should also be carried out in S.W. Africa. It produced a plan for dividing the territory into eleven separate areas, each ultimately to have its own elected legislative council. A map was published showing the ten non-white 'Bantustans' arranged like a horse-shoe round the northern part of the territory and with several smaller 'homelands' in the south. The 100,000 whites would continue to occupy most of the areas at present settled by them, but by allocating Crown lands and purchasing farms from whites, the total land to be occupied by non-whites would be increased from 21,607,000 hectares to 32,629,000 hectares. The commission suggested the following 'homelands': Ovamboland, 239,300 population; Okavangoland, 28,800; Kaokoveld, 9,200; Damaraland, 44,300; Hereroland, 35,300; East Kaprivi, 15,800; Tswanaland (population not known, but small); Bushmanland (population also small); Rehoboth Gebiet, 11,257; and Namaland, 34,800. It was recommended that the 'white' area should be governed as at present by an Administrator and Legislative Assembly, and that South Africa should take over certain functions at present performed by the Legislative Assembly. The African 'Bantustans', with their Commissioners and Territorial Councils, would be placed under the general control of the South African Department of Bantu Affairs, while the 'homelands' for the coloured communities would fall under the Department of Coloured Affairs in the Republic.

The Commission went on to recommend a five-year development plan to cost £78,000,000. This would include irrigation and conservation schemes in the northern areas, with a project for hydroelectric power; roads, housing and agricultural and industrial schemes of various kinds. The Commission's recommendations were approved by the Legislative Assembly at Windhoek in March 1964. The South African Minister of Bantu Administration was sent to consult Africans in the territory and he asked to meet the chiefs of all the tribes. The Herero chiefs refused to attend any meetings and there were hostile demonstrations by some sections of the Nama tribe. The Ovambos announced that they would accept the apartheid proposals on condition that this meant they would be given complete independence, separate from South Africa. The South African Parliament voted £10,000,000 as a first instalment for the development plan, but Dr. Verwoerd later announced that the entire project would be held in suspense until the International Court had given its judgment on S.W. Africa.

Such, then, have been the main developments of the international dispute with South Africa over S.W. Africa, which has dragged on for more than a decade and has implications as significant for the United Nations as was the case of Abyssinia for the League of Nations. In this ten years, while the arguments about apartheid have been going on, the political situation in S.W. Africa has undergone a radical change. All twelve seats in the Legislative Assembly at Windhoek were held by the United Party in 1946. When the Nationalists won power in South Africa in 1948 the Government of Dr. Malan restored franchise rights that had been taken away from the German community during the war. Furthermore, the apartheid policies of the Nationalist Party appealed increasingly to the non-German section of the white population of S.W. Africa, who were mostly Afrikaans-speaking. The result was that when elections were held in 1950 the Nationalists won fifteen out of eighteen seats in the enlarged Legislative Assembly of S.W. Africa and all six seats in the South African Parliament. As the years passed and the dispute with the U.N. continued, so did the whites of S.W. Africa tend to close their ranks ever more tightly around the Nationalist Party.

Chapter 19

The Future

T HE STORY of South Africa can have only one ending. The apartheid order will be destroyed and the non-white people will gain their political and economic freedom. Their preponderance and their economic indispensability assure them of this. What is far more difficult to forecast is how and by what means this inevitable conclusion will be reached. Will there be a period of violence and revolution? Will the white masters eventually lose control through corruption and internal dissent? Will they be prepared to abandon apartheid when it becomes palpably obvious to everybody in South Africa that it has, in fact, failed? Or will the outside world intervene to bring about a change? Nobody can say. The story of South Africa, therefore, is rather like a Greek tragedy, where the climax can be sensed from the beginning but there is tension and uncertainty as to how the drama will unfold.

One of the ironies of the South African situation is the fact that very few of those who support the apartheid policy really believe that it can succeed. At the back of their minds is a niggling feeling that it is no longer possible to apply it on a fair basis. It is no longer possible to divide the land and assets of the Republic equitably. That might have been attempted 100 years ago but it cannot be done today. A sad thing about apartheid is that it has been deliberately and for political reasons identified with the Afrikaans *volk*. For in reality the Afrikaners are a kindly, resolute, industrious and intelligent people. They have proved themselves to be able administrators and civil servants. They run the highly complicated government of South Africa in a competent way. They operate the airways, railways, Iscor, Sasol and the other State undertakings in an efficient manner. They are justly proud of these achievements and most of them are anxious to be liked and admired by the rest of the world. English-speaking South Africans deserve less respect. Most of them are prepared to tolerate apartheid though they are more cynical about it. The Afrikaner evolved the policy of apartheid under the compulsion of strong historic, political and sociological forces that for the most part did not apply to the

English, who could have stopped apartheid and prevented the present situation from arising had they really wanted to do so. Today the English section finds itself in a political trap and its reaction is to turn aside and concentrate on making money.

There are, of course, exceptions – both Afrikaans and English – and those individuals and groups who have the courage to stand outside the white laager deserve nothing but praise. They stand in imminent danger of being crushed between the laager and the forces closing in upon it. Most outstanding opponent of apartheid is Mr. Harry Oppenheimer, head of the biggest mining and industrial group of companies in Southern Africa. Mr. Oppenheimer is a member of the Progressive Party, which has only one representative in Parliament and which stands for 'equal rights and opportunities for every individual on a basis of merit, irrespective of race or colour'. Mr. Oppenheimer unequivocally rejects apartheid, job-reservation and the colour-bar. He has tried to introduce family-life for Africans on the gold-mines and has seen to it that wages and working conditions for Africans are improved wherever possible in the great economic empire that he controls. Through De Beers, the Anglo-American Corporation and Rhodesian Anglo-American, he has the biggest influence over the world's diamond market, the gold industry, and about half the copper mines of Northern Rhodesia. He dominates the coal industry of South Africa, and he or his nominees sit on the boards of dozens of secondary industries. As an individual he is friendly, diffident, cultured and highly intelligent. He reads extensively, has the finest private library in South Africa, and through his contacts and economic intelligence services is probably the best-informed civilian in the Republic. He sat for some years in the parliament at Cape Town and was soon regarded as the most forceful and impelling speaker on the opposition side. He plays an adroit cat-and-mouse game with the Nationalist hierarchy and he owes his immunity from too sharp an attack by the Government to the immensely important role he plays in maintaining international financial confidence in South Africa.

Next to Mr. Oppenheimer and his associates the most important influence ranged against apartheid is that of organised commerce. Though most chambers of commerce have been careful not to involve themselves too obviously in political controversy, they have not hesitated to criticise aspects of apartheid which have appeared to them to restrict business or to retard economic development. They have protested against the pass-laws, job-reservation, restrictions on trading, the red-tape of apartheid, and influx control. Organised industry has been more cautious and less vocal, preferring to deal directly with government departments. But occasionally there have been forthright denunciations of apartheid policies by prominent industrialists at Chamber of Industries conventions.

The English-language Press has been another strong and insistent critic of the apartheid policies of the Government. Outstanding in this regard have been the *Rand Daily Mail* in Johannesburg edited by Laurence Gandar; the *Evening Post* in Port Elizabeth edited by John Sutherland, and the *Daily Dispatch* in East London, edited for many years by Jock Barber. These journals have not hesitated to campaign unequivocally against apartheid. Most of the other English-language newspapers also oppose the Nationalist Government but tend to be less forthright in condemning apartheid, though some of them have allowed individual journalists such as Anthony Delius of the *Cape Times*, and Stanley Uys of the *Sunday Times*, to write fairly freely against the Government's racial policies.

Then, too, there is the important role being played by the Institute of Race Relations. This is a non-political fact-finding body founded some thirty years ago 'to further inter-racial peace, harmony and co-operation in South Africa by seeking the truth in all inter-racial situations and making it known, whether it be popular or unpopular with any government or any party or group', to quote a declaration of aims by the Institute itself. The Institute employs a research staff, and it commissions experts at the universities and elsewhere to investigate specific problems. It regularly publishes objective and carefully-documented reports which are quoted by the Press and are used by critics of the Government in Parliament and in other public assemblies. The Institute is financially supported by prominent persons in business, the professions and in academic circles, and it is treated with a mixture of exasperation and respect by the Government. Its operations are, however, being increasingly restricted through the growing limitations imposed by the Government on inter-racial association.

Another force against apartheid is provided by the churches. Hitherto opposition to apartheid has come only from the English-speaking churches, but there is a ferment within the powerful and influential Dutch Reformed Churches which is growing and might become important. According to figures compiled by the official Bureau of Statistics, the Dutch Reformed Churches are supported by 53 per cent of the white population and 29 per cent of the coloureds. They have given powerful backing to the Nationalist Party by providing scriptural justification for apartheid and by preaching the myth of an Afrikaner *volk* chosen by God. However, in recent years serious doubts have arisen within the ministry of the

Dutch Reformed Churches about the moral basis of apartheid. In 1962 two prominent theologians, Professor A. S. Geyser and Professor A. van Selms, challenged the principle observed by the *Nederduitsch Hervormde Kerk* of confining membership to whites. A synodal Commission found Professor Geyser guilty of heresy and he was unfrocked. He was then offered the Chair of Divinity at the University of the Witwatersrand, which he accepted, and he is playing a leading role in the movement to rally support from among Afrikaans churchmen and intellectuals against apartheid.

Meanwhile another prominent Afrikaans churchman who was at that time Moderator of the Southern Transvaal Synod of the *Nederduitse Gereformeerde Kerk*, the Rev. C. F. Beyers Naudé, was unfrocked for accepting the position of Director of the Christian Institute of Southern Africa. The Institute seeks to unite individual Christians of all races and denominations and to make Christianity more of a 'living force' than it is at present in South Africa. In defiance of the resolution depriving Mr. Naudé of his status as a minister, one of the N.G. congregations in Johannesburg proceeded to elect him an elder, but a higher authority of the Church intervened to declare the election void. Six ministers of the Church then ranged themselves alongside Mr. Naudé and the dispute had not been resolved at the time of writing this book. According to reports, between 25 and 30 per cent of ministers in the Dutch Reformed Churches have begun to express misgivings with regard to apartheid, and should the movement grow, as appears likely, the political consequences in South Africa might be far-reaching.

All the English-speaking churches have pronounced against apartheid, and one of them – the Methodist Church – has elected an outstanding African, the Rev. Seth M. Mokitimi, President. The Methodists claim the allegiance of 9 per cent of whites and 12 per cent of the total African population. The Anglicans and Roman Catholics each claim 7 per cent of the African people, of whom 5 per cent are Lutheran and 3 per cent Apostolic. Twenty per cent of Africans adhere to the numerous independent Christian sects that have cropped up among the Bantu, while 33 per cent of Africans are classified as heathen.

In October 1964 the Anglican Bishop of Pretoria, the Rt. Rev. E. G. Knapp-Fisher, announced that white and non-white parishes would be merged in any area desiring that this should be done, and that henceforth Communion would be received by all members of the Church, irrespective of race, at the hands of priests of any colour. Heads of the Anglican Church, including the former Archbishop of Cape Town, Dr. Jooste de Blank, and the former Bishop of Johannesburg, Dr. Ambrose Reeves, denounced apartheid in forthright terms and opposed laws passed to enforce it, but there has been a general reluctance on the part of the Anglican laity to support the lead given by many of their ministers. The hierarchy of the Roman Catholic Church in South Africa has condemned apartheid as 'evil and anti-Christian in character' and the Catholics refused to co-operate with the Government in implementing the Bantu Education Act. A Roman Catholic bishop, the Most Rev. Denis E. Hurley, is President of the Institute of Race Relations.

It is difficult to forecast the role likely to be played by the Christian churches in South Africa during the coming years. There is a tendency among non-whites to question the sincerity of Christians who tolerate apartheid while professing to oppose it on moral or religious grounds. An ominous feature of the disturbances that took place in several African townships at the Sharpeville crisis (page 195) was the number of churches that were burnt down. Fears have been expressed that non-whites in South Africa may turn to Islam, but as yet there are no signs of such a movement. Some 6 per cent of coloureds, most of whom are Malays, and 21 per cent of Asians are Moslems, but very few Africans are Moslems. However, there is a growing realisation among leading churchmen that the future of Christianity in South Africa is bound up with the manner in which the churches respond to the moral challenge of apartheid. The trend among almost all denominations with the exception of the Afrikaans churches is towards greater unity and a more solid front against race-discrimination. Given time to consolidate, this movement could become significant.

Finally, there are the opposition political parties. The largest, the United Party, cannot be counted as a force against apartheid since it upholds the principles of white domination and segregation. It continues to exist mainly because a large section of English-speaking South Africans cannot yet bring themselves to vote Nationalist. There is always the hope that it might have a 'halfway role' to play should anything happen to Dr. Verwoerd. No responsible observer in South Africa considers that the United Party is likely to be returned to power through the ballot-box, but there is always the possibility that it might, in a grave political crisis, form a coalition with the less extreme section of the Nationalists, as happened in 1933.

Such a crisis could be produced by a severe economic recession, or a wave of riots and protest demonstrations such as took place during the Sharpeville emergency, or a general strike, or some other form of disturbance. It might be caused by external pressures, such as a clash with one or more neighbours of the Republic, or international action over the South-West Africa issue, or a war. A United Party-Nationalist coalition, under such circumstances, would be unlikely to abandon the basic policy of white domination, and could only be of a transitory kind.

A far more likely development would be the absorption of the United Party into the Afrikaner *volksbeweging* (people's movement), represented by the Nationalist Party, and the emergence of a one-party system such as existed in the Transvaal Republic of Paul Kruger's time. The one-party system was visualised in the draft republican constitution drawn up by the Nationalist Party in collaboration with the Ossewa Brandwag before these two movements fell out with one another in 1941, as related in Chapter 11. Dr. Verwoerd has never denied charges, made publicly, that he played a leading role in drafting this constitution, nor has he repudiated any of its provisions. For tactical reasons it suited Dr. Verwoerd to make as few changes as possible in the existing Union Constitution when South Africa became a republic in 1961, but leading Nationalists have made no secret of their belief that when the time appears propitious, the constitution will be changed to make it more in tune with Afrikaner traditions.

In a recent speech Dr. Verwoerd forecast that a day would come when the need for separate political parties would disappear. The day may, in fact, arrive sooner than many people realise. The trend among whites in South Africa is to move into the Nationalist *laager*. Support for the Nationalist Government increased in recent parliamentary by-elections and in the Provincial Council elections in March, 1965. When a national emergency was declared at the time of Sharpeville the United Party gave almost full support to the Government. At another similar or more serious crisis it might suit Dr. Verwoerd to broaden his government by including leading members of the United Party, and from that point it would be a simple step, by mutual consent, to introduce a non-party regime.

The future of the two smaller political parties in South Africa, the Progressives and Liberals, is more difficult to forecast. Both of them, as explained earlier in this book, oppose apartheid in principle and stand for the political and economic integration of all races. The Progressive Party has recruited members from among the Africans, Asians and coloureds, and has elected non-whites to its policy-making committees. It has formed branches in African townships in Johannesburg and Cape Town. During 1964 the Party organised a drive among coloureds in the Cape Province to register on the voters' roll and by the end of the year more than 12,000 were reported to have responded. These activities were viewed by the Nationalists with strong disapproval, and in September, 1964, while addressing the Transvaal Congress of the Nationalist Party, Dr. Verwoerd declared : 'We cannot allow that white parties meddle in the politics of the Bantu, coloured, and Indians.' Early in 1965 it was announced that the Government planned to introduce legislation prohibiting white-controlled political parties from playing any part in elections for non-white bodies and providing that only recognised coloured parties would be allowed to nominate candidates to represent coloureds in Parliament and the Cape Provincial Council.

The Liberal Party is even more severely harassed by the Government. Its national president, Mr. Alan Paton, has had his passport taken away, and banning orders have been served on the deputy national president, a national vice-president and the chairman of the Cape Division. The national chairman and national treasurer have been prohibited from attending meetings. At least fifteen Liberals were arrested under the 90-day detention law, while twelve others are reported to have been warned by magistrates to cease their political activities under pain of house-arrest. Security police have raided the homes of large numbers of Liberals. According to a statement issued by the Natal Provincial Committee of the Liberal Party in September, 1964, the police had made threats, not only to Party members, but also to their wives and mothers, to the effect that unless the individual concerned gave up his activities on behalf of the Party, he would be detained, banished, or deported. Security police made a point of attending meetings held by the Liberal Party and recording the proceedings. Members of the public thus intimidated ceased attending meetings and in many cases resigned from the Party, the statement added.

With access to non-whites increasingly restricted and the political trend among whites in the direction of the apartheid *laager*, the Progressive and Liberal Parties will be hard-put to survive. Many observers believe that the Liberal Party will be banned. Or the Government might, under certain circumstances, be tempted to introduce legislation in Parliament declaring it an offence to advocate integration, thus making it virtually impossible for either the Liberal or Progressive Parties to carry on.

No political movements of any consequence are allowed to exist among non-whites. The Nationalists have from time to time tried to organise parties favourable to their point of view but all such attempts were quickly discredited. The two most important movements among Africans, the African National Congress and the Pan-African Congress, have both been banned and nearly all their leaders have either been banned, imprisoned or have left the country. Amnesty International reported in November 1963 that 1,200 African political refugees from the Republic and S.W. Africa had passed through Bechuanaland since 1960. A united front of African National Congress and Pan-African Congress leaders in exile has been formed outside the Republic, with offices in London, Dar-es-Salaam and Algiers. Inside the Republic the A.N.C. went underground when it was banned, working through a movement known as *Umkonto we Sizwe* (spear of the nation). At the same time the banned P.A.C. continued underground with a body known as Poqo. Various acts of sabotage since 1961 have been attributed to either Spear of the Nation or Poqo, or the Communist Party, also operating underground. However, towards the end of 1964, following a series of arrests, detentions and trials, the police claimed that these subversive movements had been stamped out and that the situation was well under control. Whether that was so, or this was merely a lull before more intensive and more skilfully organised operations were launched, remained to be seen. The police have been greatly assisted by the fact that there appears to be no dearth of informers among non-whites.

The most potent force working inside South Africa against apartheid is the relentless, almost unseen pressure of economics. For the plan to succeed it is essential to reduce the number of Africans in the so-called 'white' areas, especially in the main urban areas. Dr. Verwoerd is trying desperately to do this through influx-control and by cutting down opportunities for employing Africans, for example, as domestic servants. There is an elaborate structure of labour bureaux and it is illegal to engage an African excepting through an official labour bureau. No African may leave his reserve or the rural area where his family lives, or even the magisterial district where he happens to work, to enter another in search of work, without first obtaining a permit to do so. And there are rigorous provisions for endorsing Africans out of the urban areas, where they are treated officially as migrants. This procedure runs contrary to two powerful economic forces working from opposite sides. First there is the constantly-increasing demand in the towns for more and more African labour. Then there is the pressure of rising populations in the reserves and rural areas, which are impoverished and overcrowded. The natural and logical thing is for the surplus population of the reserves to be drained off the land and absorbed into industries – the well-known 'drift to the towns'

that takes place in every industrial country of the world. Dr. Verwoerd hopes to stem the tide by developing the reserves and by
siting white-owned factories on the borders of the reserves. Special
economic inducements are offered to move or start up such 'border'
industries, but though there has been a modest response it is per-
fectly clear that this expedient cannot possibly absorb enough workers to ease the pressure on the towns.

Thus a problem of poverty and unemployment is developing
among Africans in the reserves. A somewhat similar situation is
developing in the white-owned rural areas where almost all the
agricultural labour is supplied by Africans. The point of population
saturation has long been passed in a great many districts. In the
interest of sound agriculture, let alone any question of politics, the
total number of Africans and their families living on a great many
farms ought to be reduced, but where could these Africans go? The
reserves, as we have said, are already congested and Africans are
not allowed to enter the towns excepting under strict limitations.
This problem affects 31·2 per cent of the total African population
of the Republic, more than three millions in comparison with the
507,000 whites who live alongside them on the same farms. The
Government has begun to enforce its system of registration and
labour bureaux in the rural areas and sooner or later jobs and
somewhere else to live will have to be found for the surplus Africans. This situation, combined with the pressure of population in
the reserves, is clearly explosive. Already there have been rumblings
and unrest in the rural areas and reserves and it is not difficult to
visualise what may happen when there are droughts and when
crops fail.

As for the towns, there is not the slightest likelihood of reducing
the ratio of Africans to whites, even through the most rigorous application of influx-control together with a white immigration scheme
on the largest possible scale. Immigrants are wanted mostly for
skilled jobs and it has been calculated that every new opening given
to a white in a skilled job creates a demand for three Africans as
unskilled labour. Official census figures showed that 26·7 per cent
of the total African population in the Republic lived in the 'white'
towns in 1951. By 1960 the percentage had risen to 31·8 and it is
going up inexorably all the time, despite all the controls. This is
the index that really measures the economic failure of apartheid.

Another cold economic factor that may one day explode under
the apartheid structure is the startling disparity in incomes and
living-standards between whites and Africans. According to a survey
in 1960 by the State Bureau of Census and Statistics, 36·9 per cent

of the white population earned £42 per head per month while 41·3 per cent earned over £84 per month. The average monthly income of all Africans in Johannesburg in 1963 was calculated by the Bantu Wage and Productivity Association to be £21 per month. In the same year the Minister of the Interior announced in Parliament that 68,000 out of 87,000 Africans employed in the Public Service were paid under £15 per month. Similarly the Railways employed 92,800 Africans in 1963 and 62,500 of them were paid under £15 per month. This gap between the earnings of whites and Africans creates an almost classical revolutionary situation and there is very little likelihood of the gap being narrowed while the apartheid policy continues to be applied.

Though they lack arms and are unorganised, Africans have a weapon ready to hand if ever they care to use it. Mines, industries, transport, commercial activity and farming operations would all come to a standstill were Africans to withdraw their labour. The fact that attempts in the past to organise protest strikes by non-whites have generally failed, and that the strike-weapon has not yet been effectively used against apartheid, does not prove that this method of attack will not be employed in the future.

There is also the constant danger of sabotage. On the charge-sheet of a case heard in 1963 no less than 222 acts of sabotage were listed. Other instances have occurred since then. Police claimed at the end of 1964 that all subversive movements had been smashed, yet many Africans were known to be undergoing special training in sabotage techniques in other countries hostile to the Republic. The prevalent opinion in South Africa, when this book was written, was that the freedom then being enjoyed from sabotage would not be of long duration.

Another point about the internal situation worth mentioning is that throughout its 18 years in office the Nationalist Government has enjoyed the exceptional good fortune of an economy that has consistently prospered, thanks to circumstances for which the State could claim no credit. First there was a marked expansion in the gold industry due to new mines coming into production. Then there was the world demand for uranium, produced by South Africa in association with gold. The market for diamonds has continued to expand, while the agricultural industry has prospered greatly as a result of high prices for wool and citrus, greater internal consumption of food, and improved techniques of crop-production. Thus the Nationalist Government, with its apartheid policy, has not yet been subjected to the stresses of an economic depression. A period of falling agricultural prices, industrial stagnation and unemployment – particularly among Africans living close to the breadline – would quickly create an almost unmanageable situation in which anything could happen. One of the inevitable effects of the apartheid system is that it places the economy in a strait-jacket, allowing little scope for resilience should an emergency arise.

A final point about the internal situation involves a simple question of geography. The map of the existing African reserves and the proposed 'consolidated' bantustans, published on page 43, should be studied closely, since it contains one of the most powerful arguments against the feasibility of the apartheid plan. The reserves, it will be seen, lie like a great horse-shoe around the Orange Free State and the high plateau of the Transvaal. They are fragmented beyond repair. The only one with any degree of contiguity is the Transkei, and its resources are so slender that it could not survive without assistance from outside. All the other proposed bantustans, including Zululand, are deeply penetrated and split apart by large areas owned by whites. The Government's land-purchasing programme is furiously opposed by the white farming-community, who are politically influential, and it makes slow progress. In the opinion of most informed observers there is not the slightest possibility of anything even vaguely like the 'consolidation' suggested by the Tomlinson Commission being achieved. And without such consolidation the Government's apartheid plan, with its separate ethnic states, becomes a farce. In some quarters it has been suggested that apartheid might be applied in a different way : that the various racial groups, each making its own laws and creating its own living-standards and separate public amenities, might share the same geographical area. But not much thought is needed to expose the absurdities of such an idea.

Turning to the external situation, the question may be asked whether there is likely to be action against South Africa by the outside world, and if so in what form. The outside world has declared its disapproval of apartheid. African states have closed their harbours and airports to South African planes and ships, and visas are being refused to South Africans. Various cultural, professional, labour, sporting and other organisations have excluded South Africans, and attempts have been made to organise economic boycotts. Diplomatic action against the Republic has been taken by a number of countries. At the United Nations, as we have related, resolutions condemning apartheid, and calling on the world to apply pressures of various kinds, have become increasingly peremptory. The issue of South-West Africa appears likely to present an opportunity for concerted international action against the Republic when the World Court gives judgment in 1965 on the case brought by Ethiopia and Liberia.

Since a direct attack upon South Africa is hardly feasible, the idea has been mooted of applying economic sanctions against the Republic. It could be either selective sanctions, such as a decision to stop buying gold, wool, sugar and certain other commodities, plus an attempt to cut off supplies of essential stocks like oil, or it could be total sanctions, which would involve a blockade. Neither course would appear to be practicable. The United Nations has demanded that an official U.N. 'presence' should be established in S.W. Africa to ensure that apartheid is no longer applied to the territory, but in face of a continued refusal by the Republican Government, what could the U.N. do? Those who may think in terms of military action do not realise how strong the armed forces of South Africa are. Annual defence expenditure in the Republic runs at £105,000,000 and there is an active force of around 19,000 and a citizen force of 50,000 plus a commando force of 51,500. The Air Force, equipped with Sabre interceptors, Mirage fighter-bombers, Shackleton maritime reconnaissance aircraft, Buccaneers, Harvards, Vampires and an assortment of helicopters, number about 4,000, and the force is well-trained. There is a navy with an active strength of 3,500 and equipped with two destroyers, six frigates, two ocean and ten coastal minesweepers plus five other seaward defence boats.

An invasion of S.W. Africa would have to be launched from the British Protectorate of Bechuanaland, or from Angola, or from the sea. Angola is run by the Portuguese, with whom the Republic has close treaty and economic relationships, and Bechuanaland could not be easily reached from outside even if the British were prepared to co-operate in an attack on S.W. Africa, which is doubtful. An attack from the sea would involve international problems which would appear to be quite beyond the capacity of the United Nations. Certainly nobody in South Africa regards S.W. Africa or the Republic as being in danger of attack from outside in the immediate future. But what does worry the Government is the possibility at some time in the future of guerilla operations directed from across the borders and supported by an African fifth-column inside the Republic or S.W. Africa. With this in view the Government in Pretoria is watching current developments in Angola, Mozambique, Southern Rhodesia and the British Protectorates with close interest. There has been a revolt in Angola which the Portuguese claim to have suppressed but which other sources believe may break out again. Reports have reached South Africa of incidents and unrest in Mozambique. The Portuguese, meanwhile, are maintaining strong forces in both territories.

There is less concern in Pretoria about the British Protectorates. The economies of Basutoland, Bechuanaland and Swaziland are almost wholly dependent upon the Republic, which is in a position to squeeze any one of the territories at any time it might wish to do so. As each protectorate moves towards independence it is likely to tread warily beside its powerful neighbour. Dr. Verwoerd is sponsoring a 'common market' plan for Southern Africa as a step towards some form of closer political association at a later date, and it will be extremely difficult for any one of the protectorates to remain outside the common market.

One other external possibility should be mentioned which could have an important bearing on South Africa. This involves global defensive strategy. South Africa commands the southern entrance to the Indian Ocean from the west, and in 1965 there were important developments affecting the Indian Ocean. Over on the eastern side there was the 'confrontation' between Indonesia and Malaysia and there was also the Chinese threat to India. The United States was deeply concerned with her position in Indo-China. Britain and the United States were re-examining their position in the Indian Ocean, and one of the projects was a network of island bases and observation-posts in this important area. There was talk of abandoning the strategy of having land bases on foreign soil, and if a decision of that kind were taken, Britain might well withdraw her naval forces from South African waters. If that were to happen, and the Americans were to withdraw from Africa as a 'sphere of influence', as many influential persons in Washington were urging, South Africa might find herself dangerously isolated and exposed.

Such, then, are the main human and economic forces involved in the South African situation when we review it today. Our summing-up suggests that the overthrow of apartheid, when it does occur, is more likely to be achieved from within the Republic than from without. Both external and internal factors will, of course, be involved, but as things stand the internal pressures are the more important. They will, however, have to increase considerably before a large enough explosion occurs. It may not be one but a whole series of explosions, and nobody can say when and where to expect them.

Yet it would be wrong to end this book at such an indefinite point. There is still the question of what future there can be for South Africa once the apartheid era has come to an end. We must not lose sight of the fact that Southern Africa is an exceptionally rich land, with an easy climate and abundant human and material resources which not even the kind of crisis necessary to overthrow apartheid could destroy. There is no question of the whites being driven out of Southern Africa any more than there is of the Africans, the coloureds and Asians allowing themselves indefinitely to be enthralled by apartheid. They will all be compelled to work together, and the amalgam should be rich.

A picture that seems likely to emerge is of a chequer-board of states, large and small, rather like the United States of America, with the Zambesi as the northern border. It was a mistake in 1910 to have adopted a unitary form of government, and when the inevitable change takes place that results in the end of apartheid, the union is almost certain to be torn apart. Dr. Verwoerd himself has begun the cutting-up process with his Bantustan concept. Nearly all the states will be non-racial, though in most the African will predominate. Basutoland, with scarcely more than a handful of whites, insists on a multiracial order, while majority opinion in the first Bantustan state, the Transkei, is in favour of equal rights for all races, though Dr. Verwoerd has decreed that only Africans shall have rights there. There might be one or two predominantly white states in Southern Africa where the more fanatical adherents of white *baasskap* will be in the majority – the Free State, for example, and perhaps a new state called 'Karoo' where the big new conservation and hydro-electric projects on the Orange River will open up extensive areas to closer settlement. The Cape Province could be split in two and the boundaries of East Griqualand, Natal, Zululand, Swaziland and the Transvaal could be rearranged on more realistic lines.

The federal government of this association of states would be multiracial and the federation itself would include the British protectorates, the southern half of Mozambique, South-West Africa and Southern Rhodesia. There would be no difficulty about obtaining capital and skilled personnel to exploit this rich storehouse of mineral resources on a scale to match the boom-years in the United States of America. No part of the world is so under-populated at the present time and has so great a potential for development.

South Africa has been described by eminent anthropologists as the cradle of mankind. It is ridiculous to suppose that a small minority of late-comers to this ancient land can compel the natural processes of evolution to stand still.

Index

*Printed in Great Britain
by Western Printing Services Limited
Bristol*